Cover/Frontispiece. Guercino. *St. Luke Displaying a Painting of the Virgin.* 1652–53. Oil on canvas. Photo. With permission of The Nelson-Atkins Museum of Art, Kansas City, Missouri (Purchase) F83-55. Photo by E. G. Schempf.

Illuminating Luke

The Public Ministry of Christ in Italian Renaissance and Baroque Painting

HEIDI J. HORNIK AND MIKEAL C. PARSONS

t & t clark

NEW YORK • LONDON

T & T Clark International, Madison Square Park, 15 East 26th Street, New York, NY 10010

T & T Clark International, The Tower Building, 11 York Road, London SE1 7NX

T & T Clark International is a Continuum imprint.

Biblical quotations marked NRSV are from the New Revised Standard Version, copyright 1989, Division of Christian Education of the National Council of Churches of Christ in the United States of America. Used by permission. All rights reserved.

Cover art: Guercino. *St. Luke Displaying a Painting of the Virgin* 1652–53. Oil on canvas. The Nelson-Atkins Museum of Art. Kansas City, Missouri (Purchase) F83-55. Photo by E. G. Schempf.

Cover design: Brenda Klinger

Cataloging-in-Publication Data is available from the Library of Congress

Printed in Malaysia

05   06   07   08   09   10   9   8   7   6   5   4   3   2   1

Contents

List of Illustrations   vii

Foreword   xi

CHAPTER ONE
Introduction   1

CHAPTER TWO
The *Baptism of Christ* by Michele Tosini (Luke 3:21–22; 4:1–13)   11

CHAPTER THREE
The *Miraculous Draught of Fishes* by Raphael (Luke 5:1–11)   49

CHAPTER FOUR
The *Good Samaritan* and *The Rich Man and Lazarus*
by Jacopo Bassano (Luke 10:30–37; 16:19–31)   83

CHAPTER FIVE
Christ in the Home of Mary and Martha by Alessandro Allori
(Luke 10:38–42)   111

CHAPTER SIX
The Prodigal Son by Guercino (Luke 15:11–32)   135

Epilogue   165

Selected Bibliography   167

Index   171

List of Illustrations

Cover/Frontispiece. Guercino. *St. Luke Displaying a Painting of the Virgin*. 1652–53. Oil on canvas. The Nelson-Atkins Museum of Art, Kansas City, Missouri.

Figure 1-1. Fra Angelico. *Christ Scorned*. 1437. Fresco. San Marco, Florence.

Figure 1-2. Drawing after *Alexamemos Worships his God*. (Original graffito in stone. c. 200. Museo Nazionale dell Terme, Rome.)

Figure 1-3. *The Raising of Lazarus*. c. 350. Marble sarcophagus. Museo Pio cristiano, Rome.

Figure 2-1. Michele Tosini. *Baptism of Christ*. c. 1565. Oil on panel. Pinacoteca Nazionale, Ferrara.

Figure 2-2. Michele Tosini. Top detail of *Baptism of Christ*.

Figure 2-3. Michele Tosini. Left detail of *Baptism of Christ*.

Figure 2-4. Michele Tosini. *Venus and Cupid*. c. 1570. Oil on panel. Galleria Colonna, Rome.

Figure 2-5. Michele Tosini. *St. Mark*. 1561. Fresco. Strozzi Chapel, Villa Caserotta, Paolini.

Figure 2-6. Michele Tosini. *St. Mary Magdalen*. c. 1570. Oil on panel. The Museum of Fine Arts, Houston. Samuel H. Kress Collection.

Figure 2-7. Michele Tosini. *Madonna and Child with Saints*. 1559–61. Oil on panel. Convent of San Vincenzo, Prato.

Figure 2-8. Michele Tosini. *Madonna and Child with St. John the Baptist*. 1545–50. Oil on panel. Palmer Museum of Art, Pennsylvania State University.

Figure 2-9. Michele Tosini. *Marriage at Cana* 1561. Fresco. Strozzi Chapel, Villa Caserotta, Paolini.

Figure 2-10. Michele Tosini and Ridolfo del Ghirlandaio. *Madonna and Child with Sts. James, Lawrence, Francis and Clare and Bishop Buonafè.* c. 1540. Oil on panel. Museo di San Salvi, Florence.

Figure 3-1. Raphael. *Miraculous Draught of Fishes.* 1515–16. Bodycolour on paper mounted onto canvas (tapestry cartoon). Victoria and Albert Museum, London.

Figure 3-2. Raphael. *Miraculous Draught of Fishes.* Tapestry. Vatican Museums, Rome.

Figure 3-3. North Wall of the Sistine Chapel with Tapestries. Vatican Museums, Rome.

Figure 3-4. South Wall of the Sistine Chapel with Tapestries. Vatican Museums, Rome.

Figure 3-5. Raphael. *Christ's Charge to Peter.* 1515–16. Bodycolour on paper mounted onto canvas (tapestry cartoon). Victoria and Albert Museum, London.

Figure 3-6. Raphael. *Ananias.* 1515–16. Bodycolour on paper mounted onto canvas (tapestry cartoon). Victoria and Albert Museum, London.

Figure 4-1. Jacopo Bassano. *Good Samaritan.* c. 1557. Oil on canvas. National Gallery, London.

Figure 4-2. Jacopo Bassano. *The Rich Man and Lazarus.* 1554. Oil on canvas. The Cleveland Museum of Art.

Figure 4-3. Jacopo Bassano. *Flight into Egypt.* 1534. Oil on canvas. Museo Civico, Bassano del Grappa.

Figure 4-4. Jacopo Bassano. *Supper at Emmaus.* 1538. Oil on canvas. Kimbell Art Museum, Fort Worth.

Figure 4-5. Jacopo Bassano. *Way to Calvary,* c. 1543–44, The Fitzwilliam Museum, Cambridge.

Figure 4-6. Jacopo Bassano. *Good Samaritan.* 1546–49. Oil on canvas. The Royal Collection.

Figure 5-1. Alessandro Allori. *Christ in the Home of Mary and Martha.* 1578–80. Oil on panel. Palazzo Portinari-Salviati, Florence.

Figure 5-2. Alessandro Allori. *Pearl Fishers*. 1570–71. Oil on slate. Palazzo Vecchio, Florence.

Figure 5-3. Alessandro Allori. View of Altar Wall. 1578–80. Fresco. Palazzo Portinari-Salviati, Florence.

Figure 5-4. Alessandro Allori.*The Magdalen Washes the Feet of Christ in the House of Simon*. 1578–80. Fresco. Palazzo Portinari-Salviati, Florence.

Figure 5-5. Alessandro Allori. *Noli mi tangere*. 1578–80. Fresco. Palazzo Portinari-Salviati, Florence.

Figure 5-6. Alessandro Allori. View of Entire Chapel. 1578–80. Fresco. Palazzo Portinari-Salviati, Florence.

Figure 5-7. Giovanni da Milano. *Christ in the House of Mary and Martha*. 1365. Fresco. Rinuccini Chapel, Santa Croce, Florence.

Figure 6-1. Guercino. *Return of the Prodigal Son*. 1619. Oil on canvas. Kunsthistorisches Museum, Vienna.

Figure 6-2. Guercino. *Return of the Prodigal*. 1627–28. Oil on canvas. Galleria Borghese, Rome.

Figure 6-3. Guercino. *Return of the Prodigal*. 1651. Oil on canvas. Museo Diocesano, Wloclawek, Poland.

Figure 6-4. Guercino. *Return of the Prodigal Son*. 1654–55. Oil on canvas. The Putnam Foundation, Timken Museum of Art, San Diego.

Foreword

THIS BOOK is the second volume of a projected trilogy entitled *Illuminating Luke* and deals with subjects from Christ's public ministry unique to Luke and painted by Italian Renaissance and Baroque artists. As with the first volume, we have incurred many debts during its composition and production. First, we would like to thank the various groups and individuals at Baylor University who, in various ways, have provided the resources necessary to research and write this book. The Lilly Horizons Grant (Institute for Faith and Learning), University Research Committee, the Sabbatical and Research Leave Committees, and the Committee for Albritton Grants for Faculty Scholarship, Department of Art — all provided material support in the form of grants, sabbaticals, and research leaves. Our dean, Dr. Wallace Daniel, and our chairs, Professor John McClanahan (Art) and Dr. Randall O'Brien (Religion), have been generous advocates of our work. Dodi Holland, Sondra Brady, Michael Koehler, and Chad Hartsock provided helpful assistance, and Jason Whitlark provided cheerful and timely assistance in locating obscure citations in the last phases of composition.

Dr. David Lyle Jeffrey, provost and vice president for academic affairs, Baylor University, himself the author and editor of numerous works that plumb the Christian exegetical tradition from the angles of literature and art, understands, like surely few other North American provosts do, the importance and difficulty of such interdisciplinary work. His enthusiasm for and faith in this project have been unabashed and constant, and we are deeply grateful. Our president, Robert B. Sloan, in his nearly ten-year tenure, has created an environment that supports, recognizes, and honors scholarship aimed at recovering and explicating various aspects of the Christian tradition. His support, too, has been unfailing.

In addition to presentations at regional and national professional societies, we are grateful for the numerous invitations to present different aspects of this project in a variety of settings. Thanks are due for the following invitations: to David Gowler to give the Pierce Lecture in Religion at Oxford College, Emory University; to Craig Bartholomew to read a paper at the Scripture and Hermeneutics Seminar (which focused on Reading Luke) at Jesus College, Oxford University; and to Graham Stanton to make a presentation to the distinguished and venerable Senior

Seminar for New Testament Studies, Cambridge University. Finally, our association with the newly formed Society of Biblical Literature consultation on The Bible and Visual Art (which Heidi co-chairs with Elizabeth Struthers Malbon) has provided new insights into religious art, and no less importantly, new friends with common interests!

We are also grateful to T & T Clark International, and especially to Henry Carrigan and his staff, for their professional competence and courtesy in bringing this book to press. To all these benefactors, we express heartfelt thanks. Parts of chapter three appeared in an earlier version as Heidi J. Hornik, "Raphael's *Miraculous Draught of Fishes* and *Christ's Charge to Peter*: Their Theological and Artistic Implications in the Sistine Chapel," *Perspectives in Religious Studies* 31 (2004): 467–88. Thanks to Scott Nash, senior editor of National Association of Baptist Professors in Religion (NABPR) publications, for permission to use this article in the current book.

In the fall semester, 2000, we taught a course on Luke and the visual arts. The course was composed of undergraduates (both art and religion majors), seminary students, and doctoral students in religion. Several students wrote papers on the scenes included in this book, thus providing initial bibliography and insights into the chosen texts and paintings. We are especially grateful to Andy Arterbury (on *Christ in the House of Mary and Martha*), Pamela Kinlaw (on *Baptism of Christ*), and Anne Vestal (on *Rich Man and Lazarus*).

This manuscript was completed in Florence, Italy, during the summer of 2004. As before, many persons made our stay a delightful experience. The staff at the Kunsthistorisches Institut was always helpful in locating hard-to-find sources. The staffs at the National Gallery and the Victoria and Albert Museum in London, The Uffizi and the Archivio di Stato in Florence, and the Pinacoteca Nazionale, Ferrara, were very generous with their assistance as we studied each of the paintings and related documents. The various departments of the Ministero dei Beni e le Attività, Culturali, Florence, offered many of the permissions and photographs needed to illustrate this volume so beautifully. Special thanks also to the following people who assisted our research and writing: Mark Evans, Angeliki Lymberopulou, Christopher Marsden, Antonio Paolucci, and Louis Alexander Waldman.

In Florence our friends Janet and Fabrizio Gheri provided much-needed respite from the daily rounds of research and writing. In New York and North Carolina, our parents, Barbara and Joseph Hornik, and John Quincy Parsons, never failed in being a constant wealth of support and encouragement as we moved our young family to Florence summer after summer.

The memory and spirit of Blanche Hester Parsons (1926–2003) is still with us, guiding our thoughts and endeavors.

When this project began, our children Mikeal and Matthew (or Michele and Matteo as they prefer to be called when residents of Italy!) were both still in diapers. Now both are boys in every sense of the word. They have been more enthusiastic about our trips to Florence than we have had the right to expect. And it has been our joy to watch as they have made the Via Gioberti neighborhood of Florence — with its fine restaurants, beautiful parks, and especially the Gelateria of the Signori Ermini — their home away from home for five summers!

Our hope for volume 1 on the Lukan infancy narratives in Italian Renaissance painting was that it might contribute to a deeper understanding of the Gospel of Luke and its subsequent reception on the part of the contemporary Christian community. That hope has not changed for this present volume. Despite whatever flaws remain in our presentation, we hope that readers may gain some sense of appreciation for the brilliance of these artists and their patrons, who commissioned and executed these visual representations of beloved scenes in Scripture. And may the Gospel be thus illuminated for and in us once again.

HEIDI J. HORNIK AND MIKEAL C. PARSONS
Baylor University, Waco, Texas
June 2004

Figure 1-1. Fra Angelico. *Christ Scorned.* 1437. Fresco. San Marco, Florence. Photo. Chiesa di San Marco, Florence.

Chapter One

Introduction

IN A RECENT ESSAY, Margaret Miles muses over what elements of the visual record of Christ's life might serve as a potential resource for contemporary Christian devotional and theological reflection for the purposes of "imitating Christ":

> What might imitation of Christ look like, feel like now? What features of Christ's life might contemporary Americans select for imitation? I expect that the aspects of Christ's life that challenge Christians today would be different from those of earlier societies. Twenty-first-century Christians might, for example, be less interested in depictions of Christ's suffering since our society has more capacity to relieve suffering, or at least to keep suffering out of sight, than did historical societies. But what about the ministry episodes of Christ's life? Meditating on these might recall Christ's integrity, his commitment to the poor and needy, and his intelligent, thoughtful analysis of the sins of his society. Ministry episodes might remind contemporary Christians of Christ's passionate commitment to living lovingly, and to figuring out what that meant, not in the abstract, but "on location." . . .
>
> These are surely images that are conspicuously missing from the media images Americans consume daily. Indeed, they are fundamentally counter-cultural, challenging the greed and individualism that characterizes American life at the beginning of the twenty-first century.[1]

Miles's suggestion is a fascinating one, made all the more novel by the fact that during the medieval and Renaissance periods, Christian devotional reflection focused primarily on the suffering of the crucified Christ. She cites as one example the work of Fra Angelico, whose cell frescoes in the Dominican monastery of San Marco, Florence, are dominated by scenes from the scourging and crucifixion of Christ (Figure 1-1). These frescoes were to serve as devotional aids as the monks contemplated their calling to imitate Christ in his suffering for the world. One may easily move from the particular example of Fra Angelico to make a more general statement about the medieval focus — one might say obsession — with the passion, especially in Italian art.[2]

Figure 1-2. Line drawing after *Alexamemos Worships his God.* (Original in Graffito in stone. c. 200. Museo Nazionale delle Terme, Rome.) Drawing. Stanley Scott with permission.

But such has not always been the case in the history of Christian art, and Miles's suggestion hearkens back to the earliest period of Christian art when focus on the passion of Jesus was much less pronounced. In fact, it may come as a surprise to those not familiar with the material evidence of pre-Constantinian Christianity to learn that explicit depictions of Jesus' suffering are totally absent from the repertoire of Christian art until very late. Possibly the earliest representation of a crucified Christ, a point hotly disputed among ancient historians, is a graffito from c. 200 on the Palatine in Rome, which shows a man worshiping a crucified and ass-headed figure, with the inscription "Alexamenos worships his god" (Figure 1-2). The meaning is obscure, but many interpret the graffito as the taunt of a pagan adversary.[3] If the crucified figure is Christ, then the earliest visual rendering is by an opponent of Christianity, not an adherent.[4] Apparently — and this is the startling fact — a crucified Christ is not depicted in representational art *by a Christian* until the fifth century, and not with regularity until the seventh.[5]

Far more prevalent in the visual record of early Christians are depictions from the public ministry of Christ, especially of Christ the miracle-worker (Figure 1-3).[6] Thomas Mathews claims that these early Christian images of Christ's miracles are not only "distinctively pacific, non-military, and non-imperial";[7] they were "ubiquitous." What was their purpose? According to Mathews, they — along with other images from Christ's public ministry, including the triumphal entry — served a particular anti-imperial ideology: "In the images of the fourth century, Christ takes the attributes and attitudes of the magician; at the same time he assumes a stance of opposition to imperial authority."[8]

Figure 1-3. *The Raising of Lazarus.* c. 350. Marble sarcophagus. Museo Pio cristiano, Rome. Photo. With permission from the Biblioteca Apostolica Vaticana.

Soon, though, these images from the public ministry of Christ gave way to a preponderance of depictions of the passion of Christ. These images often served as liturgical aids for the devotional practices of Christian pilgrims.

In this book, we attempt to take seriously Miles's call for a (re)consideration of the visual repertoire of the public ministry of Christ. Although some might construe our efforts to be the visual version of the radical reformation's call to "get back to the Bible," we are not claiming the pre-Constantinian period of early Christian art as some idyllic pictorial paradise that somehow holds the key to solving the various maladies of contemporary society. For example, while we do focus in this volume on scenes from the public ministry, we do not limit those scenes exclusively, or even primarily, to the healing ministry of Christ, as did the early Christians.[9] Nor do we wish to ignore the passion of Christ as a possible source of theological reflection and liturgical practice.[10] Nevertheless, we agree with Miles that the visual interpretation of Christ's public ministry might hold unusual, and heretofore relatively unexplored, potential for contemporary theological reflection.

Therefore we have chosen as the subjects for this volume scenes depicted in Italian Renaissance and Baroque art that were unique to Luke's version of Christ's public ministry. In this sense, this volume shares a common purpose with its predecessor, *Illuminating Luke: The Infancy Narrative in Italian Renaissance Painting.*[11] But there are differences as well. For starters, the first volume dealt with scenes taken only from the first two chapters of Luke. Of course, those chapters were particularly rich fare for artists interested in depicting scenes from the birth of Christ. The public ministry in Luke, however, covers some seventeen chapters (chaps. 3–19) of the Third Gospel. The first section of this material looks at the so-called Galilean ministry of Jesus, while a significant portion of later material is devoted to Jesus' journey to Jerusalem, which begins in Luke 9:31 and ends somewhere in Luke 19.[12] For various reasons, much of this material never captured the imagination of artists and their patrons.

Nonetheless, we have had to be very selective in our choice of scenes to illustrate. Two of our scenes, the baptism (Luke 3) and the miraculous catch of fishes (Luke 5), come from the Galilean ministry, while the others, the parable of the Good Samaritan and the Rich Man and Lazarus (Luke 10, 16), Jesus in the house of Mary and Martha (Luke 10), and the parable of the Prodigal Son (Luke 15), are taken from material in the journey narrative. We address the particular function of each scene in Luke's overall plot in the individual chapters. We have been careful to choose material that represents both the words (parables, sayings) and the deeds (baptism, miracles) of Christ, though there is, lamentably, much we have left out. Still, these scenes have been carefully chosen so that the reader will have at least a beginning sense of the history of visual depictions of, in Luke's own words, "all that Jesus began to do and say" (Acts 1:1).

Methodology

Like its predecessor, this book is not primarily an application of a theoretical model, and thus methodological considerations, while certainly present, run beneath the text like an underground stream rather than appearing constantly on or near the surface.[13] Nonetheless, our methodology is generally indebted to the vocabulary of German *Rezeptionsgeschichte*, or reception theory, especially as articulated in Wolfgang Iser's notion of the reader actualizing a text.[14]

We are interested in the reception of the biblical text in two moves. First and foremost, we attend to the way in which the artist himself has actualized the text in the production of a visual image. This part of the exercise requires that we examine the work of art in stylistic, historical, and iconographical terms.

Erwin Panofsky in his instrumental essay, "Iconography and Iconology: An Introduction to the Study of Renaissance Art," first published in 1939 and still available in his *Meaning in the Visual Arts*, also contributes to our methodological stream.[15] Panofsky allowed that "*synthetic intuition* [a sense of the meaning of the whole picture] may be better developed in a talented layman than in an erudite scholar."[16] Yet he warned against pure intuition because a work of art is a symptom of "'something else' which expresses itself in a countless variety of other symptoms, and we interpret its compositional and iconographical features as more evidence of that 'something else.'"[17] Panofsky called it "intrinsic meaning or content." Intrinsic meaning is "apprehended by ascertaining those underlying principles which reveal the basic attitude of a nation, a period, a class, a religious or philosophical persuasion — unconsciously qualified by one personality [a painter, for instance] and condensed into one work."[18] Intrinsic meaning, therefore, will inform both the "compositional and stylistic methods" and "iconographical significance" of a painting.[19] We are not unaware of the treacherous path down which we trod in order to situate each work of art in its cultural, political, and theological context and to attempt an evaluation of its intrinsic meaning.

John Shearman, an art historian, has focused the problem quite clearly: "It goes without saying, I would have thought, that we cannot step right outside our time, avoiding, as it were, all contamination by contemporary ideologies and intervening histories."[20] Nevertheless, we also agree with Shearman's conclusion:

> . . . such inevitable imperfection ought not to be allowed to discourage the exercise of the historical imagination. In the same way it goes without saying that we will not reconstruct entirely correctly, but it is a sign of an unreflexive lack of realism to suppose that because we will not get it entirely right we had better give up and do something else not subject to error.[21]

In this first move of reception history, namely, to understand the way the artist has actualized or concretized the biblical text, we have been greatly assisted by another art historian, Paolo Berdini. Berdini thinks of the interpretation of the text as a "trajectory of visualization," which he labels "visual exegesis." In Berdini's words:

> The painter reads the text and translates his scriptural reading into a problem in representation, to which he offers a solution — the image. In that image the beholder acknowledges, not the text in the abstract, but the painter's reading of the text so that the effect the image has on the beholder is a function of what the painter wants the beholder to experience in the text. This is the trajectory of visualization, and the effect of the text through the image is a form of exegesis. Painting is not the simple visualization of the narrative of the text but an expansion of that text, subject to discursive strategies of various kinds.[22]

These "discursive strategies" we take to be inextricably intertwined with the artist's social, political, and religious contexts as well as the sources and precedents at the artist's disposal in composing the image. Iconography, then, in our work is understood as part of this process of visual exegesis.

While most of our efforts are spent on this first aspect of reception history, our methodology is also explicitly hermeneutical, and herein lies our second move of reception history. We are interested in how this "visual exegesis" might enrich our understanding of Luke's Gospel and at the same time inform the contemporary faith community's interpretation of Scripture.[23] Several generations of biblical scholars have been trained in the "what it meant/what it means" hermeneutic.[24] In this model, the biblical scholar explicated what a biblical text meant in its original context, and the theologian, building on these insights, discerned what the text now means in contemporary terms.[25]

Unfortunately, this construal has operated from the assumption that we need only understand the context of the first century in which most NT texts were produced and the twenty-first century in which these texts are read. In this view, the intervening period of nearly two thousand years is mostly an obstacle to be avoided. The result, in many cases, has been to foster feelings of apathy, ambivalence, or antagonism on the part of the church toward professional biblical studies or vice versa. Between the original communication, "what it meant," and the contemporary interpretive context, "what it means," however, lies a largely neglected element, "what it *has* meant" at critical moments in the church's history. Scholars today, such as Brevard Childs, David Steinmetz, and others, write of the importance of patristic, medieval, and reformation hermeneutics, but they have limited their vision to literary texts.[26] We propose to include examples of visual interpretations as part of the "afterlife" of these stories as they are reconfigured for a different time and place. Of course, we are not the first to examine visual depictions of religious art for its theological content. For example, Jaraslov Pelikan's and Margaret Miles's efforts to track the development of the Christian tradition through analysis of both verbal and visual texts have been rightly lauded, but unfortunately seldom followed.[27] One exception is the recent work of John Drury, who examines the religious meaning of various works of art from the National Gallery, London.[28] Our project, while deeply indebted to the approach of Pelikan and Miles, differs from theirs and Drury's in scope and emphasis. We attempt to trace portrayals of individual artists of specific scenes unique to Luke's version of the public ministry. This limited scope has enabled us to examine our topic in much more detail, and hopefully has prevented us from making some of the overgeneralizations often associated with such interdisciplinary studies.

Though we allow each text and its visual depiction to determine the particular issues to be pursued, in the subsequent chapters devoted to analysis of particular images and texts, we follow a common strategy for each painting. Each of those chapters begins with an overview of the biblical passage and its subsequent interpretation, pointing out significant rhetorical features and the overarching theological argument of the text, as well as outlining a brief summary of its subsequent interpretation in the ecclesiastical literature.[29] Next, we contextualize the selected work of art by giving a brief biography of the artist, placing the work within the artist's own *oeuvre*, discussing what is known of the patronage of the specific image, and exploring important social, political, and religious factors that may facilitate our understanding of the painting. A stylistic and iconographic analysis leads into brief hermeneutical reflections about how this visual interpretation might inform the church's reading of Scripture.

In addition to beginning with a rhetorical overview of the chosen text from Luke, we place the chapters in the canonical order of Luke's presentation, rather than in the chronological order of the composition. While we give ample attention to the historical context of each painting, this canonical arrangement allows us to keep the focus on the Gospel of Luke itself and to explore the painting as a visual exegesis of that text.

Notes

1. See Margaret M. Miles, "Achieving the Christian Body: Visual Incentives to Imitation of Christ in the Christian West," in Heidi J. Hornik and Mikeal C. Parsons, eds., *Interpreting Christian Art* (Macon, Ga.: Mercer University Press, 2004), 20–21. This appeal to the public ministry is made all the more attractive, as Miles points out, by our aversion to suffering and our enhanced "capacity to relieve suffering, or at least to keep suffering out of sight."

2. See, e.g., Anne Derbes (*Picturing the Passion in Late Medieval Italy* [Cambridge: Cambridge University Press, 1996]), who traces the shift in thirteenth- and fourteenth-century Italian art from a focus of the *Christus Triumphans*, "triumphant Christ" (even in crucifixion scenes), to an emphasis on *Christus Patiens*, the "suffering Christ." See also Walter Haug and Burghart Wachinger, eds., *Die Passion Christi in Literatur und Kunst des Spatmittelaters* (Tübingen: Max Niemeyer Verlag, 1993). On the emergence of passion devotion in medieval culture, see A. A. MacDonald, H. N. B. Ridderbos, and R. M. Schlusemann, *The Broken Body: Passion Devotion in Late-Medieval Culture* (Groningen: Egbert Forsten, 1998), who claim in the preface (ix): "During the late Middle Ages, devotion to the Passion of Christ, which for centuries had been an important theme in the experience and practice of Christians, was accorded a quite new level of significance."

3. See Wolfgang Helbig, *Führer durch die offentlichen Sammlungen klassicher Altertumer in Rom* (rev. ed.; ed. Hermine Speier; Tübingen: E. Washmuth, 1966), 861–63. For other ass-headed Christs, see Andre Leclerq, "Baptême," in *Dictionnaire d'archeologie chrétienne et de liturgie* (ed. Fernand Cabrol, et al.; Paris: Letouzey et Ané, 1907), 1: col. 2041–47.

4. For an alternative interpretation, see Thomas F. Mathews, *The Clash of Gods: A Reinterpretation of Early Christian Art* (rev. and expanded ed.; Princeton, N.J.: Princeton University Press, 1999), 50.

5. This fact, of course, stands in juxtaposition to the literary record, in which from the time of the earliest Christian writer, Paul, the suffering and death of Jesus were of *central* importance. One might rightly ask why there are no images of the crucifixion in early Christian art, given their preponderance in later times. Why are there no depictions of the crucified Christ in early Christian art? Robin Jensen has offered several responses to this question (*Understanding Early Christian Art* [London: Routledge, 2000], 143–48):

- Early Christians were unwilling to represent visually the instrument of shame and stigma, especially in times of persecution and ridicule.

- Early Christian visual depictions, with their lack of attention to the "true humanity" of Jesus (expressed in his birth and death), were potentially heterodox expressions.

- Early Christian art reflects the tradition of popular Christian piety, which was more enamored with Jesus the wonderworker rather than the Christ of doctrinal and theological reflection.

- Early Christian art may be more subtle and complex than previously noticed, and it may be questioned whether there is a complete absence of crucifixion imagery, Jensen argues (contra Graydon Snyder, *Ante Pacem: Archaeological Evidence of Church Life before Constantine* [Macon, Ga.: Mercer University Press, 1985]; see now Snyder's concession in "Agape, Eucharist and Sacrifice in Early Christian Art," in Hornik and Parsons, eds., *Interpreting Christian Art*, 60, that "the crucifixion may have been portrayed by the Sacrifice of Isaac").

6. The "wand" seen here in Jesus' hand in the raising of Lazarus was a common iconographical attribute in these early Christian depictions of Christ's miracles. For a discussion of the significance of the wand, see Mathews, *The Clash of Gods*, 54–59.

7. Ibid., 62. Mathews is here attempting to refute what he calls the "emperor mystique," the view perpetuated by Andre Grabar, and subsequently widely held among historians of early Christian art, that the earliest Christian images of Christ were attempts to shape Christ in the image of the emperor.

8. Ibid., 91. For the details of his argument leading to this conclusion, see chap. 2 of his book, "The Magician."

9. One reason for this is pragmatic. Most of the Gospel healing stories that have been popular subjects in art are not unique to Luke, and conversely, the few healing stories that are unique to Luke (the raising of the son of the widow of Nain, the man with dropsy, etc.) were not popular subjects in the visual tradition.

10. Despite her comments quoted above, neither do we think that Professor Miles would eschew using visual depictions of the passion/resurrection narratives for contemporary devotional practices. Her comments demonstrate the difficulty, but not the impossibility, of such an exercise; the difficulty might actually increase the desirability of such an enterprise. In fact, we plan to devote a next volume to paintings of scenes unique to the Lukan passion and resurrection narratives.

11. Heidi J. Hornik and Mikeal C. Parsons, *Illuminating Luke: The Infancy Narrative in Italian Renaissance Painting* (Harrisburg, Pa.: Trinity Press International, 2003).

12. For the various views of the ending of the journey narrative, see David Moessner, *Lord of the Banquet: The Literary and Theological Significance of the Travel Narrative* (Minneapolis: Fortress Press, 1989).

13. The following paragraphs are taken from the introduction to Hornik and Parsons, *Illuminating Luke: The Infancy Narrative in Italian Renaissance Painting,* 5–9.

14. See Wolfgang Iser, *The Act of Reading: A Theory of Aesthetic Response* (Baltimore: The Johns Hopkins University Press, 1978), esp. 85. On the history of reception theory and especially on the contributions of Robert Jauss and Wolfgang Iser to its theoretical foundations, see Robert C. Holub, *Reception Theory: A Critical Introduction* (London: Metheun, 1984).

15. Erwin Panofsky, "Iconography and Iconology: An Introduction to the Study of Renaissance Art," in *Meaning in the Visual Arts* (Chicago: University of Chicago Press, 1955), 26–54.

16. Ibid., 38.

17. Ibid., 31.

18. Ibid., 30.

19. Ibid.

20. John Shearman, *Only Connect . . . Art and the Spectator in the Italian Renaissance* (Princeton, N.J.: Princeton University Press, 1992), 4.

21. Ibid., 4–5.

22. Paoli Berdini, *The Religious Art of Jacopo Bassano: Painting as Visual Exegesis* (Cambridge: Cambridge University Press, 1997), 35.

23. Clearly here we have moved beyond Berdini's interest.

24. See Krister Stendahl's classic formulation of this method in "Biblical Theology, Contemporary," *Interpreter's Dictionary of the Bible* (ed. George Buttrick; 5 vols.; Nashville: Abingdon Press, 1962), 1:418–32.

25. Unless noted, the texts of the Bible are from the Douay translation (originally published in 1609–10).

26. See Brevard Childs, "The *Sensus Literalis* of Scripture: An Ancient and Modern Problem," in *Beiträge zur Alttestamentlichen Theologie* (ed. Herbert Donner et al.; Göttingen: Vandenhoeck & Ruprecht, 1977), 80–93; David Steinmetz, "The Superiority of Precritical Exegesis," in *A Guide to Contemporary Hermeneutics* (ed. Donald K. McKim; Grand Rapids: Eerdmans, 1986), 65–77.

27. See Jaraslov Pelikan, *Jesus through the Centuries* (New Haven: Yale University Press, 1985); and Margaret R. Miles, *Image as Insight: Visual Understanding in Western Christianity and Secular Culture* (Boston: Beacon Press, 1985).

28. John Drury, *Painting the Word: Christian Pictures and Their Meaning* (New Haven: Yale University Press, 1999).

29. In the brief history of interpretation of the text, we are following the lead, for example, of commentators like François Bovon (*Das Evangelium Nach Lukas. 2. Teilband Lk 9:51–14.35* [Evangelisch-katholischer Kommentar zum Neuen Testament; Zürich: Benziger Verlag, 1996]) and Ulrich Luz (*Matthew: A Commentary* [trans. Wilhelm Linss; Minneapolis: Augsburg, 1989]), both of whom write of the "*Wirkungsgeschichte*" of the text, which may be roughly translated the "history of influence."

Figure 2-1. Michele Tosini. *Baptism of Christ.* c. 1565. Oil on panel. Pinacoteca Nazionale, Ferrara. Photo. Pinacoteca Nazionale, Ferrara.

Chapter Two

The *Baptism of Christ* by Michele Tosini

(Luke 3:21–22; 4:1–13)

IN A VOLUME dedicated to the public ministry of Christ, we begin where Jesus began his public ministry, with his baptism. The baptism narrative, however, does not fit neatly into the "scenes unique to the Gospel of Luke" premise that we followed in our first book.[1] Rather, the baptism of Christ appears in the Gospels of Mark (1:9–11), Luke (3:21–22) and Matthew (3:13–17). The *Baptism of Christ* by Michele Tosini, c. 1565, today in the Pinacoteca Nazionale, Ferrara (Figure 2-1) was selected because it not only depicts Jesus praying while John the Baptist holds a plate of water over his head, but it also illustrates the three temptations of Jesus by Satan.[2] This temptation story occurs in Luke (4:1–13) and Matthew (4:1–11). The temptation stories in both gospels immediately precede the inauguration of Jesus' Galilean ministry. We argue that the three temptations in the Tosini painting should be read counterclockwise from right to left (stones to bread, all the kingdoms of the world [Figure 2-2], pinnacle of the temple in Jerusalem [Figure 2-3]). This reading follows the narrative of Luke only as the order of the last two temptations in Matthew is reversed. We explore the implications of this order for both Matthew and Luke in the biblical overview of the passage below.

Overview of the Biblical Text

[21]Now it came to pass, when all the people were baptized, that Jesus also being baptized and praying, heaven was opened; [22]And the Holy Ghost descended in a bodily shape, as a dove, upon him. And a voice came from heaven: Thou art my beloved Son. In thee I am well pleased. (Luke 3:21–22, DOUAY-RHEIMS BIBLE)

[1]And Jesus being full of the Holy Ghost, returned from the Jordan, and was led by the Spirit into the desert, [2]For the space of forty days; and was tempted by the devil. And he ate nothing in those days. And when they were ended, he was hungry. [3]And the devil said to him: If thou

11

Figure 2-2. Michele Tosini. Top detail of *Baptism of Christ.*
Pinacoteca Nazionale, Ferrara. Photo. Pinacoteca Nazionale,
Ferrara.

be the Son of God, say to this stone that it be made bread. [4]And Jesus
answered him: It is written, that Man liveth not by bread alone, but by
every word of God. [5]And the devil led him into a high mountain, and
shewed him all the kingdoms of the world in a moment of time; [6]And
he said to him: To thee will I give all this power and the glory of them;
for to me they are delivered, and to whom I will, I give them. [7]If thou
therefore wilt adore before me, all shall be thine. [8]And Jesus answering
said to him: It is written: Thou shalt adore the Lord thy God, and him
only shalt thou serve. [9]And he brought him to Jerusalem, and set him
on a pinnacle of the temple and he said to him: If thou be the Son of
God, cast thyself from hence. [10]For it is written, that He hath given his
angels charge over thee that they keep thee. [11]And that in their hands
they shall bear thee up, lest perhaps thou dash thy foot against a stone.
[12]And Jesus answering, said to him: It is said: Thou shalt not tempt
the Lord thy God. [13]And all the temptation being ended, the devil
departed from him for a time. (Luke 4:1–13, Douay-Rheims Bible)

Rhetorical Shape of Baptismal Narrative

Few dispute the historicity of the account of John's baptism of Jesus. Lars
Hartman's comments are typical: "There can be no doubt that Jesus really
did join John and was baptized by him, because without the compulsion

Figure 2-3. Michele Tosini. Left detail of *Baptism of Christ*. Pinacoteca Nazionale, Ferrara. Photo. Pinacoteca Nazionale, Ferrara.

of historical facts, early Christian narrators would hardly have thought of reporting that their Lord Jesus submitted to the baptism of repentance for the forgiveness of sins."[3] Despite this widespread consensus, there are significant differences in the canonical accounts of Jesus' baptism, and a brief rehearsal of those differences will bring the distinctively Lukan features into bolder relief.[4]

In John, the Spirit's descent as a dove (presumably at the baptism) upon Jesus identifies Jesus to John in order that John may disclose his identity to Israel (John 1:31–34). The heavenly voice in Matthew seems to address the audience attending Jesus' baptism: "This is my beloved son . . ." (Matt 3:17). Furthermore, Matthew contains an exchange between John and Jesus, unique among the canonical Gospels, that evidently anticipates later discussions as to why Jesus submitted to John's baptism of repentance, even though he, Jesus, was not a sinner (see Jerome's comments below under history of interpretation): "John would have prevented him saying, 'I need to be baptized by you, and do you come to me?' But Jesus answered him, 'Let it be so now, for thus it is fitting for us to fulfill all righteousness'" (Matt 3:14–15, NRSV). Mark's baptismal narrative is "an empowering of the Son of God for his battle with Satan and the demonic powers (Mark 3:22–27)."[5] It is also the most personal of the accounts, given that the voice from heaven addresses Jesus directly: "You are my beloved son; with you I am well pleased" (Mark 1:11).

Luke's account agrees with Mark in making the heavenly voice a personal revelation ("*You* are my beloved son" — Luke 3:22) rather than a

public declaration (cf. Matthew, "*This* is my beloved son") and also in seeing the Spirit's descent as empowering Jesus in his struggle against Satan.
But several elements are distinct to the Lukan account. First, there is the
emphasis of the Holy Spirit descending upon Jesus *in bodily form* as a dove
(3:22).[6] This corporeal emphasis is paralleled by the Pentecost scene in
Acts where the Spirit descends "like the rush of a mighty wind" and "like
tongues of fire" (Acts 2:1–2). A second detail, unique to Luke, is the note
that the Holy Spirit descends (after the baptism), while Jesus was praying.
Of course, Jesus at prayer is a common theme throughout Luke (see 5:16;
6:12; 9:18, 28–29; 11:1; 22:32, 39–46; 23:46).[7]

In order to understand the meaning of the baptism of Jesus in the Third
Gospel, we must explore the significance of John's baptism as presented in
Luke. In addition to the references to John's baptism found in Luke 3:1–
20, Acts — the sequel to Luke — refers to the baptism of John on several
occasions (Acts 1:5, 21; 10:37; 11:16–18; 13:24–25; 18:24–26; 19:1–7).
The cumulative effect of these references is to underscore certain features
of John's baptism.

- It was a "repentance baptism" "in which cleansing and moral
  uprightness are tied together."[8]

- John's baptism held out "the promise of deliverance and restoration
  in the forgiveness of sins."[9]

- Finally, John's baptismal ministry meant a redefinition of the people
  of God. The "children of Abraham" would now include all those who
  bore the "fruits that befit repentance," a people that would include
  tax collectors and soldiers (who were most likely not Jewish), and
  even stones (Luke 3:8)!

As such, John's baptism, for Luke, was not *inherently* inadequate as some
have argued. Rather, in the Lukan writings it points in a Christological
direction. Thus, for example, though they all only know the baptism of
John, Apollos differs from the disciples in Ephesus (Acts 19:1–7), in that
he is able to teach accurately concerning Jesus (Acts 18:24–28), while the
disciples of John represent a distortion, because in them John's baptism
has not been "realized through faith in Jesus and reception of the Spirit."[10]

But why does Jesus submit to John's baptism? Jesus identifies with John's
baptism by participating in it. The question, of course, is what this participation means.[11] For Luke, at least, it seems Jesus came to fulfill his
messianic vocation as a representative person in the kingdom of God,
who stands in solidarity with the sinners in need of deliverance (who
have come to John for the baptism of repentance) *and* who represents

the interests of God, the universal Sovereign.[12] The baptism of Jesus and the subsequent sending of the Spirit as confirmation of his vocation as Messiah provide the context within which to understand the temptations of Christ where Jesus "faces, not the impossibility of his being a Messiah, but the possibilities of His way as Messiah; and the ways He declined were those which would have destroyed His solidarity with the people He had come to save."[13] We now turn our attention to that temptation narrative.

Rhetorical Shape of Temptation Narrative

The temptation of Jesus stands at the beginning of his public ministry in both Matthew and Luke.[14] Both Gospels mention that Jesus was in the desert for "forty" days, a period reminiscent of Israel's "forty" years of wandering in the desert. In fact, the content of the tests that Jesus not only endures, but passes, correspond to the tests that Israel faced in the wilderness, but failed. Hunger tempted Jesus, as it did Israel (Exod 16), but whereas Jesus rebukes the temptation with the words "Man is not to live on bread alone," the Israelites simply complain — first about the lack of bread (Exod 16:3) and then about the lack of variety in their diet (Num 11:6, "wherever we look there is nothing except this manna"). Jesus is tempted to test God's faithfulness as was Israel (Exod 17). But whereas Jesus rebuts Satan with the words "You are not to put the Lord your God to the test" (Matt 4:7//Luke 4:12), when Moses challenged the Israelites, "Why do you test the Lord?" (NRSV) the people continued to complain against Moses (Exod 17:2–3). Jesus is also tempted to engage in idolatrous acts by worshiping Satan, but he rebukes Satan with the words "You shall do homage to the Lord your God and worship him alone" (Matt 4:10//Luke 4:8). Israel, on the other hand, succumbed to the temptation to commit idolatry and fashioned gold in the image of a calf and worshiped it (Exod 32). For both Matthew and Luke, the specific content of the tests disclose that Jesus *is* Israel, God's son, who is called out of Egypt (see Matt 2:15) to complete Israel's exodus (see Luke 9:31).

The order of the temptations may be just as important as their specific content. Communication theorists have coined the phrase "recency effect" to refer to the way hearers and readers respond to the last information given about a character or a plot.[15] Often we are able to remember only the last thing a person said or the last deed a character performed. How a story ends leaves a lasting impression on the hearer and shapes impressions of the story as a whole. The ending of a story, then, is critical to its overall message. This is true not only of the end of an entire story, but also of the ways in which individual stories within a larger account are closed.

Recency effect plays a major role in understanding the function of the temptation narrative in both Matthew and Luke. The two storytellers record the same three temptations (often attributed to a common source, "Q"), but they do not present the temptations in the same order. The first temptation is the same in both: Jesus is tempted to turn stones into bread. The order of the next two temptations, however, is reversed:

Luke		Matthew	
Locale	*Temptation*	*Locale*	*Temptation*
1. desert	stones into bread	1. desert	stones into bread
2. "up"	worship devil	2. temple	throw self down
3. temple	throw self down	3. high mountain	worship devil

In Luke, the last temptation occurs on the pinnacle of the temple (Luke 4:9); in Matthew, the last temptation occurs on a "very high mountain" (Matt 4:8). According to the "recency effect," and assuming Matthew and Luke are competent storytellers, the last temptation of Christ in each Gospel is significant. An examination of the recurrences of the locale in the two Gospels confirms this thesis.

The last temptation in Matthew occurs on a "very high mountain" (4:8). Again, mountains in Matthew are a setting where significant events take place. This reference to a mountain is the first in Matthew, but there are several others (5:1; 14:23; 15:29; 17:1; 24:3; 28:16). Matthew 5:1 is the introduction to the Sermon on the Mount, where Jesus is depicted as the "new Moses" giving a "new law." Jesus is the Teaching Messiah. In 14:23, he is the Praying Messiah: Jesus "dismissed the crowd" and "went up the hill by himself to pray." In 15:29–31; 17:1–8, Jesus received great crowds who brought with them "the lame, blind, dumb, and crippled, and many other sufferers" and "he healed them." Jesus is the Healing Messiah. In 17:1ff., Jesus takes Peter, James, and John "up a high mountain" and is there "transfigured" "in their presence." He is the Glorified Messiah. In 24:3, he sits upon the mountain called Olivet and speaks about "the end of the age." He is the Eschatological Messiah. Finally, while Luke ends his Gospel with the disciples in the temple, Matthew ends his Gospel with the disciples going "to the mountain where Jesus had told them to meet him" (28:16), where Jesus gives them the "Great Commission," commanding them to make disciples of the Gentiles/nations. He is the Universal Messiah. Our text, Matt 4:8, fits perfectly into this pattern. In the last of the temptations of Jesus in Matthew, the devil takes Jesus to a "very high mountain" and offers him "all the kingdoms of the world in their glory" if Jesus will worship him. But Jesus responds, "You shall do homage to the Lord your God and worship him alone" (4:10). Jesus is the Obedient Messiah.[16]

In Luke's Gospel, the temple is the setting for several scenes including the opening and closing scenes. In every case but the last, the temple is the location of a conflict between God's agents and God's people.[17]

Text	God's People	God's Agent	Conflict
1:5–23	Zechariah	Gabriel	1:18–20
2:41–51	Jesus' parents	Jesus	2:48–50
19:45–48	religious leaders	Jesus	19:47

The opening scene (Luke 1:5–23) introduces the motif of conflict between the people of God and his agents. Zechariah — who, the narrator tells us, was "upright and devout, blamelessly observing all the commandments and ordinances of the Lord" (1:5–6) — is one of God's people. While in God's sanctuary, the temple, God's agent, an angel of the Lord (vv. 11, 19), appears to him. The conflict begins in 1:18 when Zechariah doubts the angel's prophecy that he and Elizabeth will have another son. The angel rebukes Zechariah, revealing to him that he is none other than Gabriel who was "sent to speak to you" (1:19). The conflict is resolved when Gabriel strikes Zechariah speechless until Elizabeth gives birth to John. This initial episode provides the type-scene for the other temple (and synagogue; cf. 4:16–30 6:6–11; 13:10–17) encounters. The tension seems to intensify with each subsequent conflict and reach a climax in the last temple conflict scene, where the tension is almost unbearable as God's people plot the death of God's agent (19:45–57).

How does the temptation narrative fit into this pattern? The last temptation occurring on the pinnacle of the temple both recalls the Zechariah episode and foreshadows the temple scene in Luke 19. Here, God's agent, Jesus, is in direct conflict not with God's people (as in Luke 1 and 19), but with God's adversary, Satan, on the pinnacle of God's house. The effect of this story is to set the other conflict scenes in a cosmic context and to make clear, at least from the narrator's point of view, that when God's people (Zechariah, the religious authorities) oppose God's agent (Gabriel, Jesus) they are choosing, perhaps unconsciously, to side with God's adversary, Satan.

The last temple scene in Luke depicts a resolution to the conflict. The Gospel concludes with the disciples returning to Jerusalem after the final departure of Jesus where they "spent all their time in the temple praising God" (24:53). By the end of the Gospel, then, the disciples have become the pious people of God, and no conflict exists between the people of God and the agent of God in God's house. They are obediently, joyously, and continually praising God in the temple.

The Baptism of Christ: History of Interpretation

By the second century the baptism of Jesus was widely discussed.[18] François Bovon suggests that there is evidence that Jesus' baptism was discussed in Jewish Christian circles even prior to the second century:

> Only in Jewish Christian writings do certain texts give evidence of older traditions about Jesus' baptism, which diverge in three different directions:
>
> 1. There is blatant embarrassment about a baptism for purification. Jesus, apparently pressured by his mother, defends himself: "Wherein have I sinned that I should go and be baptized by him?"[19]
>
> 2. Jesus fulfills Isa 11:2 through his baptism. He is the prophet who sums all prophets. Jesus is the preexistent son; he does not become God's only son through baptism but is recognized as such here.
>
> 3. The baptism is the moment at which Jesus becomes the Christ. God's Spirit unites with the human Jesus. Thus Cerinthus believed that the divine Christ in the form of a dove descended upon the human Jesus at his baptism, and from then on, Jesus proclaimed the unknown Father.[20]

Whatever the earliest reflections on the meaning of Jesus' baptism, by the fourth century the baptism was celebrated as part of the Feast of the Epiphany on January 6. The connection between Jesus' birth and his baptism, however, was made as early as the third century in the writing of Maximus of Turin:

> Today then is another kind of birth of the Savior. We see him born with the same sort of signs, the same sort of wonders, but with greater mystery. The Holy Spirit, who was present to him then in the womb, now pours out upon him in the torrent. He who then purified Mary for him now sanctifies the running waters for him. The father who then overshadowed in power now cries out with his voice. He who then, as if choosing the more prudent course, manifested himself as a cloud at the nativity now bears witness to the truth. So God says, "This is my beloved Son, in whom I am well pleased. Hear him." Clearly the second birth is more excellent than the first. The one brought forth Christ in silence and without a witness. The other baptized the Lord gloriously with a profession of divinity. From the one, Joseph, thought to be the father, absents himself. At the other,

God the Father, not believed in, manifests himself. In the one the mother labors under suspicion because in her condition she lacked a father. In the other she is honored because God attests to his son.[21]

Jesus' baptism had, so it was held, a soteriological benefit for believers. Tertullian, for example, comments: "Concerning our sacrament of water by which we are liberated to eternal life . . . We, little fishes, after the example of our ICTHUS Jesus Christ, are born in water, nor in any other way than by permanently abiding in water, are we safe."[22]

Likewise, Origen comments on the detail of the heavens being opened as a way for sins to be forgiven: "The Lord was baptized. The heavens were opened and the Holy Spirit came down upon him. . . . We should say that heaven was opened at the baptism of Jesus and for the plan of forgiving sins. These are not the sins of him 'who had committed no sin, nor was deceit found in his mouth' (1 Pt 2:22). The heavens were opened and the Holy Spirit came down for the forgiveness of the whole world's sins."[23]

Cyril of Alexandria expands the explanation of the need for Jesus' baptism, hinted at in Origen:

> But how then, they object, was he baptized and received the Spirit? We reply that he had no need of holy baptism. He was wholly pure and spotless, and the holiest of the holy. . . . Now at last we must explain God's plan of salvation. God, in his love of humankind, provided for us a way of salvation and of life. Believing in the Father, Son and Holy Spirit, and making this confession before many witnesses, we wash away all the filth of sin. . . . It was necessary, therefore, that the Word of the Father become for our sakes the pattern and way of every good work when he humbled himself to emptiness and deigned to assume our likeness. For it follows that he who is first in everything must set the example in this too. He commences the work himself in order that we may learn about the power of holy baptism and learn how much we gain by approaching so great a grace. Having been baptized, he prays that you, my beloved, may learn that never-ceasing prayer is a thing most fitting for those who have once been counted worthy of holy baptism.[24]

So also Cyprian:

> Although he himself was not a sinner, he did not disdain to bear the sins of others. Having put aside his immortality for a time, he suffered himself to become mortal, in order that though innocent he might be slain for the salvation of the guilty. The Lord was baptized by his servant, and he, although destined to grant the remission of

sins, did not disdain to have his body cleansed with the water of regeneration.[25]

Likewise Maximus of Turin, elsewhere in his sermon, follows this line of interpretation:

> Today, then, he is baptized in the Jordan. What sort of baptism is this, when the one who is dipped is purer than the font, and where the water that soaks the one whom it has received is not dirtied but honored with blessings? What sort of baptism is this of the Savior, I ask, in which the streams are made pure more than they purify? For by a new kind of consecration the water does not much wash Christ as submit to being washed.... Yet the Savior willed to be baptized for this reason — not that he might cleanse himself but that he might cleanse the waters for our sake.[26]

Medieval writers continued this focus on the moral dimensions of the baptism, emphasizing especially the humility of Christ exemplified by the baptism. Bernard of Clairvaux observed:

> Among the multitude of people He came to the baptism of John; He came like one of the people, He who alone was without sin. Who would have believed that He was the Son of God? Who would have thought that He was the Lord of majesty? Lord, how greatly you humiliated yourself; too much you hid yourself! But you could not conceal yourself from John.[27]

In the thirteenth-century *Golden Legend*, Jacobus de Voragine comments on the humility reflected in Christ's baptism while discussing the purification of Mary: "He willed also to be baptized, not that there was guilt to be purged, but that he might show the depth of his humility. Thus Christ chose to accept for himself all the remedies established against original sin, not because he had any need of them, but to manifest his humility and to show that these remedies were effective in their time."[28]

After a long meditation on the effects of Jesus' journey from Nazareth to the Jordan where he was to be baptized by John, ps.-Bonaventure also comments on the humility of Christ as exemplified in his subjecting himself to John's baptism:

> When he arrived at the Jordan, He found John, who was baptizing sinners, and a multitude, which had come for his preaching and honored him almost as Christ. Then the Lord Jesus said to him, "I pray you to baptize me together with these." And John looking at Him immediately recognized Him by virtue of the Spirit, feared, and

said reverently, "Lord, I should be baptized by you." And the Lord replied, "Remain quiet now; it is so we must fulfill every justice. Do not say this now and publicize me, for my time is not yet manifest or come, but baptize me. Now is the time for humility, and I wish to carry out every humility."

Here you will pay attention to humility, for this is the place to discuss it. And you must know that the gloss says at this point that humility has three degrees. The first is submission to a superior and not placing oneself before an equal. The second is submission to an equal and not placing oneself before an inferior. The third and highest is submission to the inferior. The third was reached at this time by Christ, who thus fulfilled every humility. See how His humility has grown since the previous chapter. Here He submitted Himself to His servant. He vilipends Himself and justifies and magnifies His servant. Consider how His humility grew in other ways. Up to now He lived as a humble, almost useless, and contemptible man; here He wished to appear as a sinner. John preached penance to sinners and baptized the Lord Jesus among them; and before them He wished to be baptized. . . . But was there not a danger here for Him who wished to preach, that He might be despised as a sinner? But the Master of humility did not want to go without humiliating Himself profoundly. Thus He wanted to appear what he was not, in his baseness and contemptibility, for our instruction.[29]

Ps.-Bonaventure contrasts the attitude of Christ with those of his readers and himself in a long excursus on humility.[30] The author then returns to the scene of the baptism and explores its salvific dimensions:

Now see carefully how the Lord of majesty undressed like every other man and entered the Jordan, into the cold waters in this period of great cold, and all for love of us. To effect our salvation He instituted the sacrament of baptism to wash away our sins. . . . In faith in baptism we are wedded to the Lord Jesus Christ. . . . Thus this festivity and this event are great and very beneficial. Today the church sings, which is united to the celestial Bridegroom, for Christ washed our sins in the Jordan for us.[31]

The Temptation Narrative: History of Interpretation

Likewise the temptation of Christ proved fertile ground for Christian meditation.[32] François Bovon has observed, "The history of the exegesis of Luke 4:1–13 is extraordinarily instructive because the life situations of the exegetes always influence their interpretation."[33]

Since Ambrose, there has been a persistent interpretation that connects the temptation narrative with an Adam typology.

> It is fitting that it be recorded that the first Adam was cast out of Paradise into the desert, that you may observe how the second Adam returned from the desert to Paradise. . . . Adam brought death through the tree. Christ brought life through the cross. Adam, naked of spiritual things, covered himself with the foliage of a tree. Christ, naked of worldly things, did not desire the trappings of the body. Adam lived in the desert. Christ lived in the desert, for he knew where he could find the lost. With their error canceled, he could recall them to Paradise. . . .
>
> So Jesus, full of the Holy Spirit, is led into the desert for a purpose, in order to challenge the devil. If he had not fought, he would not have conquered him for me.[34]

Origen draws a similar parallel with regard to the first temptation:

> . . . .since he knew that Christ was hungry, the devil came closer to him and attacked him openly. . . . He did not know that "the Son of God" had become man, for God concealed the inexpressible incarnation from him. So he assumed that Christ was a man who was pleasing to God because of his virtues. He was also jealous of him because of this honor just as he had been jealous of the old Adam. He was eager to cast this man down, just as he had cast Adam down. So he approaches Jesus and introduces the first temptation, that of gluttony, through which he had also captured the first Adam.[35]

A similar theme is found in Cyril of Alexandria: "Observe, I beg you, how the nature of man in Christ casts off the faults of Adam's gluttony. By eating we were conquered in Adam, by abstinence we conquered in Christ."[36] And Ephrem the Syrian sees the Adam typology in the third temptation, set on the temple: "[Satan] set [Jesus] up on the pinnacle of the temple. Satan wanted him to suppose that he who was a man could become God, by means of the Godly house, just as Satan had once made Adam suppose that he could become God by means of that tree."[37]

Ambrose also includes Eve in his contrast between the first and last "temptations": "Food had not persuaded Eve, nor had the forgetfulness of the commands deprived her. If she had been willing to worship the Lord alone, she would not have sought what was not due to her. So a remedy is given, which blunts the dart of ambition, so that we serve the Lord alone. Pious devotion lacks ambition."[38]

Augustine's comments, including a brief Adamic allusion in the form of the Serpent, are typical of the early interpreters' Christological focus — that is, their emphasis on the way in which the temptation narratives revealed the character of Christ:

> When the Lord had been tempted with this triple temptation — because in all the allurements of the world these three are to be found, either pleasure or curiosity or pride — what did the Evangelist say? After the devil had concluded every temptation — every kind, but of the alluring sort — there remained the other sort of temptation, by harsh and hard treatment, savage treatment, atrocious and ferocious treatment. Yes, there remained the other sort of temptation. The Evangelist knew this, knew what had been carried out, what remained, and so he said, "After the devil had completed every temptation, he departed from him until the time." He departed from him in the form, that is, of the insidious serpent. He is going to come in the form of the roaring lion. The one who will trample the lion and the cobra will conquer him. Satan will return. He will enter Judas and will make him betray his master. He will bring along the Jews, not flattering now, but raging. Taking possession of his own instruments, he will cry out with the tongues of all of them, "Crucify him, crucify him!" That Christ was the conqueror there, why should we be surprised? He was God almighty.[39]

Not all early interpreters shared this Christological focus. The Venerable Bede, for instance, saw in the temptation narratives a moral example for the faithful to follow:

> Soon after he had been baptized he performed a fast of forty days by himself, and he taught and informed us by his example that, after we have received forgiveness of sins in baptism, we should devote ourselves to vigils, fasts, prayers, and other spiritually fruitful things, lest when we are sluggish and less vigilant the unclean spirit expelled from our heart by baptism may return, and finding us fruitless in spiritual riches, weigh us down with a sevenfold pestilence, and our last state would then be worse than the first.[40]

This emphasis on finding a moral example from Christ's temptations continues through the medieval period. The author of *Meditations on the Life of Christ*, for example, draws spiritual lessons for believers from the example of Christ's temptations:

. . . while His Life was always and everywhere difficult and physically
painful, here it was especially so. With this example learn from Him
how to exercise yourself in these things. Here we are concerned with
four things that are good for spiritual exercise and assist each other in
a marvelous way, that is, solitude, fasting, prayer, and corporal suffering. Through these things we may truly arrive at purity of heart, which
is greatly to be desired, for within itself in some way it comprises all the
virtues. It includes charity, humility, patience, and all virtues, and the
removal of all vices, for with vice and lack of virtue there can be no purity of heart. . . . Solitude appears to provide the fulfillment of all these
things. One cannot pray properly with noise and clamor. . . . Therefore
follow the example of the Word and go in solitude, that is, part from
company whenever you can, and remain alone if you wish to be joined
to Him and see Him by virtue of purity of heart.[41]

Later, the Magisterial Reformer, John Calvin, would resist drawing any
direct comparison between Jesus' temptations and ours, claiming, "Fasting
brought Christ the distinction of divine glory."[42] Bovon amplifies Calvin's
logic: "Consequently, it would be mockery and detestable ridicule to imitate Christ. The temptation cannot be limited to gluttony, ambition, and
avarice."[43] Advocates of the Catholic Reformation, of course, would not be
expected to follow Calvin's mandate; in fact, one might expect such advocates (and their artists) to make direct counterclaims to such arguments,
reasserting a stream of the exegetical tradition that not only compared
Christ's baptism and temptation to the work of the first Adam, but saw in
it a potential resource for the devotional life of the baptized believer, who
was likewise "tempted in every way" (Heb 4:15).[44]

Introduction to the Life of the Artist

Michele di Jacopo Tosini was born on May 8, 1503, in Florence and lived
until October 26, 1577.[45] His father, Jacopo, was employed as a messenger for the Florentine Signoria.[46] Michele was a member of the parish of
S. Maria Novella in Florence when he wrote his testament on March 20,
1575.[47] According to the testament, Michele married a woman named
Felice, and together they had four children.[48] The testament begins with
Brother Santi, whose secular name remains unknown because that portion
of the document has been destroyed by fire. Brother Santi was a member
of the monastery of San Domenico in Fiesole at the time the testament
was written. The other son, presumed to be the eldest, is Baccio (c. 1530–
82). Baccio continued the workshop after Tosini's death. Michele also had

two daughters, both of whom became nuns. Dionora (1540–1606) entered the convent of San Vincenzo in Prato on December 31, 1553, under the direction of Caterina de'Ricci.[49] The second son, whose given name is unknown, took the name Fra Santi upon ordination into the monastery of S. Domenico in Fiesole.[50] Michele's youngest child, Lisabetta, joined the convent of S. Jacopo in Ripoli, a suburb of Florence.[51]

Ridolfo del Ghirlandaio (1483–1561), adopted father, teacher, and collaborator of Michele, was the son of Domenico Ghirlandaio.[52] At the time of the painting of the *Baptism of Christ*, c. 1565 (Figure 2-1), the Ghirlandaio workshop was under the sole guidance of Michele di Ridolfo.[53] Although Michele's artistic training began with Lorenzo di Credi (1459–1537) and continued in the shop of Antonio del Ceraiolo (d. 1525?), he received his most influential experience in the workshop of Ridolfo del Ghirlandaio. Ridolfo was known to contemporaries as one of the best draftsman in Florence and was much loved by everyone, particularly by Raphael.[54]

Giorgio Vasari (1511–74) remains the most important primary source for Michele today. Although recent scholarship warns that the writings of Giorgio Vasari must be read with scrutiny and trepidation, his statements regarding Michele's employment have proven, when compared to archival documents where available, to be highly accurate.[55] Perhaps this accuracy results from Vasari's serving as Michele's leading employment reference for the major public projects in Florence during the mid-sixteenth century. Vasari, also an employer and friend of Michele, explains the relationship between Michele and Ridolfo: Michele looked upon "Ridolfo as a father, and loved him, as one belonging to Ridolfo[;] he has always been and is still known by no other name but Michele di Ridolfo."[56] Vasari reports several collaborative works by Michele and Ridolfo during the 1530s and 1540s.[57]

Vasari states that Michele, following in the style of Ridolfo, approached the master so closely that, whereas at the beginning he received from Ridolfo a third of his earnings, they came to execute their works in company, and shared the profits equally.[58] Although Michele's works in the late 1540s and 1550s, unlike Ridolfo's, used the high *maniera* colors of Salviati, both artists continued to use the monumental compositions and figure types of Andrea del Sarto and Fra Bartolomeo.[59]

Michele's first individual works define him as a Florentine artist of the sixteenth century with the ability to observe and copy the styles of Bronzino, Salviati, and Vasari. Tosini's works from 1540 to 1560 have been critical to the dissemination of their styles in public projects as well as in private commissions.[60]

Michele's strong workshop training, familiarity with the art of his contemporaries, and participation in collaborative projects with Ridolfo del

Ghirlandaio secured the foundation necessary for him to progress towards an independent style in the 1550s, to become a participant in the major Florentine public projects of the 1560s, and to receive a broad range of private commissions in the 1560s and 1570s. Michele inherited the workshop from Ridolfo in the early 1560s.

Public Commissions

Upon the recommendation of Vasari, Michele became involved in the decoration of the Palazzo Vecchio by Cosimo I de'Medici in 1557.[61] Agnolo Bronzino (1503–72) had painted the frescoes in the Chapel of Eleonora from 1541 to 1543.[62] Francesco Salviati's (1510–63) fresco decoration in the Sala dell'Udienza had been completed twelve years earlier in 1545.[63] Through the careful study of Bronzino and Salviati and by working alongside Giovanni Stradano (1523–1605) and Giorgio Vasari, Michele learned the contemporary style of Florentine painting.[64]

Vasari also established a committee: the sculptors Montorsoli and Francesco da Sangallo, and the painters Agnolo Bronzino, Michele di Ridolfo, Ghirlandaio Tosini, and Pier Francesco di Sandro Foschi, to help him draft the constitution of the *Accademia del Disegno* in 1563.[65] Michele probably met and befriended Vincenzo Borghini, superintendent of the Foundling Hospital in Florence, the Innocenti, and the first to serve as the Duke's representative (*Luogotenente*) of the Accademia at this time through Giorgio Vasari.[66] Borghini may have also served as an advisor to this committee.

According to Vasari and Borghini, Michele was well known for his ability to attract a large number of talented artists to his shop and to train them well.[67] Michele's students are documented to have painted a major section of the catafalque for the grand funeral ceremony of Michelangelo in 1564[68] and to have participated in the painted decorations for the splendid Medici wedding of Francesco I and Giovanna of Austria in 1565.[69] A major problem with large workshops such as Michele's is distinguishing the hands of different artists.

Private Commissions

Recently, scholars have begun to study the direct influence of Michelangelo and his works of art on Mannerist artists. Michele di Ridolfo has been included alongside Pontormo and Bronzino in this group. The *Night*, *Aurora*, and *Venus* paintings by Tosini find their source in the Venus and Cupid works by Michelangelo and Pontormo.[70]

This second phase of Michele's life includes private patrons as well as religious commissions. Several of Tosini's works, namely, the *Venus and Cupid* in the Galleria Colonna, Rome (Figure 2-4), the *Adoration of the Shepherds* in

Figure 2-4. Michele Tosini. *Venus and Cupid.* c. 1570. Oil on panel. Galleria Colonna, Rome. Photo. Arte Fotografica, Rome, with permission from the Galleria Colonna, Rome.

the Museo Civici in Udine, the *Sacra Conversazione*, Church of Saints Peter and Paul in Castelnuovo Garfagnana, and the *Nativity* have been restored and/or x-radiographs made and have been illustrated alongside the results of these scientific findings.[71] Unfortunately, these studies do not offer further insight into patronage, iconography, or even dating and proper placement in the artist's oeuvre of the paintings.[72] Other documented commissions received by Michele between 1559 and 1577 included several paintings in the Monastero di S. Vincenzo, Prato, and the painted decoration of the tabernacle in the church of S. Maria della Quercia, Viterbo.[73]

A critical private commission completed by Michele Tosini and his workshop in 1561 was the chapel in the Villa Caserotta outside Florence.[74] The only contemporary reference to the Villa Caserotta is Vasari in the 1568 edition of *Le Vite*, where he states that Matteo Strozzi (d. 1541) commissioned several works of painting and sculpture.[75] Bottari, in his 1759 edition of *Le Vite*, was the first to attribute the fresco cycle in the chapel to Michele.[76] Milanesi, in 1878, maintains this attribution and states that the villa is owned by the Ganucci Cancellieri family.[77] Neither reference mentions the date of 1561 nor the exact location of the villa.[78] The chapel frescoes are in excellent condition and have undergone very little restoration except for some overpainting of the Latin inscriptions.[79] We return later to this chapel as the baptism of Christ narrative plays a fundamental part in the iconographic program of the Strozzi chapel under

Figure 2-5. Michele Tosini. *St. Mark.* 1561. Fresco.
Strozzi Chapel, Villa Caserotta, Paolini. Photo.
Heidi J. Hornik with permission.

the direction of Michele Tosini. The baptism narrative in Mark can be found clearly written on the open book of the Gospel writer on the chapel wall (Figure 2-5). This iconography of the baptism will be discussed below.

Portraiture

Portraits, both male and female, and bust-length female figures are part of the final phase of the oeuvre of Tosini.[80] This facial type was learned from Vasari during Michele's work with him in the Palazzo Vecchio in 1557. The elegant profile, long neck, small lips, and sunken eyes of St. Catherine become common to many female figures depicted by Michele, such as the securely attributed *St. Mary Magdalen* in the Museum of Fine Arts, Houston (Figure 2-6).[81] This painting illustrates the Vasarian *maniera* imitated by Michele Tosini.

Portraiture remains the most difficult area of connoisseurship for sixteenth-century painting. The male portrait type developed by Michele Tosini in the 1570s can be found in the heads of Christ and John the Baptist in the Ferrara *Baptism of Christ*, as discussed in greater detail below.

Figure 2-6. Michele Tosini. *St. Mary Magdalen.* c. 1570.
Oil on panel. Museum of Fine Arts. Photo.
With permission of The Museum of Fine Arts, Houston;
The Samuel H. Kress Collection.

Introduction to the Painting

The *Baptism of Christ* (Figure 2-1) was correctly attributed to Michele Tosini by Marco Chiarini in 1988.[82] The composition depicts John baptizing Christ and three scenes of the temptation of the devil prominently depicted from right to left in a counter-clockwise direction. The temptation scenes frame the baptism in a semicircular mode that draws the viewer's attention to them almost immediately. Michele's mature style is seen throughout the painting. The standing figures of John and Christ are reminiscent of the San Vincenzo altarpiece (Figure 2-7) in Prato, a documented work from 1559 to 1561.

The Ferrara *Baptism* and the Strozzi Chapel fresco cycle both define Michele's mature style. They serve as documents of his knowledge of the New Testament, his ability to develop and execute complex iconographic programs, and to experiment with unconventional painted narratives.

The most vivid colors of *changeant* pink and mauve are placed on the loincloth Christ wears, the front of the temple building, and on the robes

Figure 2-7. Michele Tosini. *Madonna and Child with Saints.* 1559–61.
Oil on panel. Convent of San Vincenzo, Prato. Photo. Heidi J. Hornik
with permission from the Convent of San Vincenzo, Prato.

of the figure of Christ in the temptation of the devil scenes. John's hair-
shirt has a pale blue neckline that draws attention to his strained neck
muscles and strong face. The facial figures of both men recall the four
evangelists in the Strozzi Villa Caserotta frescoes documented 1561. The
ground on which the figures stand is based partially in reality and part
in fantasy and painted in the style seen in the Penn State *Madonna
and Child with St. John the Baptist* (Figure 2-8). The elegant fingers and
profiles learned from Vasari are also depicted in the figures of Christ
and John.

The male portrait type of Michele Tosini is also found in the key figures of the *Baptism*. Michele began to develop this distinguished bearded
male figure in the 1560s. He included contemporary portraits, which can
be seen in the figures of the *Marriage of Cana* (Figure 2-9) in the documented Strozzi fresco cycle dated 1561 at the Villa Caserotta. By the time
of the *Baptism*, c. 1575, Michele's style was mature and individualized.
He never forgets his training and employment as a landscape painter. His
time in the Palazzo Vecchio under the direction of his friend Giorgio Vasari

Figure 2-8. Michele Tosini. *Madonna and Child with St. John the Baptist.* 1545–50. Oil on panel. With permission from the Palmer Museum of Art, The Pennsylvania State University.

was well spent in allowing him to formulate a name for himself and go on to commissions, both private and public, for patrons such as the Strozzi family.

Many of his mature works include neatly arranged cityscapes carefully tucked into the background and, in a way, serve as a Tosini trademark. The far left background of the Ferrara *Baptism* panel possesses such a trademark. This particular cityscape, unidentifiable with any known medieval city, fades to white in an atmospheric haze and depicts a triumphal arch, a cylindrical fortress, a long basilica, and several other buildings.

The temple of Jerusalem is necessary for the narrative, and therefore is more prominently displayed in the left middleground of the painting. Tosini has previously depicted recognizable or identifiable architecture in his paintings when it is of importance to the biblical narrative or to the patron of the commission. The Certosa of Galluzzo was depicted in the S. Jacopo altarpiece (Figure 2-10) probably at the request of the bishop who lived, worked, and was buried in the Certosa.

Figure 2-9. Michele Tosini. *Marriage at Cana.* 1561. Fresco. Strozzi Chapel, Villa Caserotta, Paolini. Photo. Heidi J. Hornik with permission.

The Baptism — A Personal Precedent

As is customary in Tosini paintings, the details of the composition are determined by the biblical narrative. The baptism of Christ appears in the gospels of Mark (1:9–10), Luke (3:21) and Matthew (3:13–17). Both Luke and Matthew give baptism stories that are followed with temptations by Satan. Although the temptations are included in this painting, Michele's previous work with the baptism narrative was in the form of the written text of yet another Gospel writer's version, namely, Mark. Michele clearly prints the text of Mark 1:9–10 on the open book of the Gospel writer in the Strozzi Chapel fresco cycle of 1561.[83] Saint Mark, to the left of the chapel's exterior door, is almost a mirror image of Luke. Luke holds a gospel book with the beginning verses of the Annunciation (Luke 1:26–28) almost entirely visible.[84]

Stylistically, these two evangelists and the details of the painting in which they are featured are characteristic of Tosini. This distinguished bearded man can be seen as a type in this cycle and also occurs in Michele's later portraits and religious work, including the *Baptism of Christ* in Ferrara.[85] The building in the upper left corner of the Mark painting is the Villa Caserotta as it appeared during the time of the Strozzi patrons, and the town in the distance may be San Casciano.[86]

Iconographically, Michele uses the biblical texts to move his narrative cycle in the Strozzi chapel and the Ferrara altarpanel. Although Mark's

Figure 2-10. Michele Tosini and Ridolfo del Ghirlandaio.
*Madonna and Child with Sts. James, Lawrence, Francis and
Clare and Bishop Buonafè*. c. 1540. Museo di San Salvi,
Florence. Photo. With permission from the Ministero dei
Beni e le Attività Culturali, Florence.

right arm partially obscures the text in the Strozzi chapel fresco, it is clearly
one of the two references to the baptism that Michele makes in the chapel
iconography. Luke 3:21, the second reference to Christ's baptism, is in-
scribed across the altar wall. The iconographic key to the program of the
chapel is found in the events associated with January 6, the date of Epiphany
in the church's liturgical calendar.[87] On this date, the Feasts of the Adoration of the Magi, the Marriage at Cana, and the baptism of Christ were all
observed in the sixteenth-century church. This holy day (with its emphasis
on Christ's baptism) was one of the most important to Florentines because
John the Baptist is the patron saint of the city.[88]

The third inscription in the Strozzi chapel, referring to the antiphon to
the Benedictus prayed at Epiphany, begins above the door on the *Adoration*
wall and continues across the altar wall and concludes above the opposite
door on the *Marriage at Cana* wall. This is the second reference to the
baptism of Christ: "Today Christ has turned to be baptized by John in the

Jordan so that he may save us."[89] Beneath the inscription and flanking the *Lamentation* altar panel are the depictions of the Evangelists Matthew and John, respectively.[90] Given the two inscriptions that refer to the baptism of Christ, a modern viewer might still expect the baptism, rather than a Lamentation, to be depicted in the altar panel.[91] But for Tosini's audience, who would have been steeped in the biblical tradition and its liturgical interpretation, the connection between Christ's baptism and his death would have seemed natural.[92]

According to the Gospel of Mark, Christ himself understood his impending death as a baptism when he asked James and John: "Are you able to drink the cup that I drink, or *be baptized with the baptism that I am baptized with?*" (Mark 10:38, NRSV, author's emphasis). Elsewhere Christ refers to his Passion as a baptism in Luke 12:50: "I have a baptism with which to be baptized, and what stress I am under until it is completed!" The identification of Jesus' baptism with his suffering and death is further strengthened by the inscription, "Christus" and "Ioanne," which flank the altar piece above the evangelists Matthew and John.[93] Like John the Baptist before him, Christ would not be recognized and would suffer at the hands of Herod (see Mark 6:14–16). The baptism is thus linked to the Lamentation, an event of the Passion. The metaphor of baptism for Christ's martyrdom was continued in postbiblical times, as witnessed by its use in the writings of John Chrysostom.[94]

Michele continues this biblical and iconographical program, based on the baptism stories, in the arch over the altar. The arch is decorated with two angels who hold banderoles with the inscription, "This is my beloved son, in whom I am well pleased" from Matt 3:17.[95] These words are spoken by God the Father during the baptism of Christ and then again during the Transfiguration (Matt 17:1–8//Mark 9:2–8//Luke 9:28–36). That God's good pleasure with Christ included not only Christ's baptism, but also his obedience to death, is made clear in Luke's account of the Transfiguration where Luke reports that Moses, Elijah, and Jesus were "speaking of his [Christ's] departure, which he was about to accomplish at Jerusalem" (Luke 9:31).[96] The inscriptions are integrated into this message. The apostle's sufferings are in continuity with Christ's suffering (Phil 1:21); the servant faithful who is distributing food must ultimately be faithful because his life depends upon it (Matt 24:45–51).

The iconography of the Ferrara baptism scene is Lukan. Christ's hands are crossed in prayer, and his eyes and head are lowered as if in prayer as well as in a position to receive the Holy Spirit through the water John is about to pour on his head. The Lukan story continues in the placement of the temptations.

The Temptations — A Personal Innovation

The Strozzi chapel, with its complex iconography, shows Tosini's grasp of painting the narratives of the New Testament. In the Ferrara panel he formulates a painting from the details of a narrative that are recognizable as being taken from the Gospel of Luke. He not only paints the familiar baptism of Christ subject but creatively paints the rarely depicted scenes of the conversations between the devil and Christ known as the temptations. The temptations are not tucked into the background but, as stated above, are displayed prominently and beg for interpretation.

The visual depictions of the three temptation scenes are in the Lukan order defined above — 4:3, desert (stones to bread); 4:5–8, up (worship the devil); 4:9–13, temple (throw self down) — in a counterclockwise reading from right to left. Incorporation of these verses of Luke (4:1–9) when Jesus is tempted by Satan after the baptism narrative, is quite original.

Artistic Sources and Precedents for the Temptation Narratives

The devil and the temptation narratives cannot be found in early Christian art and appear rarely in medieval imagery.[97] It is even more obscure when they appear with the baptism of Christ.[98] Medieval art that does illustrate the devil shows him as a grotesque beast present at Apocalypse or Last Judgment scenes.[99] Luther Link explains:

> When it came to painting the Devil, artists had a difficult time indeed. There was no literary tradition to speak of and, more vexingly, there was no pictorial tradition at all. In the catacombs and on the sarcophagi, there is *no* Devil. The lack of a pictorial tradition combined with literary sources that confused Devil, Satan, Lucifer and demons are important reasons for the lack of a unified image of the Devil and for the erratic iconography.[100]

A new type of devil emerges in the fourteenth century: — the "tempter devil."[101] This figure depicts a fiendish deceiver who, in order to swindle its victims better under cover of devotion, assumes a disguise that conceals at least part of its monstrosity. In order to inform the spectator, the artist allows some of this creature's devilish attributes to appear through its clothing.[102] As the devil becomes more human, scenes of the conversation with Christ — the temptation narratives — also become more prevalent.

The increase in Renaissance depictions of the devil are credited to two artists, Coppo di Marcovaldo's Florence Baptistery mosaics of Hell (1280) and Giotto's *Judas' Betrayal* and the *Last Judgment* frescoes in the Arena Chapel, Padua (1304–13).[103] Both were easily accessible by fellow artists. Luther Link claims that Giotto was the only artist who could paint the devil.[104] Giotto's devil, an old black hairy man, was two-dimensional and painted in the Byzantine style because evil was real to Giotto physically, psychologically, and spiritually, but the devil was not.[105] Link's study also concludes, "The only major Renaissance painter of the Devil was Giotto; and the only major Renaissance sculptor of the Devil was Donatello. . . . Donatello's Devil is no more needed than the Devil in the Giotto fresco; he was put there reflexively because of traditional iconography. Apparently the Renaissance sculptor with the most exceptional range and intensity found the Devil of no interest."[106]

Ludovica Sebregondi disagrees with Link and claims that depicted devils in the Renaissance, instead, are so numerous and varied that it seems difficult to attempt to define or classify them. Some of the reasons for so many devils include: a proliferation of anthropomorphous devils; ancient prototypes continuing to survive even when new ones were added to, or associated with, them; and representations of the devil varying according to period, location, and artistic technique.[107] All scholars agree that there was a definitive change in the appearance and prevalence of devils in late fifteenth-century Florence, and in particular with the dawning of the year 1500.[108]

The Temptation Narratives by Tosini

The possible sources for the devil available to the Florentine Tosini are clear. He certainly knew the Coppo mosaics in the Baptistery and the Fra Angelico tempera on panel in San Marco (1432–35). He was also aware of the Giotto frescoes. A probable source for his own Temptations was Botticelli's *Temptations of Christ*, the second fresco from the altar end of the north wall of the Sistine Chapel. Perugino's *Baptism of Christ* immediately precedes the Botticelli *Temptations* on the wall. Carol Lewine argues that Botticelli's *Temptations* illustrates Matt 4:1–11, the Gospel lesson of the first Lenten Sunday.[109]

It should be remembered that Domenico Ghirlandaio, the father of Michele's teacher Ridolfo del Ghirlandaio, worked alongside Botticelli and Perugino in the Sistine Chapel in the 1480s under the patronage of Pope Sixtus IV della Rovere. Tosini would have had direct contact with Botticelli's interpretation of the temptations by either visiting Rome or through the cartoons, sketches, and drawings passed down or copied in the Ghirlandaio workshop that Tosini now directed.[110]

Christ's temptations in the Botticelli painting are seen from left to right in the middle ground. Tosini reverses the order of temptations, going from right to left and also shifts the Gospel text from Matthew to Luke. Tosini's previous work in the Strozzi chapel helps explain this latter change from

the First to the Third Gospel. For Tosini, the baptism of Christ had profound allusions to Christ's suffering and death. Faced now with executing
a painting that combined both the baptism and the temptation narratives,
Tosini was faced with a problem. As was shown above, both Mark (10:38)
and Luke (12:50) explicitly connect Jesus' baptism and death, but Mark
has no extended temptation narrative. Luke and Matthew have temptation
narratives, but Matthew does not make the link between Jesus' baptism
and death. So Tosini is "left," as it were, with the Third Gospel's version.

The figure of Christ is immediately identifiable in all three temptation
scenes by his light green gown with a pink mantle covering one shoulder.
The devil is a human being with a black face.[111] He, like Christ, wears the
same attire in all three narratives. His robe buttons vertically and has a red
cloth belt cinched at the waist and red hat.[112] His bat wings are partially
visible in the first and second scenes, but certainly not pronounced.[113] In
Tosini's version, the devil is more human than monstrous, though no less
deceptive and dangerous.

The Lukan scenes read from right in a counterclockwise direction. The
Temptation by Stones appears at the right side; the Temptation by the
Kingdoms of the World is at the center; and the Temptation by High Places
is at the left. The Temptation by Stones scene shows a hunched-over devil
in discussion with an attentive Christ.

"Command these stones be made bread" are the only words spoken by
Satan in the New Testament. One might expect a very dramatic response
from Jesus but instead Tosini, like his contemporaries, shows an attentive
Christ rather than one with a confident gesture of rejection. Link general-
izes about the psychology of the event: "Usually, the confrontation between
these adversaries is rather wooden because they face one other [sic] without the slightest interaction on any pictorial level. They are simply signs:
this is Jesus and that is Satan, and Satan is tempting Jesus."[114]

In the second temptation, the devil, now upright, leads him up and
shows him all the kingdoms of the world. The devil leans back with one
outstretched arm as if to gesture to all the worlds below them while his
left arm is almost vertical at his side but with finger pointing to the kingdoms below. Jesus raises his right hand about to respond, "It is written,
'Worship the Lord your God, and serve only him.'" The devil is rejected
a second time. By positing the second temptation (for Jesus to submit
himself to Satan's authority) above the baptism, Tosini invites the reader
to contemplate the relationship between these two scenes.[115] Christ, who
willingly and humbly submits himself to the baptism of John, will not
submit himself to the authority of Satan. Furthermore, Christ's humility is
naturally extended to his obedience in death. One can easily hear an echo

of the Philippians hymn, "Christ emptied himself, taking on the form of a slave; Christ humbled himself unto death, even death on a cross" (Phil 2). Hints of adamic Christology also appear here. Adam "served" the wishes of Satan, who in medieval thought had taken the form of the Serpent, but Christ, the second Adam, adamantly refuses to serve any but the Lord God. In fact, Christ would rather die than serve Satan. By being humbly and faithfully obedient to death, Christ, as second Adam, reverses the disobedience of the first Adam, which also led to death. The salvific benefits of the second Adam's death cancel the wages of death introduced by the first. Hence the Christological focus, underscored by the juxtaposition of the second Lukan temptation over the baptismal scene. Luke himself echoes these adamic parallels by placing Jesus' genealogy (which in Luke ends with the pronouncement that Adam is "Son of God") between the baptismal and temptation narratives, an emphasis no less subtly but effectively introduced by Tosini.

The viewer moves to the third temptation where Jesus and the devil stand, literally on top of the dome of the Jerusalem temple. Both seem quite precariously perched there. The pinnacle of the temple has been transformed into a round dome on top of a centrally planned church that has sculptural niches on the upper two levels. The base of the temple is square with a rectangular door, nonsculptural pediment above it, flanked by a single Doric column. Three steps lead to the portico. Jesus is more animated in this scene as the devil points downward and suggests that if Jesus is the Son of God, he should throw himself down and be protected by his angels. Jesus is responding by raising his right hand, which holds a small, white object that may be a Jewish Tefillah as he warns the devil not to put the Lord God to the test. In the final temptation, Tosini does not depict the angels ready to minister to Christ if he jumps, because he does not, in fact, leap. Botticelli, however, does depict the angels preparing a table for Jesus, as related in Matt 4:11, and continues to paint the narrative beyond Tosini's version by showing the devil, revealed in his hairy nakedness, jumping off the cliff.

Concluding Hermeneutical Reflections

The order of the temptation narratives (desert, "up," temple) combined with the prayerful Christ help to identify Tosini's painting as a depiction of the Lukan narrative rather than Matthew. We have seen in the Strozzi chapel program and now in the Ferrara *Baptism* that Tosini enjoys and understands the variations in Gospel narratives. He does not directly draw on apocryphal stories. Instead he recognizes the characteristics unique to a particular Gospel writer and incorporates those subtleties meticulously and in an informed manner.

In Tosini's earlier works the biblical passages and/or narrative details remain secondary to the visual image tradition. This is in keeping with the contemporary understanding of the relationship between text and image. In the Ferrara *Baptism*, Tosini is more creative in his placement of the temptation narratives and selection of the Lukan account. He does not simply copy the Botticelli painting of the same subject. He does not have a direct source for this visual interpretation. Tosini is incorporating text and image at a critical time in the history of Western civilization, and most definitely did not realize all the potential ramifications for such a combination. Michele Tosini as an experienced man in his sixties displays a mature artistic style. He has seen and studied much. He continues to be an active painter and Florentine citizen for another six years. He is struggling with the multiple meanings of the baptism of Christ, first in 1561 in the Strozzi chapel and then c. 1565 in a full-size altarpiece.

In concert with the exegetical tradition, Tosini sees two axes — Christological and anthropological — in these narratives. There is something unique about Christ's baptism. In it, Christ inaugurates his messianic vocation to be both representative agent of God and to stand in solidarity with sinners. This vocation is completed when Christ undergoes his baptism of suffering and death.

But there is an anthropological dimension to these scenes as well. In baptism we participate in the humility and suffering of Christ (see history of interpretation above). But temptations do come, more often in the garb of an exotic and strange tempter than a monstrous and grotesque figure. There is a certain "appeal" to Tosini's devil that might make resisting his temptations more difficult. Yet Tosini suggests that participation with Christ in baptism is the key not only to participation in his humility and suffering, but also provides the basis to overcome temptation and ultimately, through the cross, to defeat death itself.

Notes

1. Heidi J. Hornik and Mikeal C. Parsons, *Illuminating Luke. The Infancy Narrative in Italian Renaissance Painting* (Harrisburg, Pa.: Trinity Press International, 2003).

2. In the history of art, these two scenes are typically treated as separate and are rarely depicted together; on Jesus' baptism, see Gertrud Schiller, *Iconography of Christian Art* (trans. Janet Seligman; Greenwich, Conn.: New York Graphic Society, 1971), I.127–42, and Louis Réau, *Iconographie de l'art Chrétien* (Paris: Universitaires de France, 1957), II.2, 295–304; on the temptation narratives, see Schiller, I.143–45; Réau, II.2. 304–10. For the few scenes where the narratives are combined, see Schiller, I.142–43.

3. Lars Hartman, *"Into the Name of the Lord Jesus": Baptism in the Early Church* (Edinburgh: T & T Clark, 1997), 21. The standard treatment remains George Beasley-Murray, *Baptism in the New Testament* (Grand Rapids: Eerdmans, 1973). For other literature on Jesus' baptism (in addition to the standard commentaries and other essays cited below), see: Richard Erickson, "The Jailing of John and the Baptism of Jesus: Luke 3:19–21," *Journal of the Evangelical Theological Society* 36 (1993): 455–66; Günther Schwarz, " 'Wie eine Taube'? (Markus 1,10 par Matthäus 3,16; Lukas 3,21.22; Johannes 1,32)," *Biblische Notizen* 89 (1997): 27–29; Ben Aker, "New Directions in Lucan Theology: Reflections on Luke 3:21–22 and Some Implications," *Faces of Renewal* (Peabody, Mass.: Hendrickson, 1988), 108–27; Charles Dennison, "How Is Jesus the Son of God: Luke's Baptism Narrative and Christology," *Calvin Theological Journal* 17 (1982): 6–25.

4. On these differences, see especially Charles H. Talbert, *Reading Luke: A Literary and Theological Commentary on the Third Gospel* (rev. ed.; Macon, Ga.: Smyth & Helwys, 2002), 41–42.

5. Talbert, *Reading Luke*, 41.

6. On the various suggestions regarding the symbolism of the dove, see Leander E. Keck, "The Spirit and the Dove," *New Testament Studies* 17 (1970–71): 41–67. Although many baptismal scenes in the visual arts contain the image of a dove, it is impossible to attribute this element to Luke's Gospel, because all four Gospels mention a dove and because its visualization would demand its appearance in "bodily form." The element is missing in Tosini's version, a point to which we return later.

7. A point made by Talbert, *Reading Luke*, 42. Tosini picks up this element, we argue; see below.

8. Joel Green, "From 'John's Baptism' to 'Baptism in the Name of the Lord Jesus': The Significance of Baptism in Luke-Acts," in *Baptism, the New Testament and the Church* (ed. Stanley E. Porter and Anthony R. Cross; JSNTSS 171; Sheffield: Sheffield Academic Press, 1999), 163.

9. Ibid., 165.

10. Ibid., 169; cf. also Robert C. Tannehill, *The Narrative Unity of Luke-Acts: A Literary Interpretation* (2 vols.; Philadelphia: Fortress, 1986), 2:233–34.

11. On the various explanations, see Beasley-Murray, *Baptism in the New Testament*, 45–67.

12. On this dual role (as representative "man" in solidarity with sinners and as agent of the sovereign God), see ibid., 57–58. While Beasley-Murray (50–54) is probably right that Luke did not intend to suggest foreshadowings of Jesus' suffering in the baptismal narrative (though cf. Luke 12:50), that connection was made, as we shall see, in the subsequent history of interpretation, an interpretation that evidently had some influence on Michele Tosini.

13. Ibid., 60.

14. Among the recent literature on the temptation narratives (and in addition to the standard commentaries), see David Hester, "Luke 4:1–13," *Interpretation* 31 (1977): 53–59; Nicholas Taylor, "The Temptation of Jesus on the Mountain: A Palestinian Christian Polemic Against Agrippa I," *Journal for the Study of the New Testament* 83 (2001): 27–49; Robert Brawley, "Canon and Community: Intertextuality, Canon, Interpretation, Christology, Theology, and Persuasive Rhetoric in Luke 4:1–13," *Society of Biblical Literature Papers* 31 (1992): 419–34; Kim Paffenroth, "The Testing of the Sage: 1 Kings 10:1–14 and Q 4:1–13 (Lk 4:1–13)," *Expository Times* 107 (1996): 142–43; Christoph Kähler, "Satanischer Schriftgebrauch: Zur Hermeneutik von Mt 4,1–11/Lk 4,1–13," *Theologische Literaturzeitung* 119 (1994): 857–67; Hugh Humphrey, "Temptation and Authority: Sapiential Narratives

in Q," *Biblical Theology Bulletin* 21 (1991): 43–50; William Richar Stegner, "The Temptation Narrative: A Study in the Use of Scripture by Early Jewish Christians," *Biblical Research* 35 (1990): 5–17; Wilhelm Wilkens, "Die Versuchungsgeschichte Luk 4:1–13 und die Komposition des Evangeliums," *Theologische Zeitschrift* 30 (1974): 262–72; Dale Allison, "Behind the Temptations of Jesus: Q 4:1–13 and Mark 1:12–13," *Authenticating the Activities of Jesus* (Leiden: Brill, 1999), 195–213; Christopher Tucket, "The Temptation Narrative in Q," *Four Gospels 1992* (Louvain: Peeters, 1992), 479–507; François Bovon, "The Role of the Scriptures in the Composition of the Gospel Accounts: The Temptations of Jesus (Lk 4:1–13 par) and the Multiplication of the Loaves (Lk 9:10–17 par)," *Luke and Acts* (New York: Paulist, 1992), 26–31, 215–16.

15. See especially Menakhem Perry, "Literary Dynamics: How the Order of a Text Creates Its Meaning," *Poetics Today* 1 (1979): 35–64, 311–61.

16. On the theological significance of mountains in Matthew (but with different emphases), see Terence L. Donaldson, *Jesus on the Mountain: A Study in Matthean Theology* (JSNTSS 8; Sheffield: JSOT Press, 1985). This rhetorical effect is found in other literature as well. In Nathaniel Hawthorne's *The Scarlet Letter*, the scaffold scenes occur at the beginning, middle, and end. In the first scaffold scene, the sin of Hester Prynne is publicly disclosed and she is thrown into prison. In the second, Hester and Dimsdale meet in the middle of the night on the scaffold, Dimsdale confesses what Hester already knows, and the sky, some say, illuminates in the shape of a giant "A." In the final, climatic scene, the ailing Dimsdale ascends the scaffolding steps during a procession and discloses publicly his relationship with Hester just before he dies. Here the scaffold is the locus of revelation, public and private. So it is with mountains in Matthew; the mountain is the place of revelation. Obedient, teaching, praying, healing, glorified, eschatological, universal — these are characteristics of the Messiah that Matthew reveals in mountain scenes. It all begins with the temptation narrative. The last temptation of Christ in Matthew is the first of a series of disclosures, public and private, about the nature of Jesus' messiahship.

17. On this, see Mikeal C. Parsons, *The Departure of Jesus in Luke-Acts: The Ascension Narratives in Context* (JSNTSS 21; Sheffield: JSOT Press, 1987).

18. For more on the history of interpretation of the baptism of Christ, see Daniel A. Bertrand, *Le baptême de Jesus: Histoire de l'exegese aux deux premiers siècles* (Beiträge zur Geschichte der biblischen Exegese 14; Tübingen: Mohr-Siebeck, 1973); Bovon, *Gospel of Luke,* 1:131–32; Josef Strzygowski, *Iconographie der Taufe Christi* (Munich: Verlag von Theodor Riedel, 1895); Gunter Ristow, *Die Taufe Christi* (Recklinghausen: Verlag Aurel Bongers, 1965). See also Andre Leclerq, "Baptême" in *Dictionnaire d'archéologie chrétienne et de liturgie* (ed. Fernand Cabrol et al; Paris: Letouzey et Ané, 1907), 1:col.2041.

19. Jerome (*Adversus Pelagianos dialogi III* 3.2; PL 23.570B–571A) attributes this quotation to the Gospel of the Nazarenes. Edgar Hennecke provides the English translation for the Gospel of the Nazarenes in *New Testament Apocrypha II: Writings Related to the Apostles; Apocalypes and Related Subjects* (2 vols.; ed. William Schneemelcher; trans. R. RcL. Wilson; rev. ed.; Louisville: Westminster/John Knox, 1992), 1:160.

20. Bovon, *Luke,* 131.

21. Maximus of Turin, *Sermons* 13A; Ancient Christian Writers 50:34. Many of the following references are cited also in Arthur A. Just Jr., *Luke* (ed. Thomas C. Oden.; Ancient Christian Commentary on Scripture 3; Downers Grove, Ill.: InterVarsity Press, 2003). We use the translations found there, but in every case possible we have also consulted the text in its original language.

22. Tertullian, *On Baptism.*

23. Origen, *Homilies on the Gospel of Luke,* 27.5; Fathers of the Church 94:114.

24. Cyril of Alexandria, *Commentary on Luke, Homily 11*, Corpus Christianorum: Series Latina 80–81.

25. Cyprian, *The Good of Patience*, 6; Fathers of the Church 36:268.

26. Maximus of Turin, *Sermon 13A.3*; Ancient Christian Writers 50:35.

27. Bernard, *Sermones I in epiphania Domini* in *Patrologiae cursus completes*, series Latina (ed. J.-P. Migne; hereafter cited as PL), CLXXXIII, col. 145. This quotation is found also in the *Golden Legend*; see below.

28. Jacobus de Voragine, *The Golden Legend: Readings on the Saints* (trans. William Granger Ryan; Princeton, N.J.: Princeton University Press, 1993), 1:144.

29. Ps.-Bonaventure, *Meditations on the Life of Christ: An Illustrated Manuscript of the Fourteenth Century* (trans. Isa Ragusa and Rosalie B. Green; Princeton, N.J.: Princeton University Press, 1961), 106–7.

30. Ibid., 107–13.

31. Ibid., 114.

32. On the history of interpretation of Luke 4:1–13, see Bovon, *Luke*, 1:146–47; Klaus-Peter Koppen, *Die Auslegung der Versuchunggsgeschichte unter besonderer Berucksichtigung der Alten Kirche: Ein Beitrag zur Geschichte der Schriftauslegung* (Beiträge zur Geschichte der biblischen Exegese 4; Tübingen: Mohr-Siebeck, 1961); M. Steiner, *La tentation de Jésus dans l'interpretation patristique de Saint Justin a Origene* (Études bibliques; Paris: Gabalda, 1962).

33. Bovon, *Luke*, 1:146.

34. Ambrose, *Exposition of the Gospel of Luke*, 4.7.14; *Exposition of the Holy Gospel According to Saint Luke with Fragments on the Prophecy of Isaias* (trans. T. Tomkinson; Etna, Calif.: Center for Traditionalist Orthodox Studies, 1998), 115–16.119.

35. Origen, *Fragments on Luke*, 96; Fathers of the Church 94:165–67.

36. Cyril of Alexandria, *Commentary on Luke*, 12; Corpus Christianorum: Series Latina, 88.

37. Ephrem the Syrian, *Commentary on Tatian's Diatessaron*, 4.8B–C; *Saint Ephraem's Commentary on Tatian's Diatessaron: An English Translation of Chester Beatty Syriac MS 709* (trans. and ed. C. McCarthy; Journal of Semitic Studies Supplemental 2; Oxford: Oxford University Press, 1993), 87–88.

38. Ambrose, *Exposition of the Gospel of Luke*, 4.33–34; *Exposition of the Holy Gospel According to Saint Luke with Fragments on the Prophecy of Isaias* (trans. T. Tomkinson; Etna, Calif: Center for Traditionalist Orthodox Studies, 1998),126–27.

39. Augustine, *Sermon*, 284.5; *The Works of St. Augustine: A Translation for the Twenty-First Century* (ed. J. E. Rotelle; Hyde Park, N.Y.: New City Press, 1990), 3 8:91.

40. Bede, *Homilies on the Gospels* (trans. Lawrence T. Martin and David Hurst; Cistercian Studies 110 and 111; Kalamazoo, Mich: Cistercian Publications, 1991),1.12; Cetedoc 1367, 1.12.174; *Homilies on the Gospels* 1:119–20. Bede is noteworthy too for combining his comments on the temptation narratives with those on Christ's baptism, a combination we find repeated in Tosini's visual rendition.

41. Ps.-Bonaventure, *Meditations*, 117. In the meditation that follows, Ps.-Bonaventure follows the Matthean order of temptations (wilderness, temple, mountain). The author also includes a fascinating section that deals with what Christ ate after his testing was complete, suggesting that the ministering angels brought to him a meal prepared by his mother, Mary (*Meditations*, 123–27)!

42. John Calvin, *A Harmony of the Gospels Matthew, Mark and Luke* (trans. A. W. Morrison and Thomas Henry Louis Parker; 3 vols.; Grand Rapids: Eerdmans, 1972), 1:135.

43. Bovon, *Luke*, 1:146. Bovon (1:146) goes on to suggest that Karl Barth followed an interpretive path similar to Calvin's.

44. In this way, the Catholic Reformers anticipate modern interpreters of the temptation narrative who attempt to bring out "both axes of temptation, the Christological and the anthropological" (see Bovon, *Luke*, 1:147).

45. All biographical data on the artist in this article is based on the testament of the artist. See Heidi J. Hornik, "The Testament of Michele Tosini," *Paragone* 543–45 (1995): 156–67. The discovery of the testament not only reveals information regarding the personal life of the artist, new lines of patronage and commissions but also provides documentary evidence to support or dispute the claims of Tosini's biographers such as Giorgio Vasari and Sydney Freedberg. See Giorgio Vasari, *Le Opere di Giorgio Vasari: Le Vite de'più eccellenti pittori, scultori ed architettori scritte da Giorgio Vasari pittore Aretino* (1568) (ed. Gaetano Milanesi; 9 vols.; Florence: Sansoni, 1885), VI, 543–48. Vasari includes Michele in the second edition of *Le vite* in 1568, but does not discuss him in the 1550 edition.

See Heidi J. Hornik, "Michele di Ridolfo del Ghirlandaio (1503–77) and the Reception of Mannerism in Florence" (Ph.D. dissertation, Pennsylvania State University, 1990), which is the first (and only) monograph and catalogue raisonné of Michele Tosini. See also Sydney Freedberg, *Painting of the High Renaissance in Rome and Florence* (Cambridge: Harvard University Press, 1961), I, 589–90, and *Painting in Italy 1500–1600* (New York: Penguin, 1971), 239, 463.

46. Vasari-Milanesi, *Le vite*, VI, 543 n. 3.

47. It is uncertain when Michele joined the parish or whether he was born there. The baptismal records in the parish of S. Maria Novella have been lost for the year 1503.

48. Hornik, "Testament," 157, 161 n. 10. There is no existing document in the church of S. Maria Novella for this marriage.

49. Ibid., 161 n. 12.

50. Ibid., 162 n. 13.

51. Ibid., 157.

52. Vasari-Milanesi, *Le vite*, VI, 543. For the life of Ridolfo, see Vasari-Milanesi, *Le vite*, VI, 531–48; David Franklin, *Painting in Renaissance Florence 1500–1550* (New Haven and London: Yale University Press, 2001), 103–25. See also three articles by David Franklin, "Ridolfo Ghirlandaio and the Retrospective Tradition in Florentine Painting," in *Italian Renaissance Masters* (Milwaukee: The Haggerty Museum of Art, Marquette University, 2001), 17–23; "Towards a New Chronology for Ridolfo Ghirlandaio and Michele Tosini," *Burlington Magazine* 140 (1998): 445–55; "Ridolfo Ghirlandaio's Altar-Pieces for Leonardo Buonafé and the Hospital of S. Maria Nuova in Florence," *Burlington Magazine* 135 (1993): 4–16.

53. Marco Chiarini, "Una tavola fiorentina nel Museo di Ferrara (postilla per Michele di Ridolfo del Ghirlandaio," *Arte Cristiana* 76 (1988): 369–72; *La Pinacoteca Nazionale di Ferrara* (ed. Jadranka Bentini; Bologna: Nuova Alfa Editoriale, 1990), 111.

54. Vasari-Milanesi, *Le vite*, VI, 534.

55. See Patricia Lee Rubin, *Giorgio Vasari: Art and History* (New Haven: Yale University Press, 1995); Carl Goldstein, "Rhetoric and Art History in the Italian Renaissance and Baroque," *Art Bulletin* 73 (1991): 641–52; T. S. R. Boarse, *Giorgio Vasari, the Man and the Book* (Princeton, N.J.: Princeton University Press, 1979).

56. Vasari-Milanesi, *Le vite*, VI, 543. Vasari includes Michele in the second edition of *Le vite* in 1568, but does not discuss him in the 1550 edition. See Hornik, "Michele di Ridolfo," 2–3.

57. Vasari-Milanesi, *Le vite*, VI, 543–47. See Hornik, "Michele di Ridolfo," 25–56, 196–206, for a discussion of the collaborative works by Ridolfo del Ghirlandaio and Michele Tosini. See also Franklin, "Towards a New Chronology," 448–54, and specifically, 454 n. 39 for a useful "updating" of the works. S. Jacopo altarpanel with the Palmer

Museum and Museo Bandini panels, see Heidi J. Hornik, "Michele Tosini: The Artist,
The Oeuvre and The Testament," in *Continuity, Innovation, and Connoisseurship: Old Mas-
ter Paintings at the Palmer Museum of Art* (ed. Mary Jane Harris and Patrick McGrady;
University Park, Pa.: Penn State University Press, 2003), 22–37.

58. Vasari-Milanesi, *Le vite*, VI, 543.

59. The emerging talent of Michele is apparent in the altarpiece executed as a joint
work by Michele and Ridolfo (Vasari-Milanesi, *Le vite*, VI, 544), commissioned by the
Florentine, Leonardo di Giovanni Buonafé (c. 1450–1545), a Carthusian monk for the
church of S. Jacopo e Lorenzo, Via Ghibellina, Florence. The *Madonna and Child with
Sts. James, Lawrence, Francis, Claire and Bishop Buonafé* is today located in the Museo di
San Salvi, Florence. New archival information published by Franklin, "Towards a New
Chronology," 455, confirms a completion date of 1544. Several smaller panels by Michele
Tosini are derived from this altarpiece. Two panels depicting the Madonna and Child
with Saint John the Baptist are known. One is located in the Palmer Museum of Art,
Pennsylvania State University, and the other was most recently located in the Museo
Bandini, Prato. For a comparison of the S. Jacopo altarpanel with the Palmer Museum
and Museo Bandini panels, see Hornik, "Michele Tosini: The Artist, the Oeuvre and the
Testament," 24. For a discussion of their dependence on the Porta a Pinti *Madonna and
Child* by Andrea del Sarto, see Hornik, "Michele di Ridolfo," 46–49.

60. Michele became so adept at the style of these masters, scholars continue to battle
with problems of attribution. Confusion between the hands of Michele, Salviati, and Vasari
are most prevalent in portraiture. For an attribution discussion of the *Portrait of a Florentine
Nobleman*, St. Louis City Art Museum, see Nora W. Desloge and Laura Lewis Meyer, *Italian
Paintings and Sculpture* (St. Louis: St. Louis Art Museum, 1988), 46–51. More recently, see
Hornik, "Michele di Ridolfo," 346–48.

61. See Ettore Allegri and Alessandro Cecchi, *Palazzo Vecchio e I Medici, guida storica*
(Florence: S.P.E.S., 1980), 143–53, for an extensive discussion of the decoration of the Sala
di Cosimo I. See Archivio di Stato, Firenze. Fabbriche Medicee, N.7, c. 28v qtd. incorrectly
in Allegri and Cecchi, 153. (The date and the archival reference are both inaccurate.)
See Edmund Pillsbury, "The Sala Grande Drawings by Vasari and His Workshop: Some
Documents and New Attributions," *Master Drawings* 14 (1976): 139. For a discussion of
the iconography and documents related to the ceiling of the Sala Grande, see Kurt Forster,
"Metaphors of Rule. Political Ideology and History in the Portraits of Cosimo I de'Medici,"
Mitteilungen des Kunsthistorisches Institut in Florenz 15 (1971): 65–104, and Allegri and
Cecchi, *Palazzo Vecchio e I Medici*, 235–67.

62. Janet Cox-Rearick, *Bronzino's Chapel of Eleonora in the Palazzo Vecchio* (Berkeley:
University of California Press, 1993), 60.

63. Freedberg, *Painting in Italy 1500–1600*, 439.

64. See Allegri and Cecchi, *Palazzo Vecchio e I Medici*, 143, for the artists working in
the Sala di Cosimo I between 1556 and 1559.

65. Vasari-Milanesi, *Le vite*, VI, 658. See Archivio di Stato, Firenze. Accademia del
Disegno, N. 24, c. 15 for original document. See Karen-edis Barzman, *The Florentine
Academy and the Early Modern State: The Discipline of Disegno* (Cambridge: Cambridge
University Press, 2000), 29–31; Barzman, "The Florentine Accademia del Disegno: Liberal
Education and the Renaissance Artist," *Leids Kunsthistorisch Jaarboek* 5–6 (1986–87): 26
n. 2; for Tosini, see Hornik, "Michele di Ridolfo," 65–77.

66. See Archivio di Stato, Firenze. Accademia del Disegno, N. 157, c. 9; Archivio di
Stato, Firenze. Mediceo, N. 497, c. 907. Borghini writes to Cosimo I several times regarding
the foundation of the academy.

67. Vasari-Milanesi, *Le vite*, VI, 547.

68. Ibid., VI, 656.

69. Ibid., VI, 547. See *L'apparato per le nozze di Francesco de'Medici e di Giovanna d'Austria nelle narrazioni del tempo e da lettere inedite di Vincenzo Borghini e di Giorgio Vasari* (ed. Piero Ginori Conti; Florence: Leo S. Olschki, 1936), 141–46.

70. Most recently, see Franca Falletti and Jonathan Nelson, *Venere e Amore: Michelangelo e La Nuova Belezza Ideale = Venus and Love* (Florence: Giunti, 2002), 166–67. The Venus painting, Nelson rightly states, is based on the Michelangelo-Pontormo model, while the figures of Night and dawn find their specific source in the Michelangelo Medici Chapel figures of the same subject. See also Philippe Costamagna, "Nuovi studi. Rivista di arte antica e moderna," in *La collection de peintures d'une famille fiorentine étable à Rome: L'inventaire après décès du duc Anton Maria Salviati dressé en 1704* 8 (2000): 177–233.

71. For the Galleria Colonna, see Angela Negra, *Venere e Amore di Michele di Ridolfo del Ghirlandaio. Il mito di una Venere di Michelangelo fra copie, repliche e pudiche vestizioni* (Rome: Campisano Editore, 2001). For three studies recounting the restoration of the *Adoration of the Shepherds*, in Udine, see *Udine. Bollettino delle civiche istituzioni culturali* (Udine: Artis Grafiche Friulane) 3, no. 4 (1998): 36–74. For the *Sacra Conversazione*, see Pietro Luigi Biagioni, Sandro Baroni, Barbara Segre, and Marcello Spampinato, *Un capolavoro del cinquecento: la "Sacra conversazione" nel Duomo di Castelnuovo di Garfagnana* (Bagni di Lucca: Pastregno, 1999), 9–31. For the Badia di Passignano paintings, see Maria Clelia Galassi, "The Re-use of Design-Models by Carta Lucida in the XVth Century Italian Workshops: Written Sources and an Example from Michele di Ridolfo del Ghirlandaio," in *La peinture dans les Pays-Bas au 16e siècles. Pratiques d'atelier infrarouges et autres méthodes d'investigation* (Leuven: Uitgeverij Peeters, 1999), 206–12.

72. The brief synopsis of the artist's life in these publications is for the most part accurate but does not reflect a scholarly research study of either the artist or the painting.

73. See also Hornik, "Michele di Ridolfo," 205–6, 207, 224, and Roberta Villani, "Contributo a Michele di Ridolfo del Ghirlandaio," *Antichità viva* 21 (1982): 19–22.

74. Heidi J. Hornik, "The Strozzi Chapel by Michele Tosini: A Visual Interpretation of Redemptive Epiphany," *Artibus et Historiae* 46 (2002): 97–118.

75. Vasari-Milanesi, *Le vite*, VI, 59; VII, 595.

76. Ibid., VI, 548 n. 2.

77. Ibid.

78. Claudia Beltramo Ceppi and Nicoletta Confuorto, *Il primato del disegno* (Milan: Electa, 1980), 146.

79. The original panel has been removed from the altar wall and is undergoing restoration at the time of this writing. Unfortunately, it has been replaced by a twentieth-century painting of a different theme.

80. For recent work on portraiture that includes attributions to Tosini, see three recent articles by Philippe Costamagna, "De l'idéal de beauté aux problèmes d'attribution. Vingt ans de recherche sur le portrait florentin au XVIe siècle," *Studiolo. Revue d'histoire de l'art de l'Académie de France à Rome* 1 (2002): 192–220; "Il ritrattista," in *Francesco Salviati (1510–1563) o la Bella Maniera* (ed. Catherine Monbeig-Goguel; Milan: Electa, 1998), 47–52; "Mécènat et Politique Culturelle du Cardinal Giovanni Salviati," in *Francesco Salviati et la Bella Maniera: Actes des colloques de Rome et de Paris (1998)* (ed. C. Monbeig-Goguel, P. Costamagna, and M. Hochmann; Rome: École française de Rome, 2001), 227.

81. See C. Wilson, *Italian Paintings. XIV–XVI Centuries in the Museum of Fine Arts, Houston* (Houston: Museum of Fine Arts, 1996), 266–71, for an entry on this Tosini painting. Wilson's synopsis of Tosini's life and scholarship is less accurate than her quite detailed study of the *St. Mary Magdalen*. Especially helpful is her discussion of the infrared reflectograms taken of the painting.

82. Previously, the painting was attributed to Giulio Romano by N. Barbantini, *La Galleria del duca Francesco Massari Zavaglia a Ferrara. Catlogo delle opere* (Venice, n.p., 1910), 53–54 and to Stefano Falzagalloni by G. Medri in a brief guide written in 1940 and cited by Barbantini, 54. These guides reconstruct the provenance of the painting beginning in a private collection from Lombardy in 1910.

83. Hornik, "The Strozzi Chapel by Michele Tosini," 115 n. 55.

84. Ibid., 114 n. 51. For the illustration of Luke, see the cover of Hornik and Parsons, *Illuminating Luke: The Infancy Narrative in Italian Renaissance Painting.*

85. For a discussion of male portraits and further bibliography, see Hornik, *Continuity, Innovation*, 30–31, 36–37.

86. Lumachi, *Guida di San Casciano*, 84, suggests that the villa at the time of Matteo Strozzi appears in the background of the Saint John fresco to the right of the altar.

87. The feast of the Epiphany, God's manifestation in Jesus Christ, dates back to the third century. The earliest celebrations were probably in Egypt, where it replaced a festival of Isis, the main point of which was the virgin birth of Aion, on January 6. The changing of water into wine, a Dionysiac miracle, was celebrated in conjunction with this festival. The Christians reinterpreted the miracle, referring it to baptism; this may have been the reason that the miracle of Cana was also celebrated at Epiphany. See Gertrude Schiller, *Iconography of Christian Art* (trans. Janet Seligman; 2 vols.; Greenwich, Conn.: New York Graphic Society, 1971–72), 1:95. During the celebration of the Epiphany, the antiphon to the Benedictus at Lauds unites the Baptism with the Adoration and the Marriage at Cana. *Catholic Encyclopedia*, V, 506; Hugo Kehrer, *Die heiligen drei Könige in Literatur und Kunst* (Leipzig: A. Seemann, 1908–9), I, 46–49. For a discussion of the historical linking of the Baptism of Christ and the Adoration of the Magi, see Marilyn Aronberg Lavin, *Piero della Francesca's 'Baptism of Christ'* (New Haven: Yale University, 1981), 64–67. See also Josef A. Jungmann, *The Early Liturgy to the Time of Gregory, the Great* (South Bend, Ind.: University of Notre Dame Press, 1959), 149–51; Ludwig Eisenhofer and Josef Lechner, *The Liturgy of the Roman Rite* (Freiburg: Herder; Edinburgh-London: Nelson, 1961), 224–28.

88. For a discussion of the Epiphany as "The Feast of First Appearances," see Lavin, 123; Thomas Martone, "Book Review of *Piero della Francesca's 'Baptism of Christ'* by Marilyn Aronberg Lavin," *Art Bulletin* 70 (1988): 523–28.

89. Hornik, "The Strozzi Chapel by Michele Tosini," 100.

90. Ibid., 107–8.

91. The choice later to replace the altar panel with an innocuous Madonna with Child completely destroys the iconographic program of the chapel.

92. Hornik, "The Strozzi Chapel by Michele Tosini," 107–8.

93. Ingeniously, they also form part of the inscription, which, continuing from the door on the left and concluding on the opposite wall, emphasizes this comparison and reads, "Today Christ turned to be baptized by John in the Jordan."

94. John Chrysostom, *Homilies on the Gospel of Saint John* (trans. J. H. Parker; Oxford: Oxford University Press, 1848–52), 2.5.2 (8.146D).

95. Hornik, "The Strozzi Chapel by Michele Tosini," 118 n. 126. The inscription reads: HIC EST FILIVS MEVS DILECTVS IN QVO MIHI [BENE] CONPLACVI. Matt 3:17 (Latin, 1565): HIC EST FILIUS MEUS DILECTUS IN QUO MIHI BENE COMPLACUI. Matt 3:17: "This is my beloved Son, in whom I am well pleased."

96. Ibid., 118 n. 127.

97. Schiller, *Iconography*, 1, figs. 389–91, illustrates perhaps the first three works of art that depict temptation narratives: on two manuscript pages from psalters and an ivory book cover, respectively. For further discussion of the Stuttgart psalter, see Schiller, fig. 389. On the color and nakedness of the devil, see Luther Link, *The Devil: A Mask without a*

Face (London: Reaktion Books, 1995), 52–53. See Link, *Devil*, 72–73, for an assessment of why the devil does not appear prior to the ninth century in art.

98. There are no indications that any of the scenes illustrated in Schiller in the preceding note were taken from Luke's account of the event, and none of them includes the baptism of Christ scene.

99. Link, *Devil*, 38–40.

100. Ibid., 44–50. Ludovica Sebregondi, "The Devil in Fifteenth- and Sixteenth-Century Florentine Engravings," *Demons: Mediators between This World and the Other* (ed. Ruth Retzoldt and Paul Neubauer; Frankfurt am Main: Peter Lang, 1998), 111, finds that the medieval devils can be easily categorized by types. This is in contrast to the Renaissance, when so many appear it is difficult to classify them with the same facility.

101. Sebregondi, "The Devil in Fifteenth- and Sixteenth-Century Florentine Engravings," 111.

102. Ibid., 112.

103. Lorenzo Lorenzi, *Devils in Art: Florence, From the Middle Ages to the Renaissance* (Florence: Centro Di della Edifimi srl, 1997), 9, 60.

104. Link, *Devil*, 145–46.

105. Ibid., 146.

106. Ibid. This is not entirely true, as one may see from the Duccio, *Temptations of Christ*, Frick Collection, also dating from the fourteenth century. See Lorenzi, *Devils in Art*, 50–51, for a discussion of the Duccio.

107. Sebregondi, "The Devil in Fifteenth- and Sixteenth-Century Florentine Engravings," 111.

108. Lorenzi, *Devils in Art*, 59–61; Link, *Devil*, 70–73.

109. Carol F. Lewine, *The Sistine Walls and the Roman Liturgy* (University Park, Pa.: Penn State University Press, 1993), 33.

110. Although Tosini is documented (Hornik, "Michele di Ridolfo," 207, 428) as having worked on the decoration of three sides of a tabernacle for the Dominican church of Santa Maria della Quercia in Viterbo, twenty miles outside Rome, during 1569–70, we are not able to document Tosini's presence near or in Rome prior to this commission.

111. Link (*Devil*, 73) states that a different theme begins in the fifteenth century and is fully developed in the sixteenth: "Now the Devil becomes more and more human, until he is barely distinguishable from his opponent, Michael." In the case of the Tosini painting, the opponent is Christ himself—another human. For the convention of the devil wearing a monk's habit, see Schiller, *Iconography*, I:143. Link (*Devil*, 70) argues that the source for many 'costumed' devils is the mystery play of liturgical drama.

112. Réau (II-2, 308) notes that Satan is disguised in robes of a Franciscan monk in Botticelli's *Temptation*. It is not possible to identify the robes in the Tosini as being of a certain order. For a discussion of the well-known convention of the devil wearing a monk's habit, see Schiller, *Iconography*, 1:143.

113. Link, *Devil*, 68. Dante, *Inferno*, describes Lucifer as having "two immense outspread wings — not feathered wings, but resembling those of a bat" (final canto, lines 49–50). Link also credits Giotto with "inventing" the "bat-winged devil."

114. Link, *Devil*, 79.

115. Because of the change from literary to visual medium, Tosini is able to do something that Luke himself was not; he is able to focus on the middle temptation (see discussion above under rhetorical shape of the baptismal narrative).

Figure 3-1. Raphael. *Miraculous Draught of Fishes.* 1515–16. Bodycolour on paper mounted onto canvas (tapestry cartoon). Victoria and Albert Museum, London. Photo. With permission from the Victoria and Albert Museum / The Royal Collection.

Chapter Three

The *Miraculous Draught of Fishes* by Raphael

(Luke 5:1–11)

RAPHAEL'S CARTOON (Figure 3-1) of the *Miraculous Draught of Fishes* was painted as the design for a tapestry (Figure 3-2) to hang on the wall of the private chapel of the pope in Rome, the Sistine Chapel.[1] The decoration of the frescoed walls in the 1480s, ceiling in the beginning of the 1500s, and the woven tapestries of the 1510s affirm the authority of the papacy through an iconographic program representing the Primacy of Peter and Apostolic Succession. Both of these doctrines have their foundation in the trust Peter places in Christ when Christ directs Peter to cast his net despite the latter's skepticism. Christ performs the miracle in Peter's boat and afterwards says to Peter that he will make him a "fisher of men" (in the very familiar language of the King James Version) or "from now on you will be catching people" (Luke 5:10, NRSV). According to tradition, these words imply the role Christ intends for Peter as leader of the apostles.

At the end of the miracle the first disciples leave their boats and follow Christ. In the traditions that developed, all subsequent disciples, priests in the Roman church, were invested with spiritual authority transmitted from the apostles, but the pope's supreme authority, spiritual and temporal, was transmitted from Peter who, according to this tradition, was chosen by Christ as the Vicar on Earth.[2]

This chapter examines the biblical text, its subsequent interpretation, and Raphael's depiction of that text. A brief biography of the artist, the patron, the commission, and the iconographic program of the Sistine Chapel allows us to understand the work in its original context and location: — the first chapel of Christendom.

Overview of the Biblical Text

[1]And it came to pass, that when the multitudes pressed upon him to hear the word of God, he stood by the lake of Genesareth, [2]And saw two ships standing by the lake: but the fishermen were gone out of them and were washing their nets. [3]And going into one of the ships that was Simon's, he desired him to draw back a little from the land. And sitting, he taught the multitudes out of the ship. [4]Now when he had ceased to speak, he said to Simon: Launch out into the deep and let down your nets for a draught. [5]And Simon answering said to him: Master, we have labored all the night, and have taken nothing: but at thy word I will let down the net. [6]And when they had done this, they enclosed a very great multitude of fishes, and their net broke. [7]And they beckoned to their partners that were in the other ship, that they should come and help them. And they came, and filled both the ships, so that they were almost sinking. [8]Which when Simon Peter saw, he fell down at Jesus' knees, saying: Depart from me, for I am a sinful man, O Lord. [9]For he was wholly astonished, and all that were with him, at the draught of the fishes which they had taken. [10]And so were also James and John, the sons of Zebedee, who were Simon's partners. And Jesus saith to Simon: Fear not: from henceforth thou shalt catch men. [11]And having brought their ships to land, leaving all things, they followed him. (Luke 5:1–11, DOUAY-RHEIMS BIBLE)

Before exploring the meaning of Luke 5:1–11 in its present canonical context, this story can be compared to two other very similar stories recorded in John 21:1–11 and Mark 1:16–20.[3] First, we examine the parallel story in John. Rudolf Bultmann was one of the first scholars to suggest that Luke 5:1–11 represented the retrojection of a post-resurrection appearance story (John 21:1–11) into the public ministry of Jesus.[4] Bultmann's theory may or may not be the best explanation of the literary phenomena. However one explains the literary parallels between John 21 and Luke 5, we would do well to begin our study by considering these shared details.

Raymond Brown has described ten points of similarity between Luke 5 and John 21: (1) disciples who fish all night in vain; (2) Jesus ordering the disciples to cast a net; (3) the extraordinary catch of fish; (4) the effect(s) on the net; (5) Simon Peter reacts to the catch; (6) Jesus is addressed as "Lord"; (7) other fishermen who take part in the catch are silent; (8) at the end of the story, one or more of the fishermen "follow" Jesus (see John 21:19, 22); (9) the catch of fish symbolizes a successful missionary

Figure 3-2. Raphael. *Miraculous Draught of Fishes.* Tapestry. Vatican
Museums, Rome. Photo. Courtesy of the Vatican Museums, Rome.

enterprise; (10) the use of the name "Simon Peter" (which occurs only
here in Luke).[5]

In contrast, Alfred Plummer observed seven points of dissimilarity:
(1) in Luke, Jesus is immediately recognized by the fishermen; (2) in Luke,
Jesus is in a boat, not on shore; (3) in Luke, there is no mention of Peter
and the Beloved Disciple (John?) being in the same boat; (4) in Luke,
Peter is an active participant in the catch of fish; (5) in Luke, the net is
breaking (in John, it is not torn); (6) in John, the fish, which are caught
close to shore, are dragged to it; and (7) in John, Peter rushes through the
water to the Lord (whom he has only recently denied); in Luke, he begs
Jesus to depart from him.[6]

Despite these differences, most modern commentators agree that Luke
and John present different versions of the same miracle, although not all
accept Bultmann's hypothesis of Luke's retrojecting a post-resurrection
story into the public ministry. C. H. Dodd, for example, contends that
few of the elements expected in an appearance story are found in the
Lukan account.[7] On the other hand, there is little evidence in the gospel

tradition for post-resurrection scenes being derived secondarily from the public ministry, whereas it seems a fairly common, and perhaps inevitable, practice for early Christian writers to shape their narratives about the pre-risen Jesus in light of post-resurrection stories (cf. Matt 16:16b–19).[8]

While it is possible that by the time Luke inherited the story it had become a simple miracle story, which he fashions into the call of Peter, "the post-resurrection setting for the original episode . . . seems more plausible."[9] Simon's reaction of calling Jesus "Lord" suggests an original post-resurrection setting, and his confession of unworthiness is strange in its Lukan context. An apology for his fishing expertise or lack thereof would seem more appropriate in Luke 5, whereas the reaction of sinfulness more plausibly arises in a context in which he has done something of which he is ashamed (e.g., denying his Lord).[10] Whether or not the story was originally set in a post-resurrection context, subsequent interpretation of the story in both literature and art depicted the scene in explicit Christological tones, appropriate to a risen and glorified Christ, and paid special attention to the ecclesial significance to the call of Peter.

Similarities also exist between Luke's account and Mark's account. Assuming the two-source theory that Luke and Matthew used Mark and another document known as "Q," many scholars treat Luke 5:1–11 as a transposition of Markan material; that is, Luke has diverged from the Markan order of episodes in this instance to place the story of the "call of the disciples" in a different place in his gospel.[11] Joseph Fitzmyer has identified at least seven of these Lukan transpositions of Markan episodes, offering in each instance an explanation for the change.[12]

1. The imprisonment of John the Baptist (Mark 6:17–18) is moved to Luke 3:19–20 "in an effort to finish off the story of John before the ministry — and even baptism! — of Jesus."

2. Jesus' visit to Nazareth (Mark 6:1–6) becomes in Luke the occasion for Jesus' inaugural sermon at the beginning of his public ministry in Luke (Luke 4:16–30).

3. Our text, the call of the disciples (Mark 1:16–20) in Luke 5:1–11, "acquires a more psychologically plausible position, depicting disciples attracted to Jesus after a certain amount of ministry and preaching by him."

4. The summary about the crowds who followed Jesus (Mark 3:7–12) and the choosing of the Twelve (Mark 3:13–19) are inverted in Luke 6:12–16, 17–19 in order to achieve a "more logical setting and audience for the Sermon on the Plain (6:20–49)."

5. The episode about who constitutes Jesus' "real" family (Mark 3:31–35) is shifted to Luke 8:19–21 to provide "an illustration of the relationship between the word of God and disciples who hear it." The placement of the passage in Luke also has the effect of muting the criticism of Jesus' family of flesh, a point prominent in Mark with its connection of Jesus' family standing "outside" with those "outsiders" who hear but do not understand Jesus's message and mission.

6. The prediction of Jesus' betrayal at the Last Supper (Mark 14:18–21) "becomes part of the discourse after the meal in Luke 22:21–23, being joined to three other sayings (22:24–30, 31–34, 35–38)."

7. Luke inverts the Sanhedrin's questioning of Jesus (Mark 14:55–72//22:54c–71) in an effort to "unite the material about Peter" and "to depict only once [the] appearance of Jesus before the Sanhedrin."

We accept Fitzmyer's characterization of Luke 5:1–11 as a transposition of Mark 1:16–20, but we would like to offer a slight emendation to Fitzmyer's explanation that the story's placement in Luke gives it a more "psychologically plausible position."

Rather than seek a psychological reason for the change, the ancient Progymnasmata (handbooks of rhetorical exercises for schoolchildren), along with the rhetorical handbooks (Quintilian, *Institutio Oratoria*, IV.2.32; *Rhetorica ad Alexandrum*, 30.143b.1–4; Cicero, *De Inventione*, I.21.29–30), may provide the context for understanding the Lukan version as an example of "rhetorical plausibility."[13] According to Theon, author of the earliest extant Progymnasmata, plausibility was a highly desired quality of ancient narrative. He observed: "for the narrative to be credible/plausible, one must use words that are suitable for the persons and the subject matters and the places and the occasions/contexts; in the case of the subject matters those that are plausible and naturally follow from one another. One should briefly add the causes of things to the narration and say what is unbelievable in a believable way" (84.19–24; Patillon, 46).[14]

In the Markan version of the story, Jesus has hardly begun his ministry when he sees two pairs of brothers fishing. He calls these presumably complete strangers, who inexplicably follow without hearing his teaching or witnessing his miraculous power. The rendering of the story sounds somewhat far-fetched, and perhaps Mark intends it so. Nonetheless, Luke makes changes in the story to "tell the unbelievable in a believable way." Among the healings that precede the call of Simon is the healing of Simon's mother-in-law. The audience is led to believe Simon knows of her miraculous recovery. This fact makes more understandable Simon's willingness to allow Jesus on board his boat and to teach from it. Simon, in

Luke, is not welcoming a stranger on board, but acknowledging the holy man who had already healed a family member.

While one might view Luke's redaction as a distortion of Mark's rhetoric, no longer does it seem implausible in the Lukan account that these fishermen would leave everything and follow Jesus. The audience would have little difficulty in believing that the fishermen follow Jesus.[15] Theon's comments on plausibility suggest that the audience would have conceived of this plausibility in rhetorical terms, however much those of us living in the early twenty-first century might wish to speak of this plausibility in psychological terms.

A Brief History of Interpretation of Luke 5:1–11

Early on in the liturgical tradition, Luke 5 was the Gospel text for the fourth Sunday after Pentecost. Although the story of the Stilling of the Storm (Mark 4:35–41//Matt 8:23–27) is more central still to this concept of the church as boat or ship, Luke 5 did subsequently contribute to the development of the image. This image of the church as a ship is ancient.[16] In fact, many scholars see in Matthew's reworking of Mark's account of the stilling of the storm already a move to allegorize the ship in the storm as the *ecclesia pressa*, the oppressed or persecuted church.[17] Matthew seems to have pushed the story in this direction with several subtle changes in his account. The story follows on a passage about discipleship (Matt 8:18–22) and begins by observing that when Jesus stepped into the boat, "his disciples followed" (8:23). The disciples, fearful of the storm, address Jesus: "Save us, Lord; we are sinking!" (8:25). The theological connotations of "save" and "Lord" are obvious. Likewise, the response of Jesus to the disciples is slightly different, and, unlike Mark, the rebuke occurs before the stilling of the storm: "Why are you such cowards? How little faith you have!" (8:26). Jesus' disciples, fearful of the storm raging outside their boat, petition the "Lord" to "save them." Jesus, in turn, rebukes them for having so little faith. How easily Matthew's community could appropriate this story to their own context, whether of persecution of the church by outside forces or more personal crises of faith. In either case, Matthew's point is that Jesus had the power and authority to still the storm, rescue the disciples, and bring the boat safely to its destination.

In the *Apostolic Constitutions* (a second- or third-century Christian text), the nautical metaphor for the church is extended. In advice to bishops, the author writes:

> When thou callest an assembly of the Church, as one that is the commander of a great ship, appoint the assemblies to be made with all possible skill, the deacons as mariners to prepare places for the brethren with all due care and decency. And first, let the building be long, with its head to the east, with its vestries on both sides at the east end, and so it will be like a ship. (*Apostolic Constitutions*, ii.57; ANF)

Tertullian and Hippolytus of Rome were among the first to use the symbol of the ship for the church, but they were not the last.[18] Similar claims are made in the Epistle of Clement to James, Chrysostom, Peter Chrysologus, and Gregory of Nazianzus, among others.[19]

The church as ship was also a favorite image in early Christian art. In the Catacomb of Domitilla, there are two ships, one with a dove holding a sprig of olive in its beak (recalling Noah's ark), and the other a ship with a dove, with an inscription, *Genialis in pace*.[20] The Catacomb of Callixtus, clearly echoing Matt 8, shows a ship in a storm with two principal figures, one standing in prayer and supported by a figure in a cloud, while another sinks in the waves, lost by lack of faith. Post-Constantinian Christian architecture also reflected this understanding. "The very shape of the church, with a long nave, i.e., *navis*, ship, and with, in the early forms, an apse at one end with the bishop's throne in it, may be likened to a ship with helmsman steering it."[21]

For this last point, the role of the helmsman for the ship, Luke 5 was much more central. In fact, this text (and others) was used to establish the importance of Peter for the church. If the church is the "ship," Peter is its captain, its *gubernator*.[22] When Peter lets down his nets, according to Augustine, he preaches and converts — the nets are torn only by heretics.[23] The story of the Miraculous Draught of Fishes in Luke 5:1–11 was long recognized in the exegetical tradition as one of the principal "proofs" of the primacy of Peter. As we shall see, this tradition strongly influenced our artist's interpretation of this scene.

The Artist and the Painting

Raffaello Santi (or Sanzio; 1483–1520), known to us as Raphael, is the great assimilator of the Italian Renaissance style.[24] Unlike Leonardo da Vinci and Michelangelo, Raphael lived a brief life, most of which he spent not formulating new theories and techniques but bringing Renaissance concepts to their full potential. Yet, for several subsequent generations he remained the perfect High Renaissance artist. He was exposed to

courtly life at an early age by his father, who was held in high esteem
as a poet, chronicler, and painter in the Montefeltro court in Urbino.[25]
Giorgio Vasari, contemporary biographer, writes that Raphael was placed
in Perugino's (c. 1445–1523) shop c. 1500.[26] Raphael's figures embody
nobility, dignity, and grace in a balanced, symmetrical composition. Harmony and proportion are combined with emotion and revealed in the
gestures of the figures. His painting style is consistent and elegant while
his drawing is refined and expressive.[27]

Raphael's painting style is the reason that in 1513 the newly elected
Giovanni de'Medici as Pope Leo X (1513–21) chose him to design tapestries for the walls of the pope's private chapel, the Sistine.[28] The ten
tapestries, woven in Brussels from cartoons made by Raphael, were to
hang beneath the frescoes commissioned by Pope Sixtus IV della Rovere (1471–84) in the early 1480s.[29] Very few visitors today realize that
the Sistine Chapel decoration is incomplete without the tapestries. The
iconographic importance of the tapestries to the Sistine Chapel program
rivaled Michelangelo's ceiling (1508–12) commissioned by Pope Julius II
(1503–13), in fame and beauty during the sixteenth century. An anonymous author describes the Sistine during his 1523 visit to the Vatican
Palace:

> On the left appears the Chapel of Sixtus IV, built at enormous ex-
> pense (for Sixtus was truly magnificent in the construction of public
> works) . . . and Julius II decorated this chapel with an admirable work
> of painting by Michelangelo, outstanding for his skill in painting
> and sculpture; and many judge that nothing in our age is more per-
> fect than this. And soon afterwards Leo X enhanced the chapel,
> through the genius of the celebrated architect and painter Raphael
> of Urbino, with tapestries woven with gold and splendid colours; they
> hold everyone's attention by the incomparable beauty of the work
> and compel every mind to admiration.[30]

The tapestries were stolen after the sack of Rome in 1527, and some
time passed before they were recovered. In honor of the five hundredth
anniversary of the artist's birth, 1983 was designated Raphael Year. During
this celebratory year the tapestries were rehung in the position for which
they were intended.[31]

The Patron and the Commission

The cartoons were not Raphael's first encounter with papal patronage.
He painted frescoes on the walls in the papal apartments or stanze of
the Vatican Palace for Pope Julius II (1503–13) and continued working

on that project during the time of his successor Leo X. The first two
rooms, the Stanza della Segnatura (1508–12) and the Stanza d'Elidoro
(1512–14) made Raphael one of the most celebrated artists in Europe.
His ability to fresco narrative scenes, both historical and legendary, that
had a special significance to furthering the designs of ambitious popes
made him very popular. Pope Leo X expanded Raphael's role by making him one of the architects of St. Peter's. Raphael completed the final
room, Stanza dell'Incendio (1514–17), with the aid of his assistants.[32]
At the same time that Raphael was decorating the Stanza dell'Incendio,
the pope had commissioned him to make tapestry designs for the Sistine
Chapel.

After Julius II's death in February 1513, the young Giovanni de'Medici
was elected Pope Leo X on March 11. The mood in Rome was concil-
iatory toward the group of cardinals and clergy who attempted a schism
to overthrow Julius II two years earlier.[33] Although some aspects of the
personalities of the two popes may have differed, they both shared ambition. Michelangelo completed the Sistine ceiling commission given under
Julius II just three years before Raphael was commissioned by Leo X to
design the tapestries. John Shearman draws this analogy: "But just as Leo-
Augustus (to use an image of the period) succeeded Julius-Caesar on the
throne of Saint Peter, so — and quite appropriately — the eloquence of
Raphael once complemented the *terribilità* of Michelangelo in the first
chapel in Christendom."[34]

The first documented payment to Raphael was dated June 15, 1515,
and is believed to be the beginning of the project. The only other record
to Raphael describes the closing of the account on December 20, 1516.[35]
Raphael received one thousand ducats.[36] Raphael's assignment was to prepare ten large colored cartoons. Scholars believe all of the designs and the
most significant portions of the painting were done by Raphael himself.[37]
The original set of ten cartoons was sent to Brussels to be woven in the
shop of Pieter van Aelst at a cost of fifteen thousand ducats.[38] On December 26, 1519, seven of the tapestries were put on display in Rome.[39]
Raphael may have seen the completed set by the time of his death in 1520,
but Shearman states, "Leo X unquestionably had the satisfaction before
his death on December 1, 1521."[40]

Provenance of the Cartoons and the Tapestry Sets

As was the custom, the cartoons were retained in the weaver's studio. In
1534, Francis I of France purchased three tapestries from the cartoons as
the first pieces of a set of ten; another set of nine scenes (omitting the
St. Paul in Prison) was woven for Henry VIII (this series is now in Berlin);

a third set, also consisting of nine tapestries, was prepared for Phillip II of Spain and is now in Madrid.[41] All of these sets were presumably under the auspices of van Aelst.[42] The set for Henry VIII and Francis I, like the original Vatican set, used gold and silver thread extensively.

The Sistine Chapel and the Tapestry Narratives

The narrative scenes of the original tapestry program were tailored to continue the iconography of the *Capella papalis*. The proper titles for the Sistine are *Capella palatina* and *Capella magna* (or *maior*) in the Vatican. Together with the Basilica of St. Peter's, the chapel was the primary location for the liturgical feasts of the pope and his court. St. Peter's was the premier church of Christendom, and the chapel represented Christ's vicar on earth, the pope. The manifestation of the *Maiestas Papalis* occurred not only in the magnificence of these structures and the money spent on the gold and silver threads used to weave the tapestries but also in the narratives painted on the walls under Sixtus, the ceiling under Julius, and the tapestries under Leo. Paris de Grassis served as the master of ceremonies of the *Capella papalis* under Julius II and Leo X.[43]

Building, Decoration, and Chapel Iconography

Shortly after 1473, Sixtus IV replaced the original chapel that Pope Nicholas III (1277–80) built on this site.[44] It was dedicated to the Virgin of the Assumption on that feast day, August 11, 1483.[45] The altar of the chapel is in the west, and the entrance is in the east. The walls are divided into three horizontal levels. These levels are interrupted by

Figure 3-3. North Wall of the Sistine Chapel with Tapestries. Photo. Courtesy of the Vatican Museums, Rome.

Figure 3-4. South Wall of the Sistine Chapel with Tapestries. Photo. Courtesy of the Vatican Museums, Rome.

five vertical pilasters, resulting in a pattern of six horizontal bays.[46] Each of the bays of the uppermost level contains a window flanked on either side by a portrait of a pope. The second level contains the large narrative painting commissioned by Sixtus IV and executed between 1481 and 1483. The tapestries were designed for the lowest level. During the time of Sixtus there were fictive tapestries with emblems of the pope painted onto the walls. This pattern continued across both the entrance and altar walls until Michelangelo painted the *Last Judgment* in 1536–41. The ceiling may or may not have been painted before Michelangelo's frescoes (1508–12).[47]

The chapel itself was divided in two by a chancel screen or *cancellata*. It was originally placed closer to the altar than it is today. Shearman claims that "its original position on a step just a little over half-way down the chapel is clearly marked by an inset marble strip on the floor."[48]

The iconographic program of the Sistine begins with the sixteen (fourteen extant) narrative frescoes of the 1480s.[49] Scenes from the life of Christ illustrated on the north wall (Figure 3-3) are paralleled with those from the life of Moses on the south wall (Figure 3-4). The cycle ends with Perugino's *Christ Giving the Keys to Peter* (Matt 16:18–19) that legitimizes the history and authority of the pope as a descendant of Peter, the rock on which Christ builds his church. Latin inscriptions above the narratives assist the viewer in understanding the complex relationships.[50] The similar roles of Moses, Christ, and the pope (by virtue of apostolic succession) as leader, lawgiver, and priest are apparent.

The subjects of the ceiling frescoes are taken from the first nine chapters of Genesis. The *Creation of Eve* is strategically placed in the center of the nine bays. The dedication of the chapel to Mary as the new Eve and a symbol of the church are also quite deliberate iconographic references.[51]

The theme of papal authority is continued through the placement of the life-of-Peter tapestries beneath the scenes from the life-of-Christ frescoes on the north wall. The narratives of Paul's life woven into tapestries are located beneath the painted life of Moses on the opposite wall. Sharon Fermor explains the selection of these tapestry narratives: "Peter and Paul are portrayed as the twin founders of the Christian church, with special missions to convert the Jews and Gentiles respectively. They are also presented as the joint sources of the Pope's own authority and the tapestries were certainly intended to have a personal and political dimension for Leo in his role as Pope."[52]

The final portion of the Sistine decoration, the painted fresco of the entire altar wall by Michelangelo (1536–41), was the idea of Clement VII de'Medici (1523–34) and continued by Pope Paul III Farnese (1534–50). Michelangelo's *Last Judgment* destroyed Perugino's original altarpiece of the *Assumption of the Virgin* and the two 1480s frescoes, *Finding of Moses* and *Nativity of Christ*. The painting does not continue the primacy-of-the-papacy theme but instead reflects the dramatic change of direction of the Catholic Church subsequent to the Protestant Reformation. Pierluigi de Vecchi sums up the change:

> Thus the entire iconographic program of the Chapel, which had been built up in stages but with marvelous consistency, so as to express with remarkable rhetoric the ideology and belief of the Roman Curia in the last years of the 15th century and the first years of the 16th — this was now brutally mutilated on the initiative of a pope and by the hands of an artist who together had seen the increase and fruition of the ideal of the "renovatio" of the "eternal city" under the governance of St. Peter's successors, but who also had lived through the dramatic events that led, amid extreme religious bitterness and great agonies of conscience, to the toppling of the "caput mundi" and the pillage of the see of Christ's vicar, in which part at least of Christendom had identified the aspect of a "new Babylon."[53]

The Tapestries

Thematically, the tapestries depict events from the lives of Peter and Paul on the north (Figure 3-3) and south (Figure 3-4) sides of the altar and continue along the same side walls, respectively. They would cover approximately twelve hundred square feet.[54] Each tapestry series parallels the 1480s frescoes: Peter and Christ, Moses and Paul. The tapestries were not permanently on display but were put up on special occasions. Their exact order has never been determined in the scholarship, although most agree with Shearman's placement. Fermor, however, states that no record shows that they were always hung in the same sequence.[55] She offers several other tapestry cycles from the fifteenth and sixteenth centuries that are documented as being hung in a variety of ways according to such determining factors as the liturgical occasion.[56] The tapestries hung just above eye level on the lower walls of the chapel, above the stone bench provided for its occupants and below the fifteenth-century frescoes.[57]

Raphael completed cartoon designs for ten tapestries in eighteen months. The number (sixteen or seventeen) of tapestries Pope Leo X originally intended for the chapel has been the subject of some art historical debate.[58] If the tapestries were hung under each of the 1480s frescoes, then the correct number would be sixteen. Scholars agree that the ten surviving tapestries are incomplete because the number is too few to cover the entire lower space of the chapel and one too many to cover the area inside the *cancellata* or chancel screen.[59]

Like the frescoes of the 1480s, the tapestries also contain inscriptions that reveal their relevance to the papacy. Raphael designed cartoons, now lost, for fictive bronze bas-relief borders below the pictorial scene.[60] These showed scenes from Pope Leo's religious and secular life.[61] Cartoons for vertical borders have also been lost, but they depicted *The Seven Liberal Arts*, *The Seven Virtues*, *The Hours*, *The Seasons*, *The Elements*, and *The Labours of Hercules*. The exact placement of these borders cannot be determined, but some remain intact on the extant tapestries.[62]

As one faces the altar, the Peter scenes are placed below the Christ frescoes and begin on the right side of the altar and move clockwise onto the side wall in the following order: *Miraculous Draught of Fishes* (Luke 5:3–10), *Christ's Charge to Peter* (Matt 16:18–19; John 21:15–17), *Healing of the Lame Man* (Acts 3:1–11), *Death of Ananias* (Acts 5:1–6). The scene on the left side of the altar is the *Stoning of Stephen* (Acts 7:54–60). Continuing on the side wall, in a counterclockwise direction are the Paul scenes, hung below the Moses frescoes. The Paul compositions are:

Conversion of Saul (Acts 9:1–9), *Blinding of Elymas* (Acts 13:6–12), *Sacrifice at Lystra* (Acts 14:8–18), *Paul in Prison* (Acts 16:23–26), and *Paul Preaching at Athens* (Acts 17:15–34).[63]

Audience

Understanding the audience for these works is important to understanding the works and their setting. The chancel-screen, which was placed closer to the altar than it is presently in the chapel, separated two groups of visitors.[64] The clergy who were allowed to be on the altar side (the papal entourage) included the College of Cardinals, generals of the monastic and mendicant orders, patriarchs and visiting archbishops, and bishops.[65] Other, less distinguished members of the audience included the resident theologian, the sacristan, the majordomo of the papal household, the chamberlain, secretaries, notaries, and auditors. Certain distinguished laity and visitors of the pope were also allowed on this side of the chancel-screen.[66] Servants, pilgrims, and other spectators were seated on the outside of the screen. Although most of the distinguished guests and even some of the laity could identify the individual scenes on the ceiling and walls of the chapel, the full range of meanings and the complexity of the narrative cycles were probably only understood completely by certain members of the group.[67]

The *Miraculous Draught of Fishes*, including the lateral border depicting Leo's entry into Rome for the Conclave of 1513 and election to the papacy, is 18′ x 19′.[68] The cartoon, a gouache on paper, is 10.5′ x 12.8′. It is believed to have hung to the right of the altarpiece of Perugino's *Assumption of the Virgin* beneath the lost *Nativity of Christ*. [69]

Sources and Technique

The Raphael cartoons are the first set of tapestry cartoons on paper known to survive.[70] They are extremely large drawings; without sources, hypothesizing how Raphael might have constructed them is difficult.[71] The cartoons were prepared with the understanding that the composition would eventually be reversed, given the tapestry weaving technique then used in Brussels. Shearman explains: "In this technique the weaver worked, looking through the horizontal warps at the Cartoon, upon that side of the tapestry which was destined to be the back."[72] This compositional reversal was not a new process for Raphael, because he had already experienced it in making designs for engravers and mosaists.[73]

Contemporary sources such as Vasari's *Lives* (1550, 1568) and Giovan Battista Armenini's *On the True Precepts of Painting* (1586) do not give much information on the construction of cartoons but do consider them to be valuable and worth saving.[74] Vasari does discuss fresco cartoons that may offer the closest comparison.[75] Scholars have studied the techniques used for the fresco cartoons of Leonardo and Michelangelo but most useful for our comparison are probably those that Raphael himself designed for the *Stanze* in the Vatican apartments produced just prior to the tapestry cartoons.[76]

Raphael made large cartoons for the Stanze frescoes. The cartoon for the lower portion of *The School of Athens*, made for Pope Julius II c. 1510, survives in the Ambrosiana, Milan.[77] It reveals Raphael's inventive use of preparatory designs and how the cartoon functioned in organizing the fresco's masses of light and shade. The cartoon has been pricked through to make secondary cartoons for use on the wall. Leonardo and Michelangelo may also have implemented this idea of using a secondary cartoon to prevent damage to the original.[78]

Two significant differences distinguish a fresco cartoon and a tapestry cartoon. Fermor states: "First, the (fresco) cartoons were probably not destined to be cut up and used, or subjected to the exigencies of direct use in the fresco process, let alone those of the weaving process. Second, and perhaps most important, all were executed largely in dry media such as chalk or charcoal, less likely to put a strain on the paper surface than the bodycolor used by Raphael in the tapestry cartoons."[79] Raphael's Sistine cartoons were painted; this made them heavier than fresco cartoons, and they were to be cut up for the weaver's loom. The sheets were relatively small, about 12″ x 19″, which means that numerous sheets were glued together to form a sheet 11′9″ x 14′8″.[80] Glue at regular intervals provided additional strength to the paper.[81]

The cartoons were not always cut with consideration of the design itself, but Fermor believes that for this reason, combined with the evidence of how the cartoons were shipped (rolled rather than folded), the weavers made the cuts.[82] Fermor's theory is that the cartoons were reinforced with canvas behind the cut areas either when they were reintegrated to allow Francis Cleyn to make copies in the 1620s or when they were temporarily exhibited at Hampton Court and the Tower of London late in the seventeenth century.[83] The cartoon strips were permanently reintegrated and adhered to a canvas backing in the 1690s by the restorers, Cooke and Walton.[84] This backing makes it almost impossible to see a watermark to help identify the paper supplier that Raphael used.[85] During the restoration of the 1690s, the strip-linings on the *Miraculous Draught of Fishes* cartoon were meticulously trimmed and cut back so that the excess canvas could be removed. Fermor reports, "The paper edges were also trimmed so that the cartoon strips could be neatly abutted."[86]

Almost all of the outlines of the cartoons (figures, landscapes, objects) have been pricked. In the *Miraculous Draught of Fishes*, both the figures and almost the entire landscape (the leafy tree at the extreme edge of the landscape background for an unknown reason was not) have been pricked.[87] This process is not related to weaving but instead to their being copied. Recent technical examination reveals that the pricking holes go through the original paper but not through the canvas backing of the 1690s. Although a precise dating of the process is difficult, certainly it occurred prior to the Cooke and Walton reintegration. The question then becomes: did the pricking occur before or after they were cut by the weaver, Pieter van Aelst in Brussels — a question that Fermor dealt with extensively, but which is not necessarily important to the discussion at hand.[88]

Form

Several formal elements (figure style and color) of the original cartoons have been changed. Although the overall composition remains essentially the same, the other elements have changed over time; we must rely on extensive technical processes to understand and visualize the cartoon in its original state. Observations regarding Raphael's intentional continuity of compositional elements appearing in the cartoon and intended for the final tapestry of the *Miraculous Draught of Fishes* are examined.

Composition and Figure Style

Sharon Fermor and John Shearman agree that the *Miraculous Draught of Fishes* was the first cartoon in the series produced by Raphael.[89] They find Raphael's hand greatest in this composition. It is the only cartoon not having a fully finished *modello* that survives.[90] Yet, recent technological investigations reveal that the most detailed underdrawing of any cartoons also occurs in the *Miraculous Draught of Fishes*. Raphael manipulated the figures (their poses, gestures, and foreshortening) several times to get the precise compositional rhythm and relationship between figures and landscape.[91] This spontaneity leads scholars to believe that Raphael worked directly onto the cartoon, without detailed studies.[92] At least seven drawings associated with this cartoon survive in the scholarship, three of which Paul Joannides identifies as preparatory studies by Raphael.[93]

The center of the composition contains the narrative scene at hand (Luke 5:1–11) and is the earlier of the two miraculous draughts of fishes described in the Gospels. The miracle has occurred as Christ sits calmly in the first of the two boats that is low in the water with the weight of deep-water fish.[94] Shearman identifies Christ's head as a portrait whose type is derived from the *Vera effigies* on a lost emerald cameo from the treasury of Constantinople reproduced in a number of bronze medals in the later 1400s.[95] Christ's blessing gesture, right hand raised with fingers extended and palm facing outwards, is directed at the kneeling Peter. Peter's hands are clasped in prayer and astonishment as he leans towards Christ. The recent technical processes, especially X-radiographs, help distinguish the hand of the artist from his assistant. Particularly noteworthy in the *Miraculous Draught* is the head of St. Peter. Pope-Hennessy stated that the head of St. Peter was certainly done by Raphael and Raphael alone.[96]

A standing Andrew, confused at the abundance of fish present in their boat, is positioned on the right and moves toward Peter. Andrew's arms are extended out from alongside his body with both hands open in surprise. Skill and delicacy of the drawing of Andrew is evident in the reflectograms.[97]

A second boat, slightly behind and to the left of Christ's boat, shows two disciples pulling in a second catch and a third disciple sitting with an extended oar, cropped from the picture plane. Their boat also has an abundance of fish present indicating the exact moment of the narrative chosen by Raphael.

The boats create a strong, horizontal division in the center of the cartoon. The shore, a triangular shape of land with foliage and three birds, is painted in the lower right corner. Diagonally across the composition in the upper left corner, Raphael balances the shore with a hilly landscape. Also visible in the distant landscape is the crowd to whom Christ had been preaching.

Shearman identifies this topography as the western tract of the Leonine wall that rises over the summit of the *Mons Vaticanus* and overlooks the *Vallis inferni*. The proposed view from the Via Aurelia is quite different today, but Shearman finds the Raphael towers to be architecturally distinctive and offers a very specific directional orientation for their location. He also compares them to historical description and engravings of the towers.[98] This topography unites the *Miraculous Draught of Fishes* with the *Charge to Peter* (Figure 3-5). John White observes:

> When the tapestries of the *Miraculous Draught of Fishes* and *Christ's Charge to Peter* were reversed in tapestry, the rising, flower-strewn bank ran on exactly from one scene to the next. The bow of the boat cut off behind the figure of Christ in the *Miraculous Draught of Fishes* appears pulled to the shore in the succeeding scene. Even the tip of the promontory above the seated Christ is continued in the background hills of *Christ's Charge to Peter*.[99]

The proportions of the figures may find their source in Masaccio's Peter cycle frescoed in S. Maria del Carmine, Florence. The massive bulk and dramatic gesture are combined in the figures who stand approximately eight feet, more than two-thirds the total height of the narrative scene.[100]

Color

Raphael used a glue-based watercolor over a charcoal preparation. He was very conscious of tone and, according to Fermor, "provides the weavers not simply with colour guides in the form of thin washes of colour, but with fully coloured and carefully calculated designs."[101] Unfortunately much of the cartoons have faded and discolored over the years, which Fermor attributes to Raphael's use of madder lakes (fugitive pigments produced in a variety of shades from pink to red and purple to brown), indigo (dark blue), or orpiment (bright gold-yellow).[102] Fermor concludes that the overall color range of the cartoons would have been "richer, warmer and more varied than it now appears."[103] Evidence of fading in the *Miraculous Draught of Fishes* occurs in the color of Christ's robe. It is now white but its reflection in the water remains the original red and is shown as red in the tapestry.[104] Some of the heads have been repainted and others retouched. The joins in the strips of paper have been colored in.

Iconography

Any consideration of Raphael's iconography must begin with John Shearman's magisterial study of the cartoons. Given the placement and purpose of the tapestries (to decorate the Sistine Chapel under the pontificate of Leo X), Shearman cautions that "we should expect ideas to be rigorously traditional, authoritative, and orthodox. We may anticipate, in other words, that if our interpretation contains any real surprises it is almost certain to be wrong."[105] Shearman's observation reinforces that the tapestries were "to hang in a space that was not private, but public even international, and thus their message — or at least their main message — would be ineffective unless it were universal, familiar and direct."[106] With these caveats in mind, let us turn to the task of interpreting the cartoon at hand.

Figures in the Boat

Two features of Raphael's cartoon make it certain that he intends to depict the scene from Luke 5 and not John 21. First, the tapestry was intended to stand as the first in the Peter cycle, suggesting that the reference is to

Figure 3-5. Raphael. *Christ's Charge to Peter.* 1515–16. Bodycolour on paper mounted onto canvas (tapestry cartoon). Victoria and Albert Museum, London. Photo. With permission from the Victoria and Albert Museum / The Royal Collection.

an event early in the public ministry of Christ and not to a later post-resurrection appearance. But this position in the overall program is not in itself fully persuasive, because in the next tapestry, the *Charge to Peter*, there is clearly a conflation between Matt 16, which occurs during the public ministry, and John 21, again a post-resurrection scene. In the *Charge to Peter*, the Apostle Peter is clearly holding the keys mentioned in Matt 16. This point is so prominent that since 1517, the piece has regularly been referred to as the *Donation of Keys*.[107] Yet, the resurrected Christ is in view here; Christ has white robes and the marks of the Stigmata.[108] Furthermore, sheep, which play so prominently in the Johannine passage ("Do you love me more than these?" "Yes, Lord, you know I love you." "Feed my sheep."), are, of course, entirely missing from the Matthean passage but present here behind Jesus in the cartoon. Finally, John specifically mentions that seven apostles are present at the post-resurrection appearance recorded in John 21, while Raphael has included eleven in his rendition.[109] Shearman's conclusion seems on target: "The subject, then, is a conflation of the texts Matthew xvi.17–19 and John xxi.15–17, which corresponds to and expresses the orthodox interpretation of the second as the moment of fulfillment of the promise contained in the first: 'Et tibi *dabo* claves regni caelorum'"[110] ("and to you I *will* give the keys to the kingdom of heaven").

Obviously then, the placement of the *Miraculous Draught of Fishes* at the beginning of the Peter cycle does not *a priori* rule out a conflation of

texts (Luke 5:1–11 and John 21:1–11) in a manner analogous to the combination of Matt 16 and John 21 in the *Charge to Peter*. Our second feature,
however, does seem to exclude John 21 from immediate consideration as
a primary or direct literary source.

In the cartoon, when the action takes place, both Jesus and Peter are
in the boat. Only in Luke, however, do the two figures remain in the boat
during the climatic moment of the story. In John, by the end of the story
neither Jesus (who was walking on the water) nor Peter (who, when he
recognized who Jesus was, leapt out of the boat) is in the boat. Depictions
of this scene are frequent and perhaps extend back into the art of the
catacombs.[111] The peculiar position of the figures in the boat here in our
cartoon, along with its position as the first in the Peter cycle, suggests
Luke 5, and not John 21, is Raphael's immediate inspiration.

We may say the same about the relationship between Luke 5 and
the calling of the apostles recorded in Matt 4:18–22 (//Mark 1:16–20).
Though some have assumed that Raphael's cartoon draws from both
Matthew and Luke,[112] Shearman argues convincingly that such is not
the case:

> The *Miraculous Draught of Fishes* is not derived, as has been sup-
> posed, from a long tradition of representations of the Vocation of
> the Apostles in which Christ stands on the shore. These several
> representations all illustrate a different text (Matthew iv. 18–22);
> and Raphael had a particularly good reason for avoiding that tra-
> dition, and the consequent probability of confusion over the text,
> since an example of it already existed in the Sistine decorations of
> the chapel.[113]

Thus, given the large number of visual depictions in which either Jesus
or both Jesus and Peter are out of the boat,[114] Raphael's version is distinct
and allows us to conclude with some certainty that Luke 5:1–11, and not
John 21:1–11 nor Matt 4:18–22, is in view in Raphael's cartoon.

Having established that Luke 5:1–11 is, in fact, the biblical source of our
cartoon, what is the meaning of the figures in the boat? Raphael seems to
be following the dominant line of interpretation since antiquity: the ship
and Peter, both selected by Christ, represent the church and its leader,
respectively. Furthermore, this ancient tradition of identifying the boat as
the church, Peter as its leader, and the fish as its evangelical mission were
still current and popular in the literature contemporary with Raphael.
Giovanni Francesco, Christoforo Marcello, and Angelo da Vallombrosa,
all writing in the early sixteenth century, reflect this view.[115] Especially
noteworthy is a letter by Innocent III in which Christ's action of sitting in

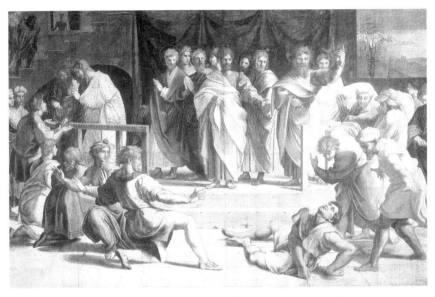

Figure 3-6. Raphael. *Ananias.* 1515–16. Bodycolour on paper mounted onto canvas (tapestry cartoon). Victoria and Albert Museum, London. Photo. With permission from the Victoria and Albert Museum / The Royal Collection.

Peter's boat was understood to signify that "Peter was given a firm throne, whether in the Lateran or the Vatican."[116] Thus, the main figures of Christ and Peter, and their setting, seated in a boat, are all to be understood within the ecclesiastical debate regarding the "primacy of Peter," and the legitimization of the papacy that it ensured — hardly surprising given the patron, Pope Leo X, and the locale, the Sistine Chapel, for which this tapestry was designed.

Position among the Tapestries

Relationship to Rest of Peter Cycle. The *Miraculous Draught of Fishes* stands as the first in the Peter cycle, which includes *Christ's Charge to Peter*, the *Healing of the Lame Man at the Beautiful Gate of the Temple*, and the *Death of Ananias* (Figure 3-6). As such, one would expect the *Miraculous Draught* to introduce themes common to the rest of the cycle, and such expectations are not disappointed.

In addition to the formal continuity between the *Miraculous Draught* and the *Charge to Peter* above, there are thematic connections. Obviously, both the *Miraculous Draught* and the *Charge to Peter* support the doctrine of Petrine authority.[117] The other two tapestries likewise bear witness to this theme. The Healing of the Lame Man is the first miracle of Peter, and as such parallels Jesus' healing ministry.[118] The miracle also establishes Peter's role as leader of the apostles (Luke 22:32).

Similarly the story of the Death of Ananias (and Sapphira) in Acts 5 establishes Peter's authority in the early Christian community.[119] Peter himself had spoken of "a prophet like Moses" whose authority could be ignored only at great peril (Acts 3), a prophecy fulfilled here in a grizzly manner. Significantly both these stories were held as examples of Peter's primacy in the thought world of the fourteenth and fifteenth centuries as well. Innocent III, for example, mentioned both Peter's miracle working ministry (and specifically the fact that he was first among the apostles to perform such miracles, e.g., in Acts 3) and specifically the Ananias and Sapphira episode, as evidence of the *Primatus Petri*.[120] Poggio makes a similar claim about the Healing of the Lame Man in relationship to Peter's authority, and Torquemada does the same for the death of Ananias.[121]

Relationship to Pauline Cycle. The *Miraculous Draught* was intended to hang on the altar-wall of the chapel along with the *Stoning of Stephen*. The moment evidently depicted in the tapestry is a specific one. After his enraged audience stones him, and Stephen petitions God to receive his spirit (Acts 7:59, paralleling Luke 23:46), Stephen "knelt down and cried out with a loud voice, 'Lord, do not charge them with this sin'" (Acts 7:60). Surely, Saul, who in the tapestry presumably stood as a consenting, and therefore sinful, observer, is to be included in Stephen's petition. Likewise the subject of sin is at the forefront of the *Miraculous Draught* where Peter kneels in obvious contrition, and Raphael captures the moment where Peter confesses: "Depart from me, for I am a sinful man, O Lord" (Luke 5:8). The subject of sin, however anomalous it might seem in a cycle designed to undergird Peter's authority,[122] is nonetheless appropriate for its particular placement in the chapel, namely, near the altar where sins were forgiven through the mediation of the priest in the mass.

In the tapestries, absolution is found in the *Miraculous Draught* in Christ's upraised hand in a gesture of blessing and his commission from Scripture that the gesture is intended to recall: "Fear not: from henceforth thou shalt catch men" (Luke 5:10). In the Stoning of Stephen, forgiveness, at least for Paul, is delayed until the conversion scene, the subject of the next tapestry.[123]

So much for the connections between the first tapestry in each cycle. But what of possible connections between the *Miraculous Draught* and the Pauline cycle as a whole? As Shearman observed: "the *Primatus Petri* cannot be the main theme of the whole tapestry-sequence; had that been the intention the Petrine set would have been placed on the left wall, in the right from the point of view of the altar and the Crucifix, the point precedence overriding all other considerations."[124] Rather, he maintains: "The chosen arrangement strongly suggests, on the contrary, a balance and equal division of powers."[125] Sharon Fermor has aptly described the overall connection between the two cycles: "Peter and Paul are portrayed as the twin founders of the Christian Church, with special missions to convert the Jews and Gentiles respectively. They are also presented as the joint sources of the Pope's own authority and the tapestries were certainly intended to have a personal and political dimension for Leo in his role as Pope."[126] Thus, the two founders of the church among the Jews and the Gentiles stand as dual witnesses to the continuity and universality of the church (even in the face of recent schism) preserved in the person of the pope.[127]

Relationship to Christ Cycle. There has also been speculation about the second boat in Raphael's cartoon. Ephrem the Syrian is representative of those who took the two boats in Luke 5 to represent, in the history of salvation, Jews and Gentiles: "The two boats represent the circumcised and the uncircumcised."[128] The same kind of interpretation was made regarding the *Nativity of Christ*, beneath which fresco the *Miraculous Draught of Fishes* was originally intended to hang. Reflecting the reference in Isa 1:3 ("An ox knows its owner and a donkey *its master's stall*; but Israel lacks all knowledge, my people have no discernment"), Origen, Augustine, and Gregory of Nyssa all argued that in the story of salvation history, which the Nativity recorded, the Shepherds represented the Jews and the Magi stood for Gentiles (as the ox symbolized Jews and the ass Gentiles).[129]

Raphael and his patron, Leo X, were no doubt aware also of this tradition. In the Vatican Logge (executed 1517–19), two of Raphael's five New Testament scenes depict the *Adoration of the Shepherds* and the *Adoration of the Kings*, presumably to underscore the point that Christ appeared to both Jews and Gentiles.[130] So the Shepherds and the Magi in the fresco and the two boats in the tapestry both point to the same reality: the universality of Christ's redemption.[131]

Concluding Hermeneutical Reflections

The ancient tradition of picturing the church as a "ship" remains a compelling image, even today. The ship is an image both of vulnerability and of safety. It provides shelter to those in the storm, yet the very fact that the ship is itself exposed on the turbulent sea (and not riding out the storm in a safe harbor) symbolizes the inherent danger in the church's call to be "in the world but not of the world." Or rather, the church is called to be "on the sea" (providing a venue for deliverance for those drowning in these treacherous waters), but "not in the sea" (for a sinking ship catches no fish!).

As Maximus of Turin once wrote:

Ordinarily people are not given life on a boat but transported. Nor
are they comforted on a vessel but anxious about its journey. Notice
also that this boat is not a boat that is given to Peter to be piloted —
rather, it is the church, which is committed to the apostle to be
governed. For this is the vessel that does not kill but gives life to
those borne along by the storms of this world as if by waves. Just as
a little boat holds the dying fish that have been brought up from the
deep, so also the vessel of the church gives life to human beings who
have been freed from turmoil. Within itself, I say, the church gives
life to those who are half-dead, as it were.[132]

Navigating such deep waters requires more the steady and skillful hand
of an experienced captain than the savvy of a CEO! In the history of interpretation, Peter, of course, is given the role as "captain of the ship."[133] This
point is, no doubt, the more problematical one for Protestants.[134] Both our
text and Raphael's rendering of it, however, suggest a fine balance between
the importance of Peter and his own self-professed limitations. Certainly,
as we have seen, Raphael, by presenting a kneeling and contrite Peter,
does not gloss over Peter's sinful humanity, even though his tapestries
were designed to hang in the Pope's private chapel, the very one who
stood in the line of Peter.

Whether or not one accepts the doctrine of apostolic succession, there
is no doubting the significant role Peter played in the early church, despite his utter failure — a failure that Jesus had predicted (22:31–34).
In that same passage, however, Jesus also exhorted Peter to "strengthen
the believers" (22:32). Within its explicitly pro-papacy apologetic, we find
in Raphael's cartoon the seed for pastoral leadership today — the need,
as it were, for people called and willing to acknowledge their own sinful
inclinations and limitations, yet, who, at the same time, are called and
willing also to take up the task with Peter of steering the ship. Only with
such self-aware and strong guidance can the churchly ship prevent going
aground in the shoals of irrelevant antiquarianism, on the one side, or
rootless relativism, on the other. Only then can the church, in a constant state of vulnerability and exposure, engage in the task of "fishing
for people," which remains our calling even today, a calling Raphael so
powerfully illustrates in the *Miraculous Draught of Fishes*.

Notes

1. Literature on Raphael is vast, but we have found Roger Jones and Nicholas Penny, *Raphael* (New Haven and London: Yale University Press, 1983) to be a scholarly and accurate recent monograph. Also useful are Nicholas Penny, "Raphael," *The Dictionary of Art* (ed. J. Turner; 34 vols.; London: Macmillan, 1996), 25:896–910; Jürg Meyer ZurCappellen, *Raffael in Florenz* (Munich: Hirmer, 1996).

2. Jones and Penny, *Raphael*, 136.

3. Literature on this pericope includes: Robert Leaney, "Jesus and Peter: The Call and Post-resurrection Appearance (Lk 5:1–11 and 24:34)," *Expository Times* 65 (1954): 381–82; Klaus Zillessen, "Das Schiff des Petrus und die Gefährten vom andern Schiff zur Exegese von Luc 5:1–11," *Zeitschrift für die neutestamentliche Wissenschaft* 57 (1966): 137–39; Günter Klein, "Die Berufung des Petrus," *Zeitschrift für die neutestamentliche Wissenschaft* 58 (1967): 1–44; D. P. Davies, "Luke 5:8 Simon Petros," *Expository Times* 79 (1968): 382; J. Delorme, "Luc V.1–11. Analyse structurale et histoire de la redaction," *New Testament Studies* 18 (1971/72): 331–50; J. D. M. Derrett, "James and John as Co-Rescuers from Peril (Lk 5,10)," *Novum Testamentum* 22 (1980): 299–303; Samuel Abogunrin, "The Three Variant Accounts of Peter's Call: Critical, Theological Examination of the Texts," *New Testament Studies* 31 (1985): 587–602; Robert Fortna, "Diachronic/Synchronic: Reading John 21 and Luke 5," in *John and the Synoptics* (Leuven: Leuven University Press, 1992), 387–99. For more bibliography, see François Bovon, *Das Evangelium nach Lukas, Lk 1,1–9,50* (3 vols.; Evangelisch-katholischer Kommentar zum Neuen Testament; Zurich: Benziger Verlag, 1993), 1:227–36.

4. Rudolf Bultmann, *History of the Synoptic Tradition* (trans. John Marsh; Oxford: Basil Blackwell, 1968), 217–18. For more on the relationship of Luke 5 and John 21, see Rudolf Pesch, *Der reiche Fischfang. Lk 5,1–11/Jo 21,1–14. Wundergeschichte — Berufungserzählung — Erscheinungsbericht* (Kommentare und Beiträge zum Alten und Neuen Testament 6; Düsseldorf, 1969).

5. Raymond E. Brown, *The Gospel According to John, XIII–XXI* (Anchor Bible 29A; Garden City, N.J.: Doubleday, 1966), 1090.

6. A. Plummer, *A Critical and Exegetical Commentary on the Gospel according to S. Luke* (International Critical Commentary; New York: Scribner, 1922), 147.

7. C. H. Dodd, "The Appearances of the Risen Christ: An Essay in Form-Criticism of the Gospels," *Studies in the Gospel: Essays in Memory of R. H. Lightfoot* (ed. Dennis E. Nineham; Oxford: Blackwell, 1957), 9–35.

8. See Klein, "Die Berufung des Petrus," 34–35. Cf. also R. E. Brown et al., eds., *Peter in the New Testament* (New York: Paulist, 1973), 83–101.

9. Joseph Fitzmyer, *The Gospel According to Luke* (Anchor Bible 28–28A; Garden City, N.J.: Doubleday, 1981, 1985), 1:561.

10. Ibid., 1:561–62.

11. This is not the place to consider the merits of the various solutions to the so-called Synoptic problem, e.g., the explanations for the literary relationship between Matthew, Mark, and Luke, which best explain their verbatim and near-verbatim agreement, as well as account for the significant peculiarities to each Gospel. For the classic presentation of the two-source hypothesis, see B. H. Streeter, *The Four Gospels: A Study of Origins, Treating of the Manuscript Tradition, Sources, Authorship, & Dates* (London: Macmillan, 1924). For the two-gospel hypothesis (which argues for the priority of Matthew, or more properly the posteriority of Mark), see William R. Farmer, *The Synoptic Problem: A Critical Analysis* (New York: Macmillan, 1964); for a critique, see Christopher Tuckett, *The Revival of the Griesbach Hypothesis: An Analysis and Appraisal* (Cambridge: Cambridge University Press, 1993). For the Farrer hypothesis (which argues for the priority of Mark, and Luke's use of

both Mark and Matthew), see A. M. Farrer, "On Dispensing with Q," in D. E. Nineham, ed., *Studies in the Gospels: Essays in Memory of R. H. Lightfoot* (Oxford: Blackwell, 1955), 55–88; E. P. Sanders and M. Davies, *Studying the Synoptic Gospels* (London: SCM, 1989), 92–116 passim; and now, especially, Mark Goodacre, *The Case against Q: Studies in Markan Priority and the Synoptic Problem* (Harrisburg, Pa.: Trinity Press International, 2002). Because most scholars, whether of the two-source hypothesis or the Farrer variety, assume Luke's use of Mark, our analysis presumes Luke's knowledge of Mark 1:16–20 in his composition of Luke 5:1–11.

12. The following list, including direct quotations, is taken from Fitzmyer, *Luke*, 1:71.

13. We are indebted to the work of Derek Hogan, a Baylor Ph.D. student, for much of what follows. He and the other students in a doctoral seminar on Luke and Rhetoric in the fall of 1999 provided the initial stimulus for this section. For a fuller account of the relationship of Luke to ancient rhetoric, see Mikeal C. Parsons, *Luke: Storyteller, Interpreter, and Evangelist* (Peabody, Mass.: Hendrickson, forthcoming).

14. Theon evidently considered plausibility/persuasiveness (*pithanoi* and its cognates) as the key element to narrative: "For it is always necessary to keep what is plausible in a narrative; for this is its best quality" (79.28–29; Patillon, 40). On plausibility, see also Quintilian, *Institutio Oratoria*, IV.2.32; *Rhetorica ad Alexandrum*, 30.143b.1–4; Cicero, *De Inventione*, I.21.29–30. See also Theon's comments on plausibility/persuasiveness in the fable at 76.35–77.9. We have used the critical edition of the Greek text (along with a French translation) found in Michel Patillon and Giancarlo Bolognesi, eds., *Aelius Théon. Progymnasmata* (Paris: Les Belles Lettres, 1997). The Patillon text has replaced Leonard Spengel, ed., *Rhetores Graeci*, vol. 2 (Leipzig: Teubner, 1854–56), 59–130, as the standard critical edition. Patillon with the aid of Bolognesi has reconstructed from the Armenian manuscripts five chapters (13–17), missing from the Greek texts. For an English translation, see George A. Kennedy, trans., *Progymnasmata: Greek Textbooks of Prose Composition and Rhetoric* (Writings from the Greco-Roman World 10; Atlanta: Society of Biblical Literature, 2003).

15. In a sense, this scene also provides the plausibility for the call of Levi, later in this same chapter, which, following Mark very closely, has Levi follow immediately and presumably without any prior relationship with Jesus.

16. On this symbolism and its pagan antecedents, see Hugo Rahner, *Symbole der Kirche* (Salzburg: Otto Muller, 1964), 306–60. See also H. S. Benjamins, "Noah, the Ark, and the Flood in Early Christian Theology: The Ship of the Church in the Making," in *Interpretations of the Flood* (ed. Florentino Garcia Martinez and Gerard P. Luttikhuizen; Leiden: Brill, 1998), 134–49.

17. See Günther Bornkamm's classic study, "The Stilling of the Storm in Matthew," in *Tradition and Interpretation in Matthew* (ed. Günther Bornkamm, Gerhard Barth, and Heinz Joachim Held; trans. Percy Scott; New Testament Library; London: SCM Press, 1963), 52–57.

18. Tertullian, *De baptismo*, 12; Hippolytus, *De Antichristo*, 59.

19. See *Epistle of Clement to James*, 14, 15 (PG 2, 49); Chrysostom, *Sermo in vivificam Crucem* (PG 50, 817); Peter Chrysologus, *Sermo 8* (PL 52); Gregory of Nazianzus, *Carmini*, I.1.1–5 (PG 37, 397).

20. On the identification of Noah's ark as a prefiguring of Peter's boat in Luke 5, see Ambrose, *Sermo XI*, PL 17, col. 675.

21. Peter and Linda Murphy, *The Oxford Companion to Christian Art and Architecture* (Oxford: Oxford University Press, 1996), 488. See also the quotation from the *Apostolic Constitutions* above.

22. Ambrose, *Sermo de mirabilibus* (PL 17, cols. 675); Ambrose, *Expositio Evangelii secundum Lucam*, 4.68. See also *Glossa Ordinaria* on Luke 5:10 (PL 114, 256C).

23. Augustine, *Sermo CCXLVIII* (PL, col. 1159).

24. For documentation and early scholarship, see Vincenzo Golzio, *Raffaello nei documenti nelle testimonianze dei contemporanei e nella letteratura del suo secolo* (Vatican City: Arti Grafiche Paneto & Petrelli, 1971); Giovanni Bellori, *Descrizione delle imagini dipinte da Raffaelle d'Urbino* (Rome: Greg Famborough, 1968 [1695]); Giorgio Vasari, *Le Opere di Giorgio Vasari: Le Vite de'più eccellenti pittori, scultori ed architettori scritte da Giorgio Vasari pittore Aretino* (1568) (ed. Gaetano Milanesi; 9 vols.; Florence: Sansoni, 1885), 4:315–86.

25. Penny, "Raphael," 4–5.

26. Vasari-Milanesi, *Le vite*, 4:317. Scholars generally agree that there was some relationship between Perugino and Raphael because of the similarities of their styles and the prominence of Perugino's workshop at exactly the time Raphael is beginning his training and career, but there is no documentation. Perugino was at the height of his career in 1500, and his reputation would have been known in the area near his hometown of Perugia. For more on the relationship between Raphael and Perugino, see Jones and Penny, *Raphael*, 2–5; Penny, "Raphael," 897.

27. For the study of drawings, see Paul Joannides, *The Drawings of Raphael with a Complete Catalogue* (Oxford: Oxford University Press, 1983); Francis Ames-Lewis, *The Draftsman Raffael* (New Haven and London: Yale University Press, 1986).

28. John Shearman, *Raphael's Cartoons in the Collection of Her Majesty the Queen and the Tapestries for the Sistine Chapel* (London and New York: Phaidon, 1972). This book developed from two earlier articles; see John White and John Shearman, "Raphael's Tapestries and Their Cartoons," *Art Bulletin* 40 (1958): 193–221, 229–323. More recently Shearman addresses the cartoons and tapestries in John Shearman, *Only Connect . . . Art and the Spectator in the Italian Renaissance* (Princeton, N.J.: Princeton University Press, 1992), 202–7, 216–18, 223, 238–39, 252–53. See two studies by Sharon Fermor, *The Raphael Tapestry Cartoons: Narrative, Decoration, Design* (London: Scala, 1996), and "The Raphael Tapestry Cartoons Re-examined," *Burlington Magazine* 140 (1998): 236–50. Related to technique, see Joyce Plesters, "Raphael's Cartoons for the Vatican Tapestries: A Brief Report on the Materials, Technique and Condition," in *The Princeton Raphael Symposium* (ed. John Shearman and Maria B. Hall; Princeton, N.J.: Princeton University Press, 1990), 111–24.

29. For a discussion of the original number of planned tapestries, see Creighton Gilbert, "Are the Ten Tapestries a Complete Series or a Fragment?" in *Studi su Raffaello; atti del congresso internazionale di studii: Urbino-Firenze, 6–14 Aprile 1984* (Urbino: QuattroVenti, 1987), 533–50.

30. Shearman, *Raphael's Cartoons*, 2. This manuscript ends with an account of the election of Clement VII in November 1523.

31. John Shearman, "The Chapel of Sixtus IV: Fresco Decoration of Sixtus IV, Raphael's Tapestries," in *The Sistine Chapel: The Art, the History and the Restoration* (ed. Carlo Pietrangeli et al.; New York: Harmony Books, 1986), 88.

32. The program continues the depiction of complex intellectual subjects that incorporate events related to the pope's supremacy.

33. Shearman, *Raphael's Cartoons*, 1.

34. Ibid., 3.

35. Ibid., 3; Golzio, *Raffaello*, 38, 51.

36. Jones and Penny, *Raphael*, 135. This payment is almost equal to the amount paid to Raphael for the contemporary frescoes in the Stanza dell'Incendio of the Vatican.

37. Shearman, *Raphael's Cartoons*, 3. This assessment is based on study of the seven surviving cartoons.

38. Jones and Penny, *Raphael*, 135.

39. Ibid., 135.

40. Shearman, *Raphael's Cartoons*, 3.

41. John Pope-Hennessy, *The Raphael Cartoons* (London: Her Majesty's Stationery Office, 1966), 6.

42. Ibid. Many sets were made later by other weavers in Brussels and Paris. The Hampton Court set is dated c. 1620 and executed in the Brussels studio of Jan Raes.

43. For details related to the influence this position had on the papacy, see Shearman, *Raphael's Cartoons*, 3, 8, 11–15, 21–23, 26–30, 39, 48, 59, 80–81; Jones and Penny, *Raphael*, 133.

44. See J. B. Gatticus, *De oratoriis domesticis et de usu altaris portatilis* (ed. J. A. Assemano; Rome, 1770), 26ff. and C. Carletti, "Il 'Sancta Sanctorum,'" in *Miscellanea Giulio Belvedere* (Vatican City: n.p., 1954), 387.

45. See Ettore Camesasca's appendix to Roberto Salvini, *The Sistine Chapel* (2 vols.; New York: Harry N. Abrams, 1965), 2:178–30.

46. For a discussion of this patterning, see J. Wilde, "The Decoration of the Sistine Chapel," *Proceedings of the British Academy* 44 (1958): 61–81.

47. See Leopold Ettlinger, *The Sistine Chapel before Michelangelo: Religious Imagery and Papal Primacy* (Oxford: Oxford University Press, 1965), 15–18.

48. Shearman, *Raphael's Cartoons*, 27. For the entire discussion of the chancel screen's relevance to the positioning of the tapestries, and in turn to the number of tapestries intended, see 21–27.

49. Six scenes were placed on either side of the altar wall. According to Shearman in "The Chapel of Sixtus IV," 47, the two lost scenes, the *Finding of Moses* and the *Adoration of the Shepherds*, flanked the original altarpiece on the left and right, respectively.

50. Shearman, "The Chapel of Sixtus IV," 47–77.

51. Esther Gordon Dotson, "An Augustinian Interpretation of Michelangelo's Sistine Chapel Ceiling," *Art Bulletin* 61 (1979): 223–56, 405–29. See especially 239–40 and 242.

52. Fermor, *Raphael Tapestry Cartoons*, 10.

53. Pierluigi de Vecchi, "Michelangelo's Last Judgment," in *The Sistine Chapel: The Art, the History and the Restoration* (ed. Carlo Pietrangeli et al.; New York: Harmony Books, 1986), 180–81.

54. Frederick Hartt and David G. Wilkins, *History of Italian Renaissance Art* (Upper Saddle River: Prentice Hall and Harry N. Abrams, 2003), 565.

55. Fermor, *Raphael Tapestry Cartoons*, 15.

56. Ibid.

57. Ibid., 71.

58. Shearman, *Raphael's Cartoons*, 42–43, finds seventeen to be the ideal number to "clothe" the walls. Gilbert, "Ten Tapestries," 539 and 545, says that sixteen corresponds to the number of frescoed bays (1480s cycle), so that each painting would have a tapestry beneath it.

59. See Shearman, *Raphael's Cartoons*, 21–44; Gilbert, "Ten Tapestries," 533–50; Fermor, *Raphael Tapestry Cartoons*, 10–12.

60. For a discussion of the bas-reliefs, see Shearman, *Raphael's Cartoons*, 37–38 and 84–89.

61. Fermor, *Raphael Tapestry Cartoons*, 15.

62. Ibid.

63. The cartoons are lost for the *Conversion of Saul*, *Paul in Prison*, and *Stoning of Stephen*.

64. Fermor, *Raphael Tapestry Cartoons*, 13 n. 15.

65. Ibid.

66. Ibid.

67. Ibid.

68. Ibid., 15.

69. See diagram by Shearman, *Raphael's Cartoons*, 25.

70. Fermor, *Raphael Tapestry Cartoons*, 45.

71. Later sets of cartoons do survive but do not necessarily help us in understanding this project. Giulio Romano designed two sets of cartoons, *Fructus Belli* and *The Triumph of Scipio*, in the mid-1540s and early 1530s, respectively. For the *Fructus Belli* cartoons in the Louvre, see G. Delmarcel et al., *Autour des Fructus Belli: une tapisserie de Bruxelles du XVI siècle* (Paris: Réunion des Musées Nationaux, 1992). For the *Triumph of Scipio*, see Ernst Gombrich et al., *Giulio Romano* (Milan: Electa, 1989), 467–69.

72. Shearman, *Raphael's Cartoons*, 109 n. 67.

73. Ibid., 109; Jones and Penny, *Raphael*, 135.

74. Fermor, *Raphael Tapestry Cartoons*, 45–46. For Vasari, see n. 25 above. For Giovanni Battista Armenini, see *On the True Precepts of Painting* (1586) (ed. Edward Olszewski; New York: Burt Franklin and Co., 1977).

75. *Vasari on Technique* (ed. G. Baldwin; trans. L. Maclehose; New York: Dover, 1960).

76. For Leonardo, see Karl Frey, "Studien Zu Michelagniolo Buonarotti und zur seiner Zeit," *Jahrbuch der Koniglich Preussischen Kunstsammlungen* 30 (1909): 129. For Michelangelo, see Carmen Bambach, "Michelangelo's Cartoon for the Crucifixion of St. Peter Reconsidered," *Master Drawings* 25 (1988): 131–41. For Raphael, see Konrad Oberhuber, *Il Cartone per la Scuola di Atene* (Milan: Silvana, 1972).

77. Fermor, *Raphael Tapestry Cartoons*, 47.

78. This information from this paragraph represents the research and conclusions made by ibid., 46–48.

79. Ibid., 48.

80. Ibid., 52. See ibid., 52, for additional information related to the pioneering use of the technique of photogrammetry to determine the sizes of the sheets of paper.

81. See ibid., 51, for a more extensive discussion of how these observations resulted from transmitted-light photography. This technique provides a view through the object as a whole, and shows up areas of puncture and varying density.

82. Ibid., 56–57.

83. See ibid., 54–56, for a discussion of the presence of these canvas layers or strips that was confirmed by raking-light photography. Carbon dating locates the canvas with 99 percent certainty to between 1390 and 1640, which Fermor acknowledges is inconsistent with the later need to reintegrate the cartoons.

84. Ibid., 52.

85. Ibid., 50.

86. Ibid., 56.

87. Ibid., 60.

88. Information in this paragraph is reported by ibid., 58–60.

89. Fermor, "Raphael Cartoons Re-examined," *Burlington Magazine* 140 (1998): 236–50.

90. Ibid., 241.

91. Fermor, *Raphael Tapestry Cartoons*, 61. The underdrawing can be likened to the *pentimenti* of a panel or canvas painting of the period. Visible *pentimenti* indicate changes made by the artist at some point in the creative process.

92. Fermor, "Raphael Cartoons Re-examined," 242.

93. See Joannides, *The Drawings of Raphael*, 222–23. Joannides attributes the following to Raphael: Munich, Graphische Sammlung 8235 (fig. 355); Vienna, Albertina Bd. VI, 192 verso (fig. 356v.); Vienna, Albertina Bd. VI, 192 recto (fig. 356r.). Ames-Lewis, *The Draftsman Raffael*, 128–29, agrees with the attribution of Vienna, Albertina Bd. VI, 192 verso (fig. 137) to Raphael but attributes Albertina Bd. VI, 192 recto (fig. 138) to Raphael's assistant, Penni. Shearman, *Raphael's Cartoons*, does not illustrate Vienna, Albertina Bd. VI, 192 verso; attributes Vienna, Albertina Bd. VI, 192 recto to Giulio Romano (fig. 44); attributes Munich, Graphische Sammlung 8235 to being a copy after Raphael (fig. 43); attributes a woodcut from the Windsor Castle, Royal Library, to Ugo da Carpi after Raphael (fig. 42); attributes a *Study of Birds* with an unknown location to Giovanni da Udine, a copy (fig. 40); illustrates a variant on the Albertina Anonymous, after Giulio Romano from the Windsor Castle, Royal Library (fig. 45). Both Joannides (fig. 357) and Shearman (fig. 41) attribute Windsor, Royal Collection 12749 to Penni.

94. Shearman, *Raphael's Cartoons*, 50, discusses the identification of "deep water" fish. It should also be noted that this visual tradition differs from another similar tradition that finds its biblical source in Matt 6:18–22. This scene and tradition, known as the Vocation of the Apostles, is composed of Christ standing on the shore, rather than sitting in a boat as is done here, talking to the apostles.

95. Ibid., 50. Shearman traces Raphael's connection with the emerald portrait.

96. John Pope-Hennessy, *Raphael: The Wrightsman Lectures* (London: Phaidon, 1970), 159–60. Fermor, *Raphael Tapestry Cartoons*, 244. To support her statement, Fermor compares this head to those of the apostles in the *Death of Ananias* cartoon.

97. Fermor, "Raphael Cartoons Re-examined," 242.

98. See Shearman, *Raphael's Cartoons*, 5–51, for a discussion of this theory.

99. John White, *The Raphael Cartoons* (London: H.M.S.O., 1972), 8.

100. Hartt and Wilkins, *History of Italian Renaissance Art*, 565.

101. Fermor, "Raphael Cartoons Re-examined," 249.

102. Ibid., 249.

103. Ibid.

104. Pope-Hennessy, *The Raphael Cartoons*, 9.

105. Shearman, *Raphael's Cartoons*, 44. Shearman here lists other caveats, including the embarrassing wealth of literary sources that must be consulted and the need to interpret each individual tapestry in its relationship to the overall iconographic program.

106. Ibid.

107. Antonio de Beatis was the first to describe the tapestry this way when he wrote in July 1517 about "quando Christo dono le chiavi ad San Pietro," cited in L. Pastor, *Die Reise des Kardinals Luigi d'Aragona* (Freiburg-im-Breisgau, 1905), 117.

108. Shearman, *Raphael's Cartoons*, 55.

109. Raphael's eleven apostles are themselves problematic, because they seem to presume the post-crucifixion situation where, after betraying Jesus, Judas departed from the circle of the Twelve (permanently according to Matt 27). One presumes the presence of all twelve apostles in Matt 16, given that this scene occurs during the public ministry when Judas was still a functioning member of the apostles.

110. Shearman, *Raphael's Cartoons*, 55. For writers who conflate the two texts, see *inter alia*, Beatus Maximus, *Sermo II in natali b. Petri & Pauli* (PL 57, col. 397); Petrus Comestor, *Historia scholastica: In evangelia*, cap. Lxxxv (PL 198, col. 1581); and from the period contemporary with the cartoons, Thomas de Vio, *Commentarii in quatuor Evangelia et Acta Apostolorum*, Venice, 1530, fols. 39r., 211v.; Domenico Jacobazzi, *De concilio* (1512ff.); Giovanni Francesco Poggio, *De potestate papae et concilii* (1511–12), Rome, 1517 (?), fols. 43r., 60r.

111. Depending, for example, on whether you understand the Mosaic in S. Apollinare Nuova, Ravenna (sixth century) as depicting Peter's calling or his charge.

112. So Carl Gustaf Stridbeck, *Raphael Studies, II. Raphael and Tradition* (Stockholm: Almqvist & Wiksell, 1963), 53–60.

113. Shearman, *Raphael's Cartoons*, 118.

114. In some cases, whether the scene being depicted is that of Matt 4 or John 21 might hinge on whether or not the catch of fish would be considered "miraculous." For a discussion of other examples from the early church onward (with illustrations) of Christ standing on the shore (or walking on the water) during either Peter's calling (Matt 4//Mark 1) or his charge (John 21), see Arvid Gottlicher, *Die Schiffe im Neuen Testament* (Berlin: Gebr. Mann, 1999), esp. plates 3, 5, 6, 7, 9, 10, 12, 15, 16, 17, 18, 19, 22, 23, 37, 38, 39, 40, and 43.

115. Poggio, *De potestate pape et concilii* (1511–12; ed. Rome, 1517 [?]); Marcello, *De authoritate summi Pontificis* (Florence 1521), I.vii; Angelo da Vallombrosa, *Oratio pro concilio Lateranensi contra conventiculum pisanum* (September–October 1511; ed. R. Maiocchi, *Rivista di scienze storiche*, iv [1907]), 344–55.

116. Innocent, *Epistolae*, VII.cciii (PL 215, col. 512); cited by Shearman, *Raphael's Cartoons*, 65.

117. The connection between these two stories is made also in the literature. The sixth-century writer Arator did so in his *De actibus apostolorum*, cap. ii—an interpretation that was made available in Raphael's day by Barbosa's 1516 gloss on Arator's commentary, in *Aratoris Cardinalis Historia Apostolica cum commentaries Arii Barbosae Lusitani* (Salamanca, 1516) n. 10, fol. xvii, v.

118. This miracle is also parallel to an episode later in Acts where Paul heals a lame man (see Acts 14).

119. This is the second of several so-called "punitive" miracles in which persons are miraculously punished for their disobedience; see also the stories of Judas (Acts 1), Herod (Acts 12), and Elymas (Acts 13).

120. See Innocent III's letter to the patriarch of Constantinople recorded in *Epistolae*, Bk. II. ccix (PL 214, col. 761).

121. See Poggio, fol. 42v; Torquemada, *Summa ecclesiastica* (Salamanca, 1560), 185. Shearman, *Raphael's Cartoons*, 66, has perhaps underestimated the importance of these scenes for the primacy of Peter theme, and at any rate has labored to relate them more squarely to the doctrine of the Two Keys.

122. This emphasis on the humanity of Peter was not ignored in the literature on the *Primatus Petri*; in fact, it was put to great effect in arguing both the humility of Peter and the divine grace he was shown in being called to be Christ's vicar on earth. In this sense, focus on Peter's limitations parallels Paul's own sense of weakness (cf. 1 Cor 15:9).

123. In fact, one could argue that Paul's conversion is not actually completed until the next tapestry, *The Conversion of the Proconsul*. It is not until this point in Acts that Paul's name is changed from his Hebrew name, Saul, to his Roman name, Paul. In the biblical tradition, the change of names was associated with a call or commission; see the change of Abram to Abraham in Gen 17:5 and Jacob to Israel in Gen 32:27–28. Thus, Saul's

conversion, inextricably entwined with and not only prerequisite to his call to be apostle to the Gentiles, is not complete until he demonstrates his authority and power over evil, represented by Elymas, and converts Sergius Paulus to the Way. On this interpretation, see Susan Garrett, *The Demise of the Devil* (Minneapolis: Fortress, 1989).

124. Shearman, *Raphael's Cartoons*, 68.

125. Ibid.

126. Fermor, *Raphael Tapestry Cartoons*, 10.

127. Ephrem the Syrian, *Commentary on Tatian's Diatessaron*, 5.18; ECTD 103.

128. Augustine, *Sermones* CCXLVIII, CCLII (PL, cols. 1159, 1179); cf. also Bede, *In Luce evangelium expositio*, v (PL 92, col. 382); *Glossa ordinaria*, Luke v (PL 114, col. 256). For other texts, see Shearman, *Raphael's Cartoons*, 78 n. 192.

129. See Origen, *Homilies on St. Luke*; Augustine, *Sermons* (Migne PL 38, 1026ff; also 39:2005); Gregory of Nyssa, *Against Appolinarius* (Migne PG 45, 1138). H. Leclerq, "Mages," *Dictionnaire d'archeologie chrétienne et de liturgie* (Paris, 1931), 10.1.986, also cites Fulgentius (d. 533) as equating the shepherds with the Jews and the magi with Gentiles. For more on this interpretation of the Nativity scene, see Hornik and Parsons, "Domenico Ghirlandaio's *Nativity and Adoration of the Shepherds* (Luke 2:1–20)," in Heidi J. Hornik and Mikeal C. Parsons, *Illuminating Luke: The Infancy Narrative in Italian Renaissance Painting* (Harrisburg, Pa.: Trinity Press International, 2003).

130. On this particular point in the iconography of the Vatican Logge, see Bernice F. Davidson, *Raphael's Bible: A Study of the Vatican Logge* (University Park, Pa.: Penn State University Press, 1985), 44; Kathry Virginia Andrus-Walck, "The 'Bible of Raphael' and Early Christian Antiquity" (Ph.D. dissertation, University of North Carolina at Chapel Hill, 1986), 390–92.

131. Shearman, *Raphael's Cartoons*, 78 n. 192, tentatively suggests that the ravens in the tapestry might be taken to symbolize "the raven-sinner as the Gentile" (citing various texts in support of this view). For Shearman's suggestions regarding the possible meaning of the other birds (cranes and swans) in the cartoon, see 54–55, and on his specific identification of the deep-water fish caught in the "miraculous draught"(!), see 50 n. 33.

132. Maximus of Turin, *Sermon 110*; Ancient Christian Writers 50:238–39; cited by Just, *Luke*, 889.

133. Recovering the nautical imagery of the church as ship and its leaders as "captains" alongside other imagery embedded in the tradition (e.g., shepherd and flock) would enrich our ways of speaking about and understanding the church, its organization and leadership. Of course, the imagery has not been entirely eclipsed from the tradition, especially in music. In addition to the Southern gospel tune, "The Gospel Ship" (performed by various groups from the Kingsmen to the Carter family), consider also the African American spiritual, "Old Ship of Zion." The chorus runs:

> Sail on Old Ship Zion
> Brave what lurks in the cold dark night
> Sail on Old Ship of Zion
> Till you see that Beacon Light
> He's on board, you're not alone
> Sail on till you hear the Captain say
> "Land's in sight, You've made it home."

See Walter F. Pitts, *Old Ship of Zion: the Afro-Baptist Ritual in the African Diaspora* (New York: Oxford University Press, 1993).

134. The typical Protestant interpretation of Matt 16:13–20 is to understand the demonstrative pronoun, "this," to refer to Peter's confession rather than to Peter himself ("Upon this, I will build my church"). This interpretation does not, however, do justice to the role of Peter as leader of the apostles, as depicted in the Gospels and Acts and understood in the earliest strata of the tradition. For a more balanced approach that takes seriously the importance of both the confession and the one uttering it, see David E. Garland, *Reading Matthew. A Literary and Theological Commentary on the First Gospel* (New York: Crossroad, 1993), 168–73.

Figure 4-1. Jacopo Bassano. *Good Samaritan*. c. 1557. Oil on canvas. National Gallery, London. Photo. With permission from the National Gallery, London.

Chapter four

The *Good Samaritan* and *The Rich Man and Lazarus* by Jacopo Bassano

(Luke 10:30–37; 16:19–31)

THE PARABLES OF JESUS have captured the imagination of Christian believers across the centuries. The uniquely Lukan parables, often referred to as "L" parables (because they are drawn from a Lukan or "L" source)[1] have proven to be exceptionally rich theological fare, but two of them — the Good Samaritan and the Rich Man and Lazarus — though beloved in the literature, have attracted relatively little attention in the history of pictorial depictions, especially in Italian painting.[2] One artist, Jacopo Bassano, however, has rendered powerful depictions of both these parables, the *Good Samaritan* (Figure 4-1), National Gallery, London, and *The Rich Man and Lazarus* (Figure 4-2), Cleveland Museum of Art, and thus placed us deeply in his debt.[3] Because these two paintings served similar religious and cultural purposes in their original context, dealing with both of them in this chapter is appropriate. We provide separate overviews of the biblical text and subsequent histories of interpretation. After dealing with the life and work of the artist, we discuss the ways in which the iconography of each painting served a particular function in Venetian culture, namely, to call the church to task for failing in its obligations to care for the poor and needy of its society.[4]

Overview of the Biblical Text

[25]And behold a certain lawyer stood up, tempting him, and saying, Master, what must I do to possess eternal life? [26]But he said to him: What is written in the law? How readest thou? [27]He answering, said: Thou shalt love the Lord thy God with thy whole heart and with thy whole soul and with all thy strength and with all thy mind: and thy neighbour as thyself. [28]And he said to him: Thou hast answered right. This do, and thou shalt live. [29]But he willing to justify himself,

Figure 4-2. Jacopo Bassano, Italian, c. 1510–92. *The Rich Man and Lazarus,* c. 1550.
Oil on canvas, 176 x 251 x 12 cm. Photo. © The Cleveland Museum of Art,
Delia E. and L. E. Holden Funds, 1939.68.

said to Jesus: And who is my neighbour? [30]And Jesus answering, said:
A certain man went down from Jerusalem to Jericho, and fell among
robbers, who also stripped him and having wounded him went away,
leaving him half dead. [31]And it chanced, that a certain priest went
down the same way: and seeing him, passed by. [32]In like manner also
a Levite, when he was near the place and saw him, passed by. [33]But
a certain Samaritan being on his journey, came near him: and seeing
him, was moved with compassion. [34]And going up to him, bound up
his wounds, pouring in oil and wine: and setting him upon his own
beast, brought him to an inn and took care of him. [35]And the next
day he took out two pence and gave to the host and said: Take care
of him; and whatsoever thou shalt spend over and above, I, at my
return, will repay thee. [36]Which of these three, in thy opinion, was
neighbour to him that fell among the robbers? [37]But he said: He that
shewed mercy to him. And Jesus said to him: Go, and do thou in
like manner. (Luke 10:25–37, Douay-Rheims Bible)

In the Lukan context, the parable of the Good Samaritan is prompted
by a dialogue between Jesus and a lawyer.[5] Jesus responds to the lawyer's
question, "Teacher, what must I do to inherit eternal life?" with a question
of his own, "What is written in the Law? How do you read it?" After responding with the "correct" answer (combining Deut 6:5 with Lev 19:18)

that one should love God and "one's neighbor as himself," the lawyer, seeking to "justify himself," asks one more question: "And who is my neighbor?" (Luke 10:29).[6] Jesus responds to the question, not with another question, but with the story of the Good Samaritan.

One of the reasons for this parable's continued appeal to subsequent generations of audiences is the masterful storytelling it represents. Joseph Fitzmyer has commented:

> The storytelling devices are to be noted in the episode: the threesome in the dramatis personae (the priest, the levite, and the Samaritan [like the Englishman, the Irishman, the Scotsman]); the Palestinian details (olive oil, wine, animal, and inn); the answer of the Jewish lawyer, which studiously avoids saying "the Samaritan" and uses only "the one who showed him kindness"; and a certain built-in improbability (would a Jew normally regard a Samaritan as a model of kindness, picture him traveling in Judea, or that a Jewish innkeeper would trust him?).[7]

Beyond these "stock" elements of the storytelling trade, a grasp of certain other cultural features are necessary to understand the parable's message: the privileged status of the priest and Levite in first-century Jewish society; the taboos associated with contact with a dead (or apparently dead) body (see Num 5:2c; 19:2–13; Ezek 44:25–27; and the later tradition preserved in *m. Nazir* 7:1), and the attitude, shared by most Judean Jews, toward Samaritans (cf. John 4:9: "Jews, remember, use nothing in common with Samaritans.").[8] These details help underscore the point of the story, namely, "that a 'neighbor' is anyone in need with whom one comes into contact and to whom one can show pity and kindness, even beyond the bounds of one's own ethnic or religious group."[9]

Richard Bauckham has offered an interpretation that takes seriously the Jewish halakhic context of the parable regarding which Mosaic rule should prevail — the need for the priest to avoid corpse defilement or the obligation (for any Israelite) to assist a fellow Israelite in dire need of help.[10] In a compelling argument, Bauckham concludes that "the commandment to love the neighbor is of such importance that it must always override others in cases of conflict. Moreover, by stressing the superiority of the love commandment specifically to purity laws, the parable tends to downgrade, while not necessarily invalidating, purity concerns. . . . "[11]

Recently Ronald Hock has further illuminated the meaning of the parable in a larger Greco-Roman context by relating the Samaritan's act of compassion with the virtue of philanthropy as practiced in the ancient world and as would have been understood by an ancient audience.[12] Of

course, that such virtuous philanthropy is exhibited by a Samaritan and
not the pious Jewish layperson would have come as a surprise to the lawyer
listening to the story in Luke (and no doubt to Jesus' Jewish audience).
As Nolland observes:

> The Samaritan administered first aid, led the man on his own mount
> back to civilization, took care of him overnight at an inn, and then
> took financial responsibility for seeing to the man's full recuperation
> from his ordeal. Having seen to the man's pressing need, the Samar-
> itan went on about his business. He would come back later and pay
> any bills. . . . Perhaps . . . we find that in extremis a Samaritan will do
> very well for a neighbor![13]

The parable's conclusion, admonition of Jesus to the lawyer to follow
the example of the Samaritan, is no less a command for the audience to
do the same: "Go and do likewise!"

The Rich Man and Lazarus

[19]There was a certain rich man, who was clothed in purple and fine
linen; and feasted sumptuously every day. [20]And there was a certain
beggar, named Lazarus, who lay at his gate, full of sores, [21]Desiring
to be filled with the crumbs that fell from the rich man's table. And
no one did give him; moreover the dogs came and licked his sores.
[22]And it came to pass that the beggar died and was carried by the
angels into Abraham's bosom. And the rich man also died: and he
was buried in hell. [23]And lifting up his eyes when he was in torments,
he saw Abraham afar off and Lazarus in his bosom: [24]And he cried,
and said: Father Abraham, have mercy on me and send Lazarus,
that he may dip the tip of his finger in water to cool my tongue:
for I am tormented in this flame. [25]And Abraham said to him: Son,
remember that thou didst receive good things in thy lifetime, and
likewise Lazarus evil things, but now he is comforted and thou art
tormented. [26]And besides all this, between us and you there is fixed a
great chaos: so that they who would pass from hence to you cannot,
nor from thence come hither. [27]And he said: Then, father, I beseech
thee, that thou wouldst send him to my father's house, for I have
five brethren, [28]That he may testify unto them, lest they also come
into this place of torments. [29]And Abraham said to him: They have
Moses and the prophets. Let them hear them. [30]But he said: No,
father Abraham: but if one went to them from the dead, they will
do penance. [31]And he said to him: If they hear not Moses and the

prophets, neither will they believe, if one rise again from the dead. (Luke 16:19–31, Douay-Rheims Bible)

The parable of the Rich Man and Lazarus is part of a chapter in Luke that deals with the theme of the use and abuse of wealth.[14] The chapter might be outlined as follows:

1. The Prudent Use of Wealth by an "Unrighteous" Steward (16:1–13)

2. On the Lovers of Money and the Law and the Prophets (16:14–18)

3. The Inequity of Wealth and Poverty in This Life (16:19–31)

Verses 14–18 lie at the center of the chapter; these verses are tied into what precedes them (the parable of the dishonest manager and its interpretations) by reference to the Pharisees, whom Luke calls lovers of money.[15] They scoff at Jesus' claim that one could not serve both God and mammon. Luke 16:14–17 makes two points that the second parable in the chapter, the rich man and Lazarus, then picks up: (1) Verses 14–15 — What is prized by human beings, "the outer appearances" — is an abomination in the sight of God. Luke 16:19–25 demonstrates that wealth is no sign of one's righteousness nor is poverty proof of one's evil. So God's opposition to the self-sufficient who are insensitive to the needs of the poor is evident in the fate of the rich man. (2) Luke 16:16–17 demonstrates (a) universality of kingdom and (b) continuing validity of the law. In Luke 16:27–31, Lazarus's inclusion demonstrates inclusiveness of kingdom. Furthermore the law is still in force, especially with regard to care for poor: "they have Moses and the prophets; let them hear" (16:31). This disregard for Moses and the prophets is at the root of the problem described in the parable, not their invalidity. A closer look at the parable confirms especially this last point.

The parable itself divides into two parts, both of which were widely recognized *topoi* in the ancient world. The first part, vv. 19–26, deals with the reversal of fortunes; the second, vv. 27–31, with the general topic of the return of a recently dead person with a message for the living. Both parts have been explored in terms of their relationship to similar stories from the comparative literature of Luke's world. We take up each part in turn.

H. Gressmann was the first scholar to note parallels with an Egyptian folk story of Setme and Si-Osiris and its later Jewish derivatives.[16] In the story, a miraculously reincarnated Si-Osiris takes his father on a tour of Amente, the realm of the dead, in which they see the reversal of fortunes of a rich man and a poor beggar, whose two funerals the father and son had witnessed before their sojourn to Amente. In the realm of the dead, the rich man was in torment and pain, while the poor beggar now sat, robed in the rich man's fine garments, near the throne of the ruler of the dead. While much of the subsequent scholarship followed Gressmann in his conclusion that Luke 16:19–31, along with seven other later rabbinic tales, were dependent on this Egyptian folklore, recent scholarship has questioned the validity of many of Gressmann's claims.[17]

Richard Bauckham, building upon (but also criticizing) the work of Ron Hock, argues that the general theme of the "reversal of fortunes" was not limited to the Egyptian tale and its derivatives, but was a pervasive theme in the Greco-Roman world.[18] What is the reason for this reversal of fortunes? Unlike many of the parallel stories, the Lukan parable does not claim the reversal results from the sin of the rich man (for misusing his wealth, or acquiring it unjustly, or even neglecting the poor man at his gate)[19] nor the poor man's piety. Rather,

> what is wrong with the situation in this world, according to the para-ble, is the stark inequality in the living conditions of the two men, which is vividly and memorably conveyed simply by the juxtaposi-tion of the rich man's expensive luxury and the poor man's painful beggary (vv. 19–21). That is why there is no mention of the moral qualities of the two men. The injustice which God's justice in the next life must remedy lies in the mere facts which are stated in vv. 19–21.[20]

Jesus' words both appeal to popular notions of an eschatological reversal of fortunes and provide social commentary on the inequities and injustices of the social and economic systems of his day. Yet, the resources to resolve such inequities are already in the possession of Jesus' (and Luke's) hearers, a point made in the second half of the parable.

Here Bauckham is right to argue for the unity of the two parts of the parable. In fact, the similarity between the second half of the parable with the Egyptian folklore, so often appealed to as a parallel for the parable's first half, has largely been ignored. In both stories, a venue is imagined in which this reversal of fortunes can be reported to the realm of the living in the hopes of effecting such change.[21] The difference, and it is an important one, is that in the Egyptian and Jewish stories, the message is received by those among the living, while Abraham refuses the rich man's request that his brothers be informed of his eternal fate. A most interesting parallel occurs in the *Book of Jannes and Jambres*, a second or third century c.e. text of Jewish or Christian origins.[22]

Jannes and Jambres were the names given in Jewish tradition to the Egyptian magicians who opposed Moses (cf. CD 5.19). As punishment for opposing Moses, Jannes dies and is buried by his brother, Jambres, only to be recalled by Jambres through necromancy and the use of magic books. The soul of Jannes appears and urges Jambres to avoid his fate in Hades: "make sure you do good in your life to your children and friends; for in the netherworld no good exists, only gloom and darkness."[23]

The parallels with our parable in Luke are striking (a message from a dead brother tormented in Hades to his living relative[s], revealing his fate and urging his brother[s] to repent and avoid his fate) as are the differences (the rich man asks Abraham to send Lazarus, there is no use of necromancy, and most significantly, the request for such communication is denied). One need not assume direct knowledge of this particular story on the part of Jesus or Luke (or their audiences) in order to make the assumption that the ancient auditor of the parable of the rich man and Lazarus — given the widespread number of stories in which the recently dead (or their representative) in some fashion or another, communicate their fate to those still living — might reasonably expect the rich man's brothers to benefit from the knowledge of the fate of their recently deceased brother. The refusal of this request would surely have stopped the audience in its track. Bauckham comments:

> The unusual character of the story in the parable, therefore, is that it describes the fate of particular individuals after death, proposes a way in which this fate could have become known to the living, but then rejects it. A hearer or reader familiar with the way the folkloric motifs in the story were generally used would already before v. 26 be expecting to be told of some means by which the fates of the rich man and Lazarus became known to the living, would recognize the rich man's request in vv. 26–27 as proposing a well recognized means for this purpose, and would expect the request to be granted, the revelation to be made by Lazarus to the rich man's brothers, and most likely the brothers to repent.[24]

Abraham's refusal to grant the rich man's request via some apocalyptic revelation, in effect, thwarts all the audience's expectations, but why? Again, Bauckham's conclusions are a propos:

> By refusing an apocalyptic revelation from the world of the dead, the parable throws an emphasis back onto the situation with which it began. . . . After an excursion into the hereafter, it brings us back to the world in which the rich coexist with the destitute because they do not listen to Moses and the prophets. . . . To perceive the situation of the rich and poor as radically unjust the rich need only

to listen to Moses and the prophets. If they refuse to see how the situation contradicts God's justice on the evidence of the scriptures, no purported revelation of the fate of the dead will convince them.[25]

Subsequent interpreters who grappled with the meaning of the parable did not always grasp this basic point, but for Jacopo Bassano and his patrons, the parable (along with the Good Samaritan) did provide biting commentary on the social inequities of their own situation, a point to which we eventually return.

History of Interpretation

The fine study by Stephen Wailes, *Medieval Allegories of Jesus' Parables*, aids our survey of the history of interpretation of both the Good Samaritan and the Rich Man and Lazarus parables.[26]

The Good Samaritan

Stephen Wailes has conveniently summarized the history of interpretation of the parable of the Good Samaritan:

> In the latter part of the twelfth century, Radulfus Ardens observed that this parable demonstrates four things: the ruin of the human race, the devil's persecution, the inadequacy of the Law, and Christ's mercy (col. 2046BC). This is a good summary of the allegorical understanding one finds in the earliest sources, which enjoys remarkably consistent support throughout the Middle Ages. We understand the traveler from Jerusalem to Jericho as mankind in the figure of Adam traveling from paradise to this world because of sin; he is waylaid by forces of evil, stripped of spiritual garments, and wounded through vice and error; the religion of the Old Testament alone cannot help him, so the priest and Levite pass by; Christ is the good Samaritan who places man upon his own body and brings him to the Church; the leaders of the Church receive a spiritual trust from Christ for the care of man, with the promise of recompense for additional benefits.[27]

Of course, subtle variations in the details of interpretation are as inevitable as they are interesting. Origen is the earliest writer whose comments on the parable of the Good Samaritan are extant.[28] Origen identifies the robbers as false teachers, the wounds as vices and sins, and the stable keeper as the church's presiding angel (see Rev 2:1).[29] Origen also plays on the etymology of the word "Samaritan" as "protector" to bolster his Christological interpretation.[30]

Augustine is the next major figure whose interpretation shapes for centuries to come much of the subsequent discussion of the parable.[31] For Augustine (following Jerome), "Jericho" refers to the "moon" and "signifies our mortality, for it is born, waxes, grows old, and dies" (col. 1340). According to Augustine, the priest and Levite represent "the priesthood and the ministry of the Old Testament" (col. 1340). The Samaritan's horse is for Augustine, as for so many other early interpreters, Christ's flesh, and the placement of the injured traveler on the horse represents belief in the Incarnation (col. 1340). Augustine departs from the popular interpretation of identifying the two denarii left by the Samaritan for the care of the traveler with the Two Testaments given by Christ to Paul and the apostles for the salvation of humankind, and argues that the two denarii represent the twofold command to love neighbor and God.[32] Wailes points out that "Augustine is the first authority to focus on the idea of extra expenses in verse 35. Since the stable keeper represents the apostles, and Christ is to recompense them for any further outlays, Augustine construes these to be either the observing of the counsels of religion beyond its precepts, or the forgoing of material support that might properly be required of the Christian community. At the Judgment Christ will reward both such actions."[33] Wailes goes on to contend that in most other details, Augustine's interpretation, elaborated and modified by the Venerable Bede, "became the standard teaching on 'The Good Samaritan,' as may be seen from the Gloss and the commentary of Zacharias Chrysopolitanus, which show no significant innovations or omissions."[34]

Two interesting variations, in light of Bassano's subsequent moralizing portrayal of the parable, are those found in Gottfried of Admont and Hugh of Saint-Cher.[35] Gottfried follows the traditional interpretation through verse 30, but at that point he interprets the parable as a moral lesson on the behavior desired in a good prelate. "The priest, Levite, and Samaritan are aspects of the same figure, the prelate: the first two do not heal the fallen man because the conducting of worship and study of Scripture alone is insufficient, and only the addition of pastoral works (the Samaritan) makes the ministry efficacious."[36]

Departing from the incarnational interpretation of the horse as the flesh of Christ, Gottfried raises the question as to whether the horse belongs to the traveler or the Samaritan. If the traveler, then the action represents "corporal penance" on the part of the sinner; if the Samaritan, the action represents the priest's determination to perform penitential acts in behalf of the sinner (col. 568A). The stable is the heart of the sinner "now lowly and fetid in the knowledge of sin" (col. 568B).

Hugh of Saint-Cher offers another fascinating moral interpretation, in which the Samaritan stands for the pious layperson and, as such, may come closer to the parable's original meaning, at least in the situation of Jesus — the *sitz im leben Jesu*.[37] The traveler is a person "going down" from wealth to poverty, wellness to sickness, prosperity to adversity because "the wheel of fortune is continuously turning":

> The man falls among robbers when he seeks the worldly help of rich
> people, doctors, and lawyers; doctors (as an example) take money
> from the sick but most often do no good; these robbers "go their way"
> as sated wolves leave the corpse; the priest and the Levite show the
> wickedness of the clergy, venal and merciless. The Samaritan is the
> pious layperson who approaches the traveler both in body and spirit
> by mercy, as in visiting the sick; binds wounds by alms (*necessaria*
> *tribuendo*) and infuses the oil of compassion and wine of consolation;
> sets him on his horse through the bearing of burdens; and brings him
> to the stable of his home. Hugh explains that the home of such a
> man is called *stabulum* from *stabilitas*, which he shows in his mercy.
> The stable keeper is Christ. The layperson gives two coins to Christ
> in that he gives both his will and his ability to the needy.[38]

These ethical interpretations of the parable, while in the distinct minority in the history of interpretation, nonetheless are significant reminders of the ethical obligations placed upon the Christian believer, obligations that Bassano and his patrons seek to awaken in the dormant Venetian culture of his day.

The Rich Man and Lazarus

If moralizing interpretations of the Good Samaritan make up only a small fraction of the otherwise allegorical readings of that parable in medieval exegesis, the converse is true for the Parable of the Rich Man and Lazarus.[39] Although allegorical interpretation dates back to Augustine,[40] many commentators totally rejected the allegorical elements in favor of making the parable a moral example (e.g., *inter alia*, Peter Chrysologus, Radulfus Ardens, Bonaventure, Ludolph of Saxony).[41]

One major reason for this reluctance to allegorize the parable was the belief, held at least since Ambrose, that because Jesus gave a name to the beggar in the story (Lazarus), his words referred to a historical event rather than a parable.[42] Hugh of Saint-Cher and Bonaventure both quote the *Gloss* in claiming "this seems more to be a narrative than a parable."[43]

Both Bede and Gregory include allegorical interpretations of the parable, but both admit that it is the moral lesson of the story that should take preeminence, though they make this point in different ways. Gregory begins his interpretation with allegory but acknowledges "the moral content of this account, which is extremely necessary for you, occupies the last place in the order of our exposition because those things are often better recalled that one has heard more recently."[44] Bede, on the other hand, agreed with Gregory's assessment of the moral content of the parable but gave his ethical interpretation first.[45]

In the various moral interpretations, the message is the same. The church has an obligation to care for the poor and needy, who, like Lazarus, literally lie at their door. For example, Bruno of Segni begins his interpretation with this observation: "These words are most necessary both for the rich and for the poor, because they bring fear to the former and consolation to the latter."[46] Likewise Peter Comestor claims that "to attack their avarice he [Jesus] sets forth for them an exemplum of a rich man in purple."[47]

Closer to our artist in both space and time, Cardinal Gaetano wrote in his popular commentary on the Bible, printed in Venice in 1530, that the name of the poor man and not the rich was given in the parable "to show that the spiritual order is contrary to the terrestrial," and that the parable should be taken as an exhortation to the rich to practice philanthropy.[48]

In the context of these moralizing interpretations of both parables — the minority view for the one, the majority reading for the other — we turn our attention to the visual interpretation of these parables by the artist, Jacopo Bassano.

Life and Work of the Artist

Jacopo Dal Ponte was born c. 1510 in Bassano del Grappa and died there on February 13, 1592.[49] He was apprenticed to his father, Francesco, a painter in Bassano. He frequently traveled to Venice and was trained there by Bonifazio de'Pitati, known as Veronese (c. 1487–1553), in the first half of the 1530s. Bonifazio is known for his narrative schemes but Jacopo's work from this period, such as the *Flight into Egypt*, in the Museo Civico, Bassano del Grappa (Figure 4-3) shows an influence from Titian.[50] He continued in the family shop until his father's death in 1539. He frequently collaborated with other artists in the shop on mainly altarpieces for local churches. Public commissions utilized his skills as a narrative artist and his ability at naturalism.[51]

Figure 4-3. Jacopo Bassano. *Flight into Egypt.* 1534. Museo Civico, Bassano del Grappa. Photo. By concession of Bassano del Grappa Museum, Italy.

By 1535 he was engaged in major fresco commissions, and most scholars agree that his style had matured.[52] Yet, Jacopo's frequent visits to Venice during 1535–40s enabled him to see, and be influenced by, the late works of Pordenone (1483–1539). Bassano's *Supper at Emmaus* (Figure 4-4), to-day at the Kimbell Art Museum, Fort Worth, incorporates this influence.[53] Pordenone exposed Jacopo to the style of the day known as Mannerism.[54] Keeping up with the current style was possible not only through the works of Pordenone but through the study of a wide range of graphic materials by Titian, Dürer, Marcantonio Raimondi, and others.[55] Jacopo also had a direct influence of Mannerism from the Tuscan artists who traveled and worked in Venice during this time.[56] These painters included Francesco Salviati, Giuseppe Porta Salviati, and Giorgio Vasari. The Mannerism of Jacopo Bassano included the use of elegant forms, drawing from nature, rich color, textured fabrics, and an attention to compositional organization that differed from that of the High Renaissance. Jacopo, like many other Mannerists, was often inspired by a Renaissance painting of a popular subject but then took the subject in a new and innovative direction. This may

Figure 4-4. Jacopo Bassano. *Supper at Emmaus.* 1538. Oil on canvas. Kimbell Art Museum, Fort Worth. Photo. Copyright © 2004 by Kimbell Art Museum, Fort Worth.

be seen in the painting of the *Way to Calvary* (Figure 4-5), c. 1543–44, today located in the Fitzwilliam Museum, Cambridge, that was inspired by Raphael.[57]

Jacopo married Elisabetta Merzari from Bassano and they had four sons, who became painters, and two daughters.[58] Archival scholarship has revealed that "Jacopo Bassano was an avid reader, especially of holy scripture, and had a rigorous moral code, such that he would never paint scenes or figures that might arouse scandal." [59] Throughout his life, he lived a secluded life in the town in which he was born. He declined invitations to hold public office and to work for foreign princes.[60] He enjoyed the friendship of major artists of his day such as Tintoretto, Annibale Carracci, and Paolo Veronese.

The Good Samaritan

Jacopo frequently used biblical narratives and seemed especially to favor Luke and parable stories.[61] Jacopo also selected parables that were not part of the mainstream Italian visual repertoire. The Good Samaritan parable, as told in the paintings by Jacopo Bassano, must have been highly successful for him as he did the subject several times.[62] The Good Samaritan theme appears only in Venice in the fifteenth century in works

Figure 4-5. Jacopo Bassano. *Way to Calvary*, c. 1543-44, The Fitzwilliam Museum, Cambridge. Photo. With permission from The Fitzwilliam Museum, Cambridge.

by Veronese, Domenico Campagnola, and Palma Giovane and only after Jacopo's treatment of the narrative.[63] Arslan was the first to suggest that the source of the subject was by a northern painter, Jan van Scorel, who was in Venice in 1521.[64]

Scholars generally agree that the Hampton Court painting (Figure 4-6) was the earliest rendition of the subject and was painted 1546–49. Several other versions from the period c. 1553–56 that are all very similar to the Hampton Court painting appear in the literature.[65] The Capitoline Museum in Rome and the Kunsthistoriches Museum, Vienna house two of these paintings. The Vienna painting is among several works from this time period that de Sesso thinks show a return of Jacopo to earlier biblical subjects. This composition shows the influence of Giorgione.[66] The figures are immersed in the landscape and perspective is lacking. This tendency may be recognized as Mannerist, but Jacopo's color palette is warmer than in the earlier Good Samaritan paintings.

Two additional paintings are identified by Robert Simon, one in a private collection in New York and the other formerly in Sweden, also in a private collection.[67] A related lost canvas, formerly in Berlin, survives in photographic reproduction only.

The London painting (Figure 4-1) of a different point of the narrative is next chronologically and stylistically, c. 1557. Jacopo Bassano is able to balance color and light in his works of the 1550s. The *Good Samaritan*,

Figure 4-6. Jacopo Bassano. *Good Samaritan.* 1546–49. Oil on canvas. The Royal Collection. Photo. The Royal Collection ©2004. Her Majesty Queen Elizabeth II.

c. 1557, uses light for emphasis on the body positions of the major characters in the narrative. Bassano re-creates the parable showing the moment that the Samaritan is actually saving the traveler (coming from Jerusalem to Jericho) by preparing to put him on his donkey. The donkey is visible on the right side of the painting. The lighter color of the saddle allows the outline to be found in this darkened area.

The flasks of oil and wine used by the Samaritan that have been poured on the traveler's wounds lie to the right of the Samaritan's foot. The body of the traveler is positioned on an elevated rock that enables the Samaritan to get behind him to hold him up. The bandages, applied earlier by the Samaritan, are already red with blood that has soaked into them. Two other figures are visible on the left side of the painting. According to the narrative, they are a priest and a Levite. The second man, the Levite, holds two sticks and appears to be reading.[68] Both of the passersby wear dark clothing. In contrast, the Samaritan wears a rose-colored garment with a flask attached to his waist. The distant city has been identified as the artist's hometown of Bassano. It was a walled city at the base of the Monte Grappa that is clearly defined and visible against the aquamarine of the landscape.

Rearick discusses the only known preparatory drawing for the work:

The single known drawing (II.4. Plate III) from this transitional moment is the remarkable study for the Good Samaritan (London, National Gallery) of about 1560–61, an exploration of the form and color of the wounded robbery victim for which a free mixture of media, even including pen and a golden-toned ink in addition to the exotically opalescent blending of highkeyed rose-lilac chalks with white, suggests the volatile search for a new pictorial expression which would become more disciplined in the finished painting. A particular insight into Jacopo's working process is afforded by the first stage of black chalk outline for the semi-nude figure, essentially fixed for the upper body but at first positing both legs together and extended further to the right so that the pose resembled those of many recumbent figures in his earlier treatments of the theme (Hampton Court, Royal Collections; Rome, Capitoline Museum), only subsequently, but before the colored chalks were added, revised to the more open form which he would use in the painting.[69]

In his earlier versions of the *Good Samaritan* (Hampton Court and Rome), Jacopo chose the moment that the Samaritan was actually bandaging and ministering the compassion that Jesus speaks about in the text.[70] Art historians have examined stylistically this later switch to the elevating of the body; the iconography of this change is discussed below.

Rich Man and Lazarus

Rich Man and Lazarus (c. 1554), now in the Cleveland Museum of Art, contains "Parmigianino-like forms, transformed by the violent chiaroscuro effects," which take on a naturalistic appearance, underlined by the inclusion in the scene of certain details such as the dog in the foreground warily approaching the beggar stretched out on the ground."[71] *Good Samaritan* is more the Mannerism of Salviati than that of Parma.

The size of the painting is 146 x 221 cm (57″ x 87″) and is oil on canvas. The patron of the painting is unknown, but some have suggested that Domenico Priuli commissioned it. Priuli came from a wealthy family in Venice.[72]

Because of the concentrated light that shines upon the action, the characters in the composition appear to emerge out of a darkness. According to M. Elisa Avagnina, the characters resemble actors on a stage with a spotlight shining on them.[73] Bassano also uses the concept of *tiepedezza* or indifference in this painting. No one at the table appears to respond to, or even to notice, the beggar right before their table.[74]

Lazarus is placed prominently in the foreground, painfully raised on his elbow with his staff and water gourd cast aside.[75] The size of the figure is disproportionate to the other objects in the composition and is often discussed as an example of Bassano's Mannerist tendencies. If he were to stand, it can be assumed that his torso would appear much larger than his legs. However, in contrast to this is the evident depiction of Lazarus without any type of sores, which misses the thrust of the text of him being an ill beggar. His muscular body appears healthy under the unknown light source.

Moving in a clockwise circle, the next character encountered is the young page with his unusual stare. The eyes of this figure lead the viewer toward the indefinite object of concentration. The woman, with pale complexion, is placed in the center of the painting. She is quite noticeable in the darkness that surrounds her. Her elegant three-quarter profile is almost identical to the woman seen in *The Miracle of the Quails and The Manna* (Private Collection, Florence, c. 1550?) and *The Beheading of the Baptist* (Statens Museum for Kunst, Copenhagen, c. 1554) done also by Jacopo. She is centrally located in all three of these works. Because of her duplication from *The Beheading of the Baptist* to the woman in *The Feast of the Rich Man and Lazarus*, she is often seen as a representation of Herodias, who asks Herod for the head of John the Baptist. The robust brushstrokes and coloring make the figure seem to almost be a continuation of the tablecloth in front of her.[76]

The Rich Man or Dives is seated at the table, and in contrast to the parable, he does not wear the fine purple linen. Also, his banquet table is bare, which contradicts the text. Finally, his gaze may be in the direction of Lazarus, but his expression exhibits the continuing theme of indifference.[77]

The audience never sees the face of the lute player. The raking light across his back leads the eye of the viewer across the canvas. Once again, Bassano includes dogs. Jacopo's painting of *Two Hunting Dogs* (Galleria degli Uffizi, Florence, c. 1555) closely resembles the ones in *The Feast of the Rich Man and Lazarus*.[78]

Iconographic Analysis

Bernard Aikema sees both paintings as visual attempts to support various initiatives to enlist the church and its members in poverty relief efforts in sixteenth-century Venice. Aikema builds on the work of Brian Pullan, the author of the definitive work on the problems of poverty in fifteenth- and sixteenth-century Venice and its environs.[79] Aikema's comments about Bassano's *Good Samaritan* are helpful. He focuses on a detail not actually mentioned in the Lukan text, the preoccupation of the priest in reading as he walks down the road.

> Not mentioned in the Gospel text (Luke 10:30–37), this detail was presumably introduced in the iconography to accentuate the contrast between an ostentatious, but actually superficial religiosity on the one hand and exemplary brotherly love on the other. Jacopo also employs this motif, but does so much more emphatically than his northern colleagues. Lost in his book only a few steps from the spot where the helpless victim lies, the Levite walks to the right while the Samaritan, in the foreground, leans in the opposite direction. . . . [80]

Furthermore, both the Levite and the priest are dressed in secular garb, and the Samaritan is depicted as a peasant.[81] He comments: "Given the context, there can be no question that the pious countryman embodies *sancta rusticitas*. As such he compares favorably in this case to the lettered layman who, his theological knowledge notwithstanding, disregards God's commandment."[82]

Bassano's painting then serves as a visual echo of someone like Dominican Vincenzio Giaccaro, whose devotional book appeared in Venice in 1538. Giaccaro wrote: "I say you should be holy in heart and deed, and truly devout, and not only show and feign devotion." In this regard, the follower of Christ must learn from the parable that "we servants of the holy Samaritan with the talents we have been given, that is the charity of God and of our neighbor, can and should come to the aid of his bodily and spiritual misery."[83] For the northern Italian cities, overrun as they were with beggars, this message was especially poignant.[84]

Aikema also observes that the *Rich Man and Lazarus* contains details not emphasized in the Lukan text. The dress of none of the characters, including the rich man, is particularly lavish nor is the fare on the table especially enticing. He observes: "Indeed no one seems to be enjoying himself. In the midst of the composition a boy stares blankly straight ahead. And with the exception of one empty dish the table is bare: there is no trace of food, or for that matter any crumbs to sustain poor Lazarus. The accent is thus laid not on the wealth of the host, but on the total indifference of the rest of the company toward the beggar and, for that matter, their surroundings in general."[85]

When Jacopo painted these parables in the 1540s and 1550s, the strains of poverty on the infrastructure of Venetian society were beginning to show. These problems were exacerbated by repeated food shortages and famine during this period. Civil authorities were required to stiffen existing poor laws. In 1545, the Provveditori alla Sanita (magistrates responsible for public health) presented a major plan for dealing with the indigents, which depended upon parish relief efforts, a kind of medieval faith-based initiative.[86] Priests were encouraged to visit their flock with the pressing urgency of contributing to these collections for the poor. These efforts often appealed to the earlier influential work by the Venetian church reformer, Gasparo Contarini, who in 1516 admonished bishops that their every act should benefit their fellow human beings.[87]

Who was the specific audience for Jacopo's *Rich Man and Lazarus*? Aikema further suggests the painting was intended for someone associated with new poor-houses such as the Incurabili.[88] The Incurabili was a hospital founded in 1521 to care for syphilis and "was a tangible result of changing attitudes toward the problem of poverty and contagious disease in the early cinquecento. Spiritual reformers and lay people alike recognized that the commandment 'Love thy neighbor' had become imperative in the burgeoning cities of the Po delta, where masses of homeless paupers threatened to upset the status quo."[89]

Pullan points out that there was a medieval hospital located on a Venetian lagoon island devoted to the care of lepers and dedicated to St. Lazarus (Lazaro), patron saint of lepers.[90] By the time of Bassano's paintings, leprosy was dying out, and the hospital and others like it were devoted to the care of homeless beggars and those suffering from various maladies.[91] Thus, these two parable paintings seem to have served a particular pressing social need in sixteenth-century Venetian society.

Hermeneutical Reflections

Art as social commentary is a common feature in the modern American art community,[92] but art as an agent of the church for social change is fairly rare in modern society. Furthermore, the relationship between poverty relief in the sixteenth-century Veneto and social change effected by contemporary churches is admittedly complex. In some ways, the efforts at poverty relief in Bassano's time did not extend much beyond giving a hungry person a fish. But as Ron Sider and others have argued, in modern society expressions of charity need to be seen alongside other efforts aimed at social change.

1. *Relief* (giving a hungry person a fish) involves directly supplying food, clothing, or housing to someone in urgent need.

2. *Individual development* (teaching a person to fish) includes transformational ministries that empower a person to improve physical, emotional, intellectual, relational, or social status.

3. *Community development* (giving a person fishing equipment) renews the building blocks of a healthy community, such as housing, jobs, health care, and education.

4. *Structural change* (helping everyone get fair access to the fish pond) means transforming unfair political, economic, environmental, or cultural institutions and systems.[93]

The church in Jacopo's day provides a model for the contemporary church's engagement with issues of poverty and social change. But the model is partial and incomplete. Poverty relief must be sought in tandem with structural changes in unjust systems. Jacopo provides a model for the way art can assist in such efforts. Again, the use of art as an agent of social change is not novel; what would be distinctive would be the *church's* use of art (classical and contemporary) for such efforts.

Jacopo Bassano was a simple man by the standards of his contemporaries and ours. His reading and interpreting biblical texts and his re-creating those texts into pictorial statements, however, gave him the power to make statements and give opinions (without words) at a time of lively religious and social debate. His "readings" call for a return to a way of life more in line with the scriptural stories themselves. Jacopo assisted the efforts of poverty relief for the sick and poor. As such his work reflects the ethical emphasis so prominent in the history of interpretation for these parables and is an inspiration and a model for the church's mission today.

Notes

1. In studies of the Synoptic Gospels, material unique to the Gospel of Luke is generally referred to as "L," as material unique to Matthew is labeled "M"; on the "L," see Kim Paffenroth, *The Story of Jesus According to L* (JSNTSS 147; Sheffield: Sheffield Academic Press, 1997). The classic study of the synoptic problem in English remains B. H. Streeter, *The Four Gospels* (London: Macmillan, 1924). For other bibliography, see Scot McKnight and Matthew C. Williams, eds., *The Synoptic Gospels: An Annotated Bibliography* (IRB Bibliographies; Grand Rapids: Baker, 2000). On the "L" parables in Luke, see Jeffrey Tucker, *Example Stories: Perspectives on Four Parables in the Gospel of Luke* (JSNTSS 162; Sheffield: Sheffield Academic Press, 1994), and Mikeal C. Parsons, "Landmarks along the Way: The Function of the 'L' Parables in the Lukan Travel Narrative," *Southwestern Journal of Theology* 40 (1997): 33–47.

2. For example, Louis Réau, *Iconographie de L'Art Chretien* (2 vols.; Paris: Universitaires de France, 1957), II.2.350–52, divides the visual renditions of the parable into two categories with three subdivisions each: (1) the Triumph and Chastisement of the Rich Man (Triomphe et Châtiment du Mauvais Riche) (divided into the Feast of the Rich Man, the Death of the Rich Man, and the Rich Man in Hell) and (2) the Misery and Comfort of poor Lazarus (Misere et recompense du pauvre Lazare) (Lazarus and the dogs, Lazarus clothed in nuptial robes — very rare, and Lazarus in the bosom of Abraham). Under

the category of the Feast of the Rich Man, where Réau places Bassano's painting, Réau lists only two twelfth-century bas-reliefs, one thirteenth-century stained-glass (Virtail of Bourges), and two fifteenth-century renderings of the parable. In the sixteenth century, Leandro Bassano and Bonifazio de'Pitati join Jacopo Bassano as artists depicting this scene. There are few followers of this tradition in subsequent centuries.

3. We wish to express thanks to the staff of the National Gallery, London, who made available the dossier on their Bassano painting in July 2003.

4. This is the argument of Bernard Aikema, *Jacopo Bassano and His Public: Moralizing Pictures in an Age of Reform ca. 1535–1600* (Princeton, N.J.: Princeton University Press, 1996), which we develop and extend in this chapter.

5. For the parable of the Good Samaritan see Joseph Fitzmyer, *The Gospel According to Luke* (AB 28–28A; 2 vols.; Garden City, N.Y.: Doubleday, 1981, 1985), 2:889–90; John Nolland, *Luke* (WBC 35A–35C; 3 vols.; Dallas: Word, 1989, 1993), 2:586–88. The periodical literature on the parable is voluminous; among recent contributions, see Robert W. Funk, "Old Testament in Parable: A Study of Luke 10:25–37," *Encounter* 26 (1965): 251–67; John Dominic Crossan, "Parable and Example in the Teaching of Jesus," *Semeia* 1 (1974): 63–104; F. Scott Spencer, "2 Chronicles 28:5–15 and the Parable of the Good Samaritan," *Westminster Theological Journal* 46 (1984): 317–49; William R. Stegner, "The Parable of the Good Samaritan and Leviticus 18:5," *The Living Text: Essays in Honor of Ernest W. Saunders* (ed. Dennis E. Groh and Robert Jewett; Lanham, Md.: University Press of America, 1985), 27–38; J. Ian H. McDonald, "Rhetorical Issue and Rhetorical Strategy in Luke 10:25–37 and Acts 10:1–11:18," *Rhetoric and the New Testament* (ed. Stanley E. Porter and Thomas H. Olbricht; JSNTSS 90; Sheffield: JSOT Press, 1993), 59–73; John Kilgallen, "The Plan of the 'Nomikos' (Luke 10:25–37)," *New Testament Studies* 42 (1996): 615–19; J. I. H. McDonald, "The View From the Ditch — And Other Angles: Interpreting the Parable of the Good Samaritan," *Scottish Journal of Theology* 49 (1996): 21–37; Juan Carlos Cevallos, "The Good Samaritan: A Second Reading of the Law (Luke 10:25–37)," *Theological Educator* 56 (1997): 49–58; Frank Stagg, "Luke's Theological Use of Parables," *Review and Expositor* 94 (1997): 215–29; Richard Bauckham, "The Scrupulous and the Good Samaritan: Jesus' Parabolic Interpretation of the Law of Moses," *New Testament Studies* 44 (1998): 475–89; Robert A. J. Gagnon, "A Second Look at Two Lukan Parables: Reflections on the Unjust Steward and the Good Samaritan," *Horizons in Biblical Theology* 20 (1998): 1–11; Sylvia C. Keesmat, "Strange Neighbors and Risky Care (Matt 18:21–35; Luke 14:7–14; Luke 10:25–37)," *The Challenge of Jesus' Parables* (ed. Richard N. Longenecker; Grand Rapids: Eerdmans, 2000), 263–85; Ian A. McFarland, "Who Is My Neighbor? The Good Samaritan as a Source for Theological Anthropology," *Modern Theology* 17 (2001): 57–66. For older references, see Warren S. Kissinger, ed., *The Parables of Jesus: A History of Interpretation and Bibliography* (Metuchen, N.J.: American Theological Library Association, 1979).

6. On the relationship of Luke 10:25–28 to the parable (10:29–37), see G. Schneider, *Evangelium nach Lukas*, 247; Josepah Schmid, *Evangelium nach Lukas* (Regensburg: Friedrich Pustet, 1993), 190–91; Fitzmyer, *Luke*, 2:877–88.

7. Fitzmyer, *Luke*, 2:883.

8. Ibid.

9. Ibid., 2:884.

10. Bauckham, "Jesus' Interpretation of the Law of Moses," 475–89.

11. Ibid., 489.

12. See Ronald Hock, "Why NT Scholars Should Read Ancient Novels," in *Ancient Fiction and Early Christian Narrative* (eds. Ronald F. Hock, J. Bradley Chance, and Judith Perkins; SBL Symposium Series 6; Atlanta: Scholars Press, 1998), 121–38.

13. Nolland, *Luke*, 2:598.

14. In addition to the commentaries on Luke cited below, see the following periodical literature: Kendrick Grobel, "Whose Name Was Neves," *New Testament Studies* 10 (1964): 373–82; Henry Joel Cadbury, "A Proper Name for Dives," *Journal of Biblical Literature* 81 (1962): 399–402; Henry Joel Cadbury, "Name for Dives," *Journal of Biblical Literature* 84 (1965): 73; Otto Glombitza, "Der reiche Mann uind der arme Lazarus: Luk 16:19–31," *Novum Testamentum* 12 (1970): 166–80; Vincent Tanghe, "Abraham, son fils et son envoyé," *Revue Biblique* 91 (1984): 557–77; Larry Kreitzer, "Luke 16:19–31 and 1 Enoch 22," *Expository Times* 103 (1992): 139–42; Frank W. Hughes, "The Parable of the Rich Man and Lazarus (Luke 16:19–31) and Greco-Roman Rhetoric," in *Rhetoric and the New Testament* (ed. Stanley E. Porter and Thomas H. Olbricht; JSNTSS 90; Sheffield: JSOT Press, 1993), 29–41; Michael J. Gilmour, "Hints of Homer in Luke 16:19–31," *Didaskalia* 10 (1999): 23–33; Outi Lehtipuu, "Characterization and Persuasion: The Rich Man and the Poor Man in Luke 16:19–31," in *Characterization in the Gospels* (ed. David Rhoads and Kari Syreeni; JSNTSS 184; Sheffield: Sheffield Academic Press, 1999), 73–105; Stephen I. Wright, "Parables on Poverty and Riches (Luke 12:13–21; 16:1–13; 16:19–31)," in *The Challenge of Jesus' Parables* (ed. Richard N. Longenecker; Grand Rapids: Eerdmans, 2000), 217–39; Ferdinand O. Regalado, "The Jewish Background of the Parable of the Rich Man and Lazarus," *Asia Journal of Theology* 16 (2002): 341–48.

15. Although many have understood the logion on divorce "to move to an entirely different topic" (so Fitzmyer, *Luke*, 2:1119), we view the saying on divorce, in its current Lukan form, to fit well within the theme of the wealth (so also Nolland, *Luke*, 2:821–22). Whereas the related saying in Mark 10:2–9 addresses divorce only, here the subject is divorce and remarriage. Further, Nolland notes that some Greek Fathers often interpreted the "and" in a final sense ("dismisses in order to marry"). In Jewish law, a husband could divorce his wife if he found another more attractive. This is generally understood to mean physically more attractive, but our context suggests in the first half of v. 18 that Jesus is condemning anyone who for financial reasons (i.e., the prospective wife has a larger dowry) dismisses his wife, and though in Jewish law the wife could not initiate divorce, she could certainly provoke it. And she might well do so (by providing an inadequate meal) in order to better herself with a more wealthy paramour waiting in the wings for her to extricate herself from marriage. In either case, the pain of divorce is compounded by the potential abuse of the love of money.

16. H. Gressmann, *Vom reichen Mann und armen Lazarus: eine literargeschichtliche Studie* (Berlin: Verlag der konigliche Akademie der Wissenschaft, 1918). For the story itself, see F. L. Griffith, *Stories of the High Priest of Memphis* (Oxford: Clarendon, 1900), 42–43.

17. See especially R. F. Hock, "Lazarus and Micyllus: Greco-Roman Backgrounds to Luke 16:19–31," *Journal of Biblical Literature* 106 (1987): 448–55.

18. See Richard Bauckham, "The Rich Man and Lazarus: The Parable and the Parallels," *New Testament Studies* 37 (1991): 225–46.

19. For these various opinions, see ibid., 232.

20. Ibid. For the various ways in which communication from beyond the grave might be achieved in the ancient world as well as the possible connection between these literary accounts and actual experiences upon which some of them might rest, see ibid., 236–42.

21. On the various forms in which this communication could have been imagined to take place in the ancient world, see ibid., 242–43.

22. Cited by ibid., 241; the text is fragmented. A translation by A. Pietersma and T. R. Lutz may be found in J. H. Charlesworth, ed., *The Old Testament Pseudepigrapha* (2 vols.; Darton, Longman & Todd, 1985), 2:327–42.

23. Charlesworth, *Old Testament Pseudepigrapha*, 2.440–41.

24. Bauckham, "The Rich Man and Lazarus," 245.

25. Ibid., 246.

26. Stephen Wailes, *Medieval Allegories of Jesus' Parables* (Berkeley: University of California Press, 1987), esp. sec. 28 on the Good Samaritan and sec. 38 on *The Rich Man and Lazarus*.

27. Ibid., 210. Elsewhere (45), Wailes observes: "As understood in the Middle Ages, 'The Good Samaritan' condenses all the history of salvation into a brief tale. Within this tale is the Fall and loss of innocence, the unavailing epochs under the Old Law, the Incarnation and ministry of Christ, the Passion and Resurrection, and the establishment of the Church."

28. See Origen, *Homilies sur S. Luc* (ed. Henri Crouzel, François Fournier, and Pierre Perichon; Sources Chrétiennes 87; Paris: Éditions du Cerf, 1962), 400–410. François Bovon (*Das Evangelium nach Lukas*, vol. 2. Lk 9,51–14,35 Zürich: Benziger Verlag, 1996], 93) notes that there is indirect evidence (also from Origen) for even earlier references to the Good Samaritan in the writings of Gnostics and Marcion.

29. Origen, *Homilies sur Luc*, 404, 408.

30. Ibid., 406; cited by Wailes, *Medieval Allegories*, 211; see also Bovon, *Das Evangelium nach Lukas*, 94, who also notes that the general Christological and allegorical reading of the parable is sustained by Clement of Alexandria (*Quis dives salvetur*, 28–29) and Ambrose (*Expositio in Evangelium S. Lucae* VII, 71–84). For variations in the details of Ambrose's interpretation, see Wailes, 211. Fitzmyer (*Luke*, 2:885) labels these Christological readings based on etymology as "farfetched." Nolland (*Luke*, 2:597), on the other hand, notes: "For much of the history of the church the parable has been understood by taking the Samaritan to be Jesus, and this view has found fresh support in some modern scholarship."

31. See Augustine, *Questions on the Gospels*, II, no. 19, cols. 1340–41 in *Patrologiae cursus completes*, series Latina (ed. J.-P. Migne; vol. 35; hereafter cited as PL). In fact, at the beginning of his classic study of the parables, C. H. Dodd (*The Parables of the Kingdom* [New York: Scribner's and Sons, 1936]) cites Augustine's interpretation of the Good Samaritan as a classic example of the ways in which allegorical interpretation distorts the meaning of the parables. For more on Augustine's interpretation of this parable (along with a defense of the plausibility of Augustine's exegesis), see Roland J. Teske, "The Good Samaritan (Lk 10:29–37) in Augustine's Exegesis," in *Augustine: Biblical Exegete* (ed. Frederick Van Fleteren and Joseph C. Schnaubelt; New York: Peter Lang, 2001), 347–67.

32. Wailes (*Medieval Allegories*, 211–12) attributes this interpretation to Ambrose (*Traité sur l'Évangile de S. Luc* [ed. Gabriel Tissot; Sources Chrétiennes 45, 52; Paris: Éditions due Cerf, 1956–58], 2:35) and states that at least thirteen later sources follow Ambrose in this interpretation, while Augustine's view "is effectively abandoned after him" (Wailes, *Medieval Allegories*, 212).

33. Wailes, *Medieval Allegories*, 212; citing Augustine, col. 1341.

34. Wailes, *Medieval Allegories*, 212. For other interpretations up through and including the Reformation, see Bovon's *Wirkungsgeschichte* on this parable, *Das Evangelium nach Lukas*, 93–98.

35. The references to Gottfried and Hugh in the following paragraphs are indebted to Wailes, *Medieval Allegories*, 213–14.

36. Gottfried of Admont, *Homiliae dominicales*, no. 80, cols. 566D–67A, in PL 174. Gottfried's other sermon on the parable (Homily 81) is, according to Wailes, "completely original":

The traveler is Christ, the robbers are the Jews who persecuted him, he was stripped by the defection of his apostles at the Passion (having surrounded himself with chosen men as one puts on a garment (col 571AB), his wounds are persecutions, and he is half alive in that he died as a man. The three passers-by stand for men before the Law, under the Law, and under grace. Neither the patriarchs nor just men under the Law received Christ, but the Samaritan, representing the heathen (*gentilitas*), approached through true perception, inwardly bound his wounds through hope, infused love and fear, brought him into the stable of the heart, and so forth.

See also Giuseppe Maria Pilo, "Jacopo Bassone e la "pastorale biblica": invenzione e conseguenze nel tempo. I," *Arte Documento* 13 (1999): 168–75.

37. See Hugh of Saint-Cher, "Postils on the Gospels" in vol. 6 of *Opera omnia* (8 vols.; Lyon, 1645).

38. Wailes, *Medieval Allegories*, 214.

39. For references to other interpretations in addition to those cited here, see Ursula Wolf, *Die Parabel vom reichen Prasser under armen Lazarus in der mittelalterlichen Buchmalerei* (Munich: Scaneg Verlag, 1989), esp. 13–23.

40. On these allegorical interpretations, see Wailes, *Medieval Allegories*, 255–60.

41. Ibid., 255.

42. See Ambrose, II.105.

43. Wailes, *Medieval Allegories*, 255. "The *Gloss*," according to Wailes (*Medieval Allegories*, 45) "is a selection of phrases, sentences, and passages taken from sources as early as Tertullian and Origen and as late as authorities contemporary with the compilers. In some cases, glossators added observations of their own. It rapidly became the standard aid to Bible study throughout Latin Christendom. The *Gloss* transmits in greater or lesser detail nearly all the allegories developed for the parables through the tenth century." Wailes cites Jerome, Peter Comestor, Albert the Great, Nicholas of Lyra ("this is not said to be a parable, because according to the teachers it is the narrative of an event") and Bruno of Segni as supporting this view. For the allegorical readings of Augustine and Gregory the Great, see Wailes, *Medieval Allegories*, 253–54.

44. Gregory the Great, *XL homilarum in evangelia libri duo*, col. 1302B; PL 76; cited by Wailes, *Medieval Allegories*, 257.

45. Bede, *Bedae venerabilis opera*. Part II: *Opera exegetica. 3: in Lucae evangelium expositio, In Marci evangeliam expositio* (ed. D. Hurst; Corpus Christianorum Series Latina 120; Turnhout,: Brepols, 1960), 303–4.

46. Bruno of Segni, *Commentaria in Lucam*, col. 422C.

47. Peter Comestor, *Historia scholastica*, PL 198, col. 1589C.

48. Thomas de Vio Gaetano, *Evangelia cum comment. Caietani*. Venetiis, in aedibus Lucantonii Iunctae Florentini, 1530.

49. The major art historical sources for Jacopo Bassano include: Wart Arslan, *I Bassano* (Bologna: Casa Editrice Apollo, 1931); Alessandro Ballarin, *Jacopo Bassano* (Padua: Bertoncello Artigrafiche, 1996); William R. Rearick, *Jacopo Bassano* (Bassano del Grappa: Soc. Ed. Verci Bassano, 1986).

50. Livia Alberton Vinco Da Sesso, "Jacopo Bassano," in the *The Dictionary of Art* (ed. J. Turner; 34 vols.; London: Macmillan, 1996), 3:343–47.

51. See the fresco cycle of S. Lucia di Tezze, Vicenza that dates from 1536 to 1537. Jacopo Bassano and his workshop executed both the interior and exterior decoration.

52. Da Sesso, "Jacopo Bassano," 343.

53. This painting was originally commissioned for the Podestà of Cittadella, Cosimo da Mosto and is one of the treasures of the collection. For additional work by Jacopo Bassano in Cittadella, see Michelangelo Muraro, "Gli affreschi di Jacopo e Francesco da Ponte a Cartigliano," *Arte Veneta* 6 (1952): 42–62.

A retrospective exhibition celebrating the four hundredth anniversary of the artist's death in 1992 was shown in the Kimbell Art Museum, Fort Worth, and in Bassano del Grappa. See *Jacopo Bassano c. 1510–1590* (ed. B. L. Brown and P. Marini; exh. catalog, Fort Worth, Tex.: Kimbell Art Museum, 1993 [also in Bassano del Grappa, Museo Civico, 1992]) For the Kimbell painting, see also Ruth W. Sullivan, "Hospitality to the Divine Stranger in the Kimbell *Supper at Emmaus* by Jacopo Bassano," *Source* 14 (1995): 19–26; "Cracking the Egg: Bassano's *Supper at Emmaus*," *Source* 13 (1994): 27–35; Pietro Zampetti, *Jacopo Bassano* (Milan: Fabbri, 1994).

This anniversary inspired a large number of scholarly works including: Livia Alberton Vinco Da Sesso, *Jacopo Bassano i Dal Ponte: una dinastia di pittori Opere ne Veneto/the Dal Ponte: a dynasty of painters' work in the Venetian region* (Bassano dal Grappa: Ghedina & Tassotti Editori, 1992); *La famiglia di Jacopo nei documenti d'archivio* (ed. F. Signori and G. Marcadella; Bassano del Grappa: Archivio di Stato, 1992); Michelangelo Muraro, *Il Libro Secondo di Francesco e Jacopo Dal Ponte* (Bassano: G. B. Verci, 1992).

54. For a definition of the style known as Mannerism, see chap. 2, this volume.

55. Da Sesso, "Jacopo Bassano," 343. For a printed source for the *Good Samaritan* in the National Gallery, see Enrica Pan, *Jacopo Bassano e l'incisione: La fortuna dell'arte bassanesca nella grafica di riproduzione dal XVI al XIX secolo* (Bassano del Grappa: Ghedina & Tassotti Editori, 1992), 196.

56. Da Sesso, "Jacopo Bassano," 343.

57. Ibid.

58. Da Sesso, *Jacopo Bassano i Dal Ponte*, 36.

59. Da Sesso, "Jacopo Bassano," 343. See also Luca Bortollotti, "La pittura religiosa nella provincia veneta: Jacopo Bassano in contesto," *Venezia Cinquecento* 8 (1998): 105–46; Rosmarie Sprule, *Hirtenanbetungen von Jacopo Bassano: Annäherung an ein religionspolitisches Selbstverstandnis* (Köln: Böhlau, 1999).

60. Da Sesso, *Jacopo Bassano i Dal Ponte*, 60.

61. Patricia Meilman, "Jacopo Bassano's St. John in the Desert Altarpiece," *Venezia Cinquecento* 3 (1993): 119–39, argues that this altarpiece is specifically based on the Gospel story as told in Luke.

62. Michelangelo Muraro, "The Altarpiece in the Bassano Workshop: Patronage, Contracts, and Iconography," *Italian Altarpieces 1250–1550: Function and Design* (ed. Eve Borsook and Fiorella Superbi Gioffredi; Oxford: Clarendon Press, 1994), 231–32.

63. Robert Simon, *Important Old Master Paintings: Discoveries . . . in una nuova luce* (New York: Piero Corsini, Inc., 1988), 13.

64. Asrlan, *I Bassano*, 1:93–94. Aikema, *Bassano and His Public*, 148, and Simon, *Important Old Master Painting*, 13, agree with this suggestion.

65. Da Sesso, *Jacopo Bassano*, 347, discusses only the Hampton Court and Vienna paintings, maintaining in 1995 that both are by Jacopo Bassano.

66. Ibid.

67. Simon, *Important Old Master Paintings*, 13–20, presents a new discovery of the *Good Samaritan* by Jacopo Bassano from a private collection in New York. Simon agrees with its dependence on the Hampton Court painting as he does the *Good Samaritan* formerly in the collection of Baron Hugo Hamilton in Boo, Sweden. He agrees with the reattribution by Ludwig Baldass of the Vienna painting to Jacopo's son, Francesco Bassano. Simon also attributes the lost Berlin canvas to Francesco Bassano.

68. See below in the iconography section of this chapter for a more extensive study of why these two, and sometimes one, passersby appear to be reading in the Good Samaritan paintings by Jacopo Bassano.

69. Rearick, *Jacopo Bassano*, vol. II. Mature Drawings. 1549–1567, II.4. Plate III. Private Collection, Munich.

70. Two other paintings that are quite similar to the Hampton Court *Good Samaritan* appear in the scholarly literature. For the *Good Samaritan*, Private Collection, Sweden, see Robert Simon, *Important Old Master Paintings*, 13–20. For the *Good Samaritan*, Private Collection, New York, see Rodolfo Palluchini, "Una 'Parabola del Buon Samaritano' di Jacopo Bassano," *Arte Veneta* 41 (1987): 135–38.

71. Da Sesso, *Jacopo Bassano i Dal Ponte*, 39.

72. W. R. Rearick, "Life and Works of Jacopo dal Ponte, called Bassano," in *Jacopo Bassano c. 1510–1592* (Fort Worth, Tex.: Kimbell Museum of Art, 1992), 93.

73. M. Elisa Avagnina, "La tecnica pittorica di Jacopo Bassano attraverso le fonti," in *Jacopo Bassano c. 1510–1592* (Fort Worth, Tex.: Kimbell Museum of Art, 1992), 308–10.

74. Aikema, *Jacopo Bassano and His Public*, 49–50.

75. Rearick, "Life and Works of Jacopo dal Ponte," 94.

76. Avagnina, "La tecnica pittorica di Jacopo Bassano attraverso le fonti," 308–9.

77. Aikema, *Jacopo Bassano and His Public*, 49.

78. Avagnina, "La tecnica pittorica di Jacopo Bassano attraverso le fonti," 310.

79. Brian Pullan, *Rich and Poor in Renaissance Venice: The Social Institutions of a Catholic State, to 1620* (Oxford: Oxford University Press, 1971).

80. Aikema, *Bassano and His Public*, 48–49. This depiction of the priest's reading activity, according to Aikema, picks up on a theme found in the Netherlandish masters, Maarten van Heemskerck and Herri met de Bless, whose works are illustrated in Aikema. For a different interpretation of the reading priest's significance, see Paolo Berdini, *The Religious Art of Jacopo Bassano* (Cambridge: Cambridge University Press, 1997), 1–3. For a more general discussion of Bassano's use of texts, see Paolo Berdini, "Parola e immagine in Jacopo Bassano," *Venezia Cinquecento* 9, no. 18 (1999): 81–106.

81. Aikema, *Bassano and His Public*, 49, contrasts this with the Netherlandish masters "who dress the priest and Levite in ecclesiastical robes and cast the Samaritan as an Oriental...."

82. Ibid., 48–49.

83. Vincenzio Giaccaro, *Specchio della sincera vita Christiana*. In Vinegia. Nelle case di Pietro di Nicolini da Sabbio. A requistione di M. Lucantonio Giunta. 130v; 150r.

84. Aikema, *Bassano and His Public*, 49.

85. Ibid., 49–50.

86. Pullan, *Rich and Poor in Renaissance Venice*, 232–37.

87. Cited by Aikema, *Bassano and His Public*, 51.

88. Ibid., 52.

89. Ibid., 46. For more on the Incurabili, see Pullan, *Rich and Poor in Renaissance Venice*, 232–37.

90. Pullan, *Rich and Poor in Renaissance Venice*, 207. On the tradition that Lazarus was the patron of lepers (and the subsequent confusion with the traditions of Lazarus, brother of Mary and Martha), see George Kaftal, *Iconography of the Saints in the Paintings of North East Italy* (Florence: Casa Editrice le Lettere, 1978), 603–4. Kaftal also notes (604) that at Venice Lazarus had a church dedicated to him: "Templum D. Lazaro Mendicanti..." *The Book of Saints* (ed. Dom Bede Millard et al.; 6th ed.; London: A. C. Black, 1989), 339, notes: "The military order of St. Lazarus, founded during the crusades (one of whose duties was to take care of lepers), was named after him. Hence also the words Lazaretto,

for a hospital, Lazarene, for a man on the streets, etc. The Ethiopians keep his feast on June 21." The latter point makes Lazarus the only character in one of Jesus' parables who is both canonized and given a feast day, underscoring the tenacity of the exegetical tradition that tended to historicize the parable. On the Venetian hospital San Lazzaro, see Bernard Aikema and Dulcia Meijers, "San Lazzaro dei Mendicanti the Venetian beggars' hospital and its architects," *Bollettino del Centro Internazionale dei Studi di Architettura Andrea Palladio* 23 (1981): 189 202; Michela Maguolo and Massimiliano Bandera, *San Lazzaro degli Armeni: l'isola, il monastero, il restauro* (Venice: Marsilio Editori, 1999). On the related theme of images of Charity, see Bernard Aikema, "L'Immagine Della 'Carità Veneziana," in *Nel Regno dei Poveri: Arte e Storia Grandi Ospedali Veneziani in Eta Modern 1474–1797* (eds. Bernard Aikema and Dulcia Meijers; Venice: Arsenale Editrice, 1989), 71–98; Francesco Mozzetti, "Educare per immagini gesti di carità e attivismo caritatevole," *Venezia Cinquecento* 8, no. 16 (1998): 53–80.

   91. Pullan, *Rich and Poor in Renaissance Venice*, 208. According to Pullan, there were only five persons in the hospital for lepers in 1528.

   92. See, e.g., Richard Fitzgerald, *Art and Politics* (Westport, Conn.: Greenwood Press, 1973).

   93. Ronald J. Sider, Philip N. Olson, and Heidi Rolland Unruh, *Churches That Make a Difference: Reaching Your Community with Good News and Good Works* (Grand Rapids: Baker Books, 2002), 86.

Figure 5-1. Alessandro Allori. *Christ in the Home of Mary and Martha.* 1578–80. Oil on panel. Palazzo Portinari-Salviati, Florence. Photo. Collezione Privata Palazzo Portinari-Salviati–sede Banca Toscana, Florence.

Chapter five

Christ in the Home of Mary and Martha by Alessandro Allori

(Luke 10:38–42)

IN THE PREVIOUS CHAPTER, we focused on the parable of the Good Samaritan (and the Rich Man and Lazarus) and the subsequent history of interpretation, focusing on the example of Jacopo Bassano's interpretation of those parables. The Good Samaritan story was prompted by the lawyer's claim that the law required that one should "love the Lord God with all our hearts, souls, and minds, and your neighbor as yourself." The lawyer then goes on to ask, "Who is my neighbor?" The parable of the Good Samaritan is an attempt to address the second part of the double command to love God and neighbor by redefining who qualifies as neighbor. The next episode of Luke 10, where Jesus visits the home of Mary and Martha, explores the first part of the love command, namely, to love God.[1]

Overview of the Biblical Text

[38]Now it came to pass, as they went, that he entered into a certain town: and a certain woman named Martha received him into her house. [39]And she had a sister called Mary, who sitting also at the Lord's feet, heard his word. [40]But Martha was busy about much serving. Who stood and said: Lord, hast thou no care that my sister hath left me alone to serve? Speak to her therefore, that she help me. [41]And the Lord answering, said to her: Martha, Martha, thou art careful and art troubled about many things: [42]But one thing is necessary. Mary hath chosen the best part, which shall not be taken away from her. (Luke 10:38–42, DOUAY-RHEIMS BIBLE)

The design and structure for Luke's story about Jesus' visit in the home of Mary and Martha is straightforward, and it is told in a linear fashion.[2]

111

- Martha extends hospitality to Jesus (38).

- Mary listens to Jesus' teachings (39).

- Martha attends to the duties of hospitality (40a).

- Martha complains that Mary has neglected the duties of hospitality (40b).

- Martha asks Jesus to instruct Mary to help her (40c).

- Jesus responds that Mary has chosen the better activity (41–42).

This short story about Jesus' visit in the home of Mary and Martha is found at the end of a subunit in Luke (9:51–10:42), which is part of a larger travel narrative in Luke (9:51–19:27). Beginning with 9:51, Jesus begins his journey to Jerusalem and ultimately his death.[3] In this initial subunit, the stories and emphases appear to revolve around the act of traveling.[4] Many of the later pericopae possess more of a didactic focus. Even more specific than a travel theme, the stories in this initial subunit feature elements that are representative of the ancient Mediterranean custom of either hospitality or inhospitality.

The passage begins when Martha "welcomed him [Jesus] into her home" (Luke 10:38).[5] The language and setting of the scene are reminiscent of the customs of ancient hospitality, generally understood in the ancient world to refer to kindness shown to strangers.[6] Luke has a particular interest in issues of hospitality (Luke 7:36–46; 10:38–40; 19:1–9; Acts 9:43–11:3; 21:3–6; 21:7; 21:8–16; 28:6–10; and 28:13–14). Often, as in our text here, the host initiates hospitality (Luke 7:36; 10:38; Acts 10:23; 10:22; 28:7).

Furthermore, early Christian missionaries often pursued their evangelistic efforts within a hospitality context, prompting references to and discussion of the protocols of Christian hospitality in a wide range of literature (in addition to the Lukan passages already cited, see e.g., Rom 15:22–25; Gal 4:14; 3 John 5–8; *Did.* 11–12; Ign. *Eph.* 7.1; 9.1; Herm. *Mand.* 11.12).[7] Thus, Luke wrote in a context in which virtuous people welcomed, fed, housed, and extravagantly provided for travelers, and it is reasonable to think that the original audience viewed the scene as a typical hospitality scene, where Martha fulfilled the conventional expectations of a virtuous host. In this light, it would be difficult to imagine that the original audience understood Jesus' praise of Mary to be an implicit criticism of Martha's hospitality.[8] Of course, Jesus had the capacity to level such criticism, as we see in the story of one Simon the Pharisee, who fails to follow proper hospitality protocols (see Luke 7:36–50).

So while Martha has fulfilled the typical expectations associated with a host, Jesus reserves for her sister Mary his highest praise.[9] The contrast between the sisters' actions is striking. Martha busies herself with "the details of serving" while Mary chooses to sit at the Lord's feet and listen to what he is saying. Apparently exasperated, Martha confronts Jesus about her sister's actions, "Lord, hast thou no care that my sister hath left me alone to serve? speak to her therefore, that she help me" (Luke 10:40). Rather surprisingly, Jesus replies, "Martha, Martha, thou art careful, and art troubled about many things: But one thing is necessary. Mary hath chosen the best part, which shall not be taken away from her" (10:41–42).

The passage turns on the meaning of the "one thing."[10] At first, it would seem Jesus is instructing Martha to prepare only "one dish" for the meal, but soon this interpretation is obviously inadequate.[11] Rather, the "one thing" in Jesus' logic is the "best part" which Mary has chosen. And what is that? According to Jesus, hearing the word of God's messenger is the one thing needed (see also Luke 8:15, 21).[12] Thus, however important hospitality is in Luke as a social context for the spread of the Christian message,[13] having followers who attend to Jesus' messengers is even more important. Arterbury's comments are helpful:

> Thus, it is difficult to conclude that Martha functions as a negative example for Luke's audience. Instead, given the context of Luke 9–10, Luke's audience would have considered Martha to be a somewhat positive example for hosting traveling missionaries. Yet, Luke's audience would have also realized that Martha was being redirected. Martha was right to have welcomed Jesus, but when the duties of hospitality prevented her from hearing Jesus' message the custom had then become an obstacle. Therefore, Luke's audience most likely would have concluded that they should receive the traveling missionaries, but that in the end they should spend more time listening to the Christian message than providing Homeric style hospitality. Christian hosts should not become consumed with the duties of hospitality and thereby neglect the message of the Kingdom.[14]

This emphasis on "serving" in the context of ancient hospitality does not rule out understanding the term "service" (*diakonia*; Luke 10:40) and its cognates as an action appropriate to discipleship (see, e.g., Acts 1:17, 25; 6:1, 4; 11:29; 12:25; 20:24; 21:19).[15] Thus, both Martha and Mary are engaged in complementary actions appropriate to disciples (hospitality and instruction), though hearing the word is clearly the more important activity.[16]

Furthermore, it should be noted that not only is the host in this scene a woman, but as Fitzmyer points out, "Luke in this scene does not hesitate to depict a woman as a disciple sitting at Jesus' feet. . . . "[17] While discipleship in general, and not the role of women in particular, seems to be the focus of the passage, nonetheless it is significant that Luke presumes "the willingness of the male members of his implied audience to derive a lesson from a story in which women are important characters."[18]

Finally, this emphasis on the dual activities of discipleship — hospitality (or more generally "service") and instruction ("hearing the word") — seems to lie along the same trajectory of the exegetical tradition, which understands, as we shall see, Mary and Martha as representative of two contrasting, but complementary, lifestyles — the *vita contemplativa*, the life of contemplation, and the *vita activa*, the life of action, respectively.[19]

Subsequent History of Interpretation

The Identity of Mary

Perhaps the first conundrum to be addressed in association with the history of interpretation revolves around the identity of the one called "Mary" in this scene. Ambrose posed the question long ago: "Were there Mary, the sister of Lazarus, and Mary Magdalen, or more people?"[20] Since at least the third century C.E., some have identified (or confused) this Mary, linked with Bethany on the basis of John 11:1, with Mary Magdalen and the "sinful" woman who anointed Jesus in Luke 7:36–50. Augustine, for example, links Mary of Bethany with the sinful woman, though he is very tentative in drawing this conclusion. In his commentary on John, he writes:

> Behold this sister of Lazarus (if indeed it was she who anointed the Lord's feet with unguent, and dried with her hair what she had washed with her tears) was raised from the dead more truly than her brother — she was freed from the weight of her bad habits. . . . And of her it has been said, "For she was a famous sinner."[21]

The situation through the sixth century was quite confused. Haskins observes: "That their identity intrigued the commentators is undeniable — who they were, what they represented, their importance and their relationship to one another and, above all, to Christ. Some had identified Mary Magdalen with Luke's sinner, others with Mary of Bethany; still others identified the latter two with each other, but not with Mary Magdalen. And there were those like Ambrose, Augustine, and Jerome who were unable to decide."[22] This ambiguity was resolved, at least in orthodox circles in the West, with the following declaration of Pope Gregory the Great, made c. 591: "She whom Luke calls the sinful woman, whom

John calls Mary, we believe to be the Mary from whom seven devils were ejected according to Mark."[23] Later, in another sermon, Gregory declared: "Mary Magdalen, who had been in the city a sinner, came to the sepulcher."[24] The composite picture of Mary of Bethany, the sinful woman who anointed Jesus, and Mary Magdalen as one person was now complete.[25] Furthermore, as Haskins points out, "his [Gregory's] homily collection was highly popular during the eighth and ninth centuries, more in demand than even that of St. Augustine, and his formulation of the composite Magdalen thus passed into homiletic literature to become stock-in-trade during the Middle Ages."[26]

In the late medieval period, this "composite Mary" was at one and the same time the symbol for the penitent sinner in need of conversion (based on Luke 7), the exemplar of asceticism (based on later legends of Mary's thirty-year period of self-imposed solitude in France),[27] and the paradigm for the importance of the contemplative life (based on Luke 10:38–42).[28] Because only the last of these symbols is based directly on our text from Luke 10, we shall focus our attention in the history of interpretation on this aspect of the "afterlife" of Mary. Given, however, that Allori executed his work at a time when the composite image of Mary was still intact (despite serious attacks on its coherence), we shall refer to these other traditions where they serve to illuminate the visual exegesis of the painting.[29]

The Contemplative Life

At the conclusion to his comments on Luke 10:38–42, Joseph Fitzmyer argues, "To read this episode as a commendation of contemplative life over against active life is to allegorize it beyond recognition."[30] Despite this claim, since at least the time of Origen, Martha and her sister Mary have been identified in just this way, as the "active and contemplative forms of the religious life on the basis of Luke's account."[31]

Identifying Mary with the "soul," Origen writes, "thus when the soul has been purified morally...she is fit to pass on to the things that form the object of contemplation and mysticism; her love is pure and spiritual and will raise her to the contemplation of the Godhead."[32]

Jerome is more direct in his appeal to Mary as an example of the devotional life, peppering his interpretation with quotations from the Song of Songs:

> Be you like Mary, prefer doctrine to food. Let your sisters run about and seek how they may sustain Christ as a guest. You, having disdained the burden of this world, sit at the feet of the Lord and say, "I found him whom my soul loveth; I held him and would not let

him go." And let him answer, "My dove, my undefiled is but one, she is the choice of her that bore her," that is, heavenly Jerusalem.[33]

In a variety of sermons, Augustine expands this comparison of the active and contemplative life, first using Leah and Rachel as examples and then Martha and Mary. LaRow writes:

The salient points of this exegesis are: Martha's part is good, but Mary's is better (clxxix, 17); Martha cares for many things, Mary for one thing which will be increased in this life and perfected in the next (ciii, 5); what Martha was doing is what we do, what Mary was doing is what we hope for (civ, 4). Even Mary only signified the life of contemplation; she did not yet lay hold of it (cclv). Christ will lead those who believe to the contemplation of God, where is . . . everlasting rest and joy which shall never be taken from us. A similitude of this joy is prefigured sitting at the feet of the Lord . . . she prefigured what is to be in eternity.[34]

Like Augustine, Ambrose commends Mary without criticizing Martha, since both are examples of "virtue":

Virtue does not have a single form. In the example of Martha and Mary, there is added the busy devotion of the one and the pious attention of the other to the Word of God, which, if it agrees with faith, is preferred even to the very works, as it is written: "Mary has chosen the good portion, which shall not be taken away from her." So let us also strive to have what no one can take away from us, so that not careless but diligent hearing may be granted to us. . . . Let the desire for wisdom lead you as it did Mary. It is a greater and more perfect work. . . . Nor is Martha rebuked in her good serving, but Mary is preferred because she has chosen the better part for herself. . . .[35]

While most interpreters refused to criticize Martha's action in light of Mary's "better part," few went so far as Ephrem the Syrian, who commended Martha's love as more fervent than Mary's:

Mary came and sat at his feet. This was as though she were sitting on firm ground at the feet of him who had forgiven the sinful woman her sins. She had put on a crown in order to enter into the kingdom of the Firstborn. She had chosen the better portion, the Benefactor, the Messiah himself. This will never be taken away from her. Martha's love was more fervent that Mary's, for before he had arrived there, she was ready to serve him. "Do you not care that my sister has left me to serve alone?" When he came to raise Lazarus to life, she ran and came out first.[36]

Gregory the Great (who as we saw played a definitive role in solving the identity of the various "Marys" in the West) followed Augustine, Ambrose, and others, in using the Martha/Mary paradigm to commend the contemplative life: "Martha is not reprehended, but Mary is indeed praised; for the merits of an active life are great, but those of a contemplative life are even better."[37]

John Cassian (d. 433), who was instrumental in bringing Eastern monastic ideals to the West, wrote extensively on the contemplative life, often drawing on the examples of Martha and Mary:

> It should be our main effort . . . to cleave with our mind to the things of God and to God himself. Whatever is not this . . . should be put second, or last and judged to be hurtful. There is a lovely type of this mental attitude in the Gospel story of Martha and Mary. When Martha was performing her act of holy ministry in serving the Lord and his disciples, Mary was sitting at Jesus' feet . . . and was hanging upon his words as he taught the things of the spirit. The Lord praised Mary above Martha because she had chosen the better part and that which should not be taken away from her. . . . The Lord, you see, placed the chief good in divine contemplation. All the other virtues, however necessary and useful and good we deem them must be placed on a lower plane because they are sought for the sake of this one thing.[38]

This emphasis on Mary as exemplar of the contemplative life continued throughout the late middle ages. Jacobus de Voragine comments:

> The name Mary, or Maria, is interpreted as *amarum mare*, bitter sea, or as illuminator or illuminated. These three meanings are accepted as standing for three shares or parts, of which Mary made the best choices, namely the part of penance, the part of inward contemplation, and the part of heavenly glory. . . . Since she chose the best part of inward contemplation she is called enlightener, because in contemplation she drew draughts of light so deep that in turn she poured out light in abundance: in contemplation she received the light with which she afterwards enlightened others.[39]

In a lengthy exposition on Mary and Martha, the author of *Meditations on the Life of Christ* echoes the sentiments expressed thus far, extolling both the active and the contemplative life: "First comes the deed and then the contemplation. . . . Perhaps you desire the repose of contemplation, and you do well, but do not forget the flowers of which you read that covered the bed of the bride. Therefore take heed to surround your own similarly with the flowers of good deeds."[40]

Many of the Protestant Reformers would have nothing of this composite picture of Mary and its attendant symbolism. John Calvin, for example, argued that the Scriptures gave testimony to three separate Marys. Commenting specifically on Luke 10:38–42, he said, "Now this passage has been wickedly perverted to commend what is called the contemplative life." He goes on to say, "Christ was far from intending that his disciples should devote themselves to idle and frigid speculations. It is an ancient error that those who flee worldly affairs and engage wholly in contemplation are leading an angelic life."[41]

The Council of Trent (1554–63) reaffirmed the traditional composite picture and assigned Mary Magdalen (along with Peter and the Prodigal Son) especially the role of penitent sinner par excellence.[42] Later a Roman missal was issued in 1570 affirming the Council of Trent's position. De Boer writes, "Here the missal was not just taking up the image of Mary Magdalene which had been disseminated by Gregory the Great and others. This image emerged from the Counter-Reformation church. Over against the Reformation with its doctrine of grace, the Counter-Reformation emphasized the doctrine of penance and merits."[43]

Consequently, Mary Magdalen "remained a favorite saint of Catholics throughout the Counter-Reformation."[44] This trend can be substantiated particularly in Counter-Reformation artwork. During this time period "the iconography of the Magdalene flourished anew in southern baroque art as she became a symbol for the defense of and devotion to the sacraments, especially the sacrament of penance, against the Reformers."[45]

By the time of the Counter-Reformation, she was identified as a penitent and a saint. She simultaneously symbolized conversion, contemplation, and asceticism. In this context of theological debate and conflict, our artist, Alessandro Allori, executed his painting of *Christ in the Home of Mary and Martha* (Figure 5-1), today owned by the Banca Toscana.[46]

Life of the Artist

Alessandro Allori was born into a family of painters on May 31, 1535, in Florence.[47] His father died when he was only five years old, and Alessandro was adopted by the Florentine Mannerist painter Agnolo Bronzino (1503–72). Allori lived and trained with Bronzino from 1540 until 1554.[48] In the shop of the artist Bronzino, who had been the pupil of Pontormo,[49] Allori learned the elegance, color palette and complex compositions of *la maniera*, or style of the day, in Florence.[50] Bronzino's paintings varied from formal Medici portraits to emotionally charged biblical narratives. Allori incorporated Bronzino's name into his own as seen in the inscription of one of his paintings: "Alexander Alorius Angeli Bronzini Alumnus Faciebat A D MDLXX" (Allori, foster-son of Agnolo Bronzino, made [this] in the year 1552).

At the age of nineteen, Allori traveled to Rome where he studied for six years. Allori studied antique statuary and the works of Michelangelo and was certainly influenced by the forms and contours of Michelangelo's figures. He also developed a reputation as a portrait painter.[51]

Allori returned to Florence in 1560 as an established artist and ready to receive commissions. His *Last Judgment* for the Montauti Chapel in SS. Annunziata was very well received in 1560. He participated in the foundation of the Accademia del Disegno of Florence in 1563 and participated in the major projects of the Accademia.[52] These included the preparatory decoration for the funeral of Michelangelo in 1564 and the marriage of Francesco I de'Medici and Giovanna of Austria the next year. Allori's friendship and working relationship with the Mannerist painter Giorgio Vasari (1511–74) stimulated a Mannerist style to his paintings of this period.[53] When Vasari received the commission from the Medici family to decorate the studiolo of Francesco I in the Palazzo Vecchio, he asked Allori for assistance. Allori painted the *Pearl Fishers* (Figure 5-2) on the western wall of the Studiolo. The smooth bodies and Michelangesque poses have caused art historian Jack Spalding to comment that this painting "is almost a symbol of late Florentine *maniera*."[54]

Allori's work in the 1570s was highly Mannerist, and he was working alongside a fellow Mannerist painter, Michele Tosini.[55] They may have met through the painter's Guild of St. Luke housed in the church of SS. Annunziata. In 1571, Allori painted an oil on panel of the *Trinity* for the chapel of St. Luke in the church already decorated by Vasari, in 1565, with a panel of *St. Luke Painting the Virgin*.[56]

Allori began work for the Salviati family in 1570. He was commissioned by Alamanno Salviati to paint three large mythological paintings in the family palace in Ponte alla Badia, outside Florence. He completed work on that project in 1572. Allori was appointed director of the Florentine tapestry factory in the mid-1570s but still took on private commissions.[57] Jacopo Salviati in 1574 commissioned Allori to do fresco scenes depicting scenes from the *Odyssey* and a Mary Magdalen cycle in the family chapel of their Florentine palace.

The Salviati family were cousins to the Florentine Medici. The decoration of the Salviati palace in Florence is the project in which the *Jesus in the House of Mary and Martha* painting was created. (We return

Figure 5-2. Alessandro Allori. *Pearl Fishers.* 1570–71. Oil on slate.
Palazzo Vecchio, Florence. With permission from the Ministero dei
Beni e le Attività Culturali, Florence.

to that discussion momentarily.) From 1575 to 1576, Allori painted the
cupola of the Gaddi Chapel of Santa Maria Novella, Florence, designed
by Antonio Dosio.

Allori continued to work under the patronage of the Medici family both
in and out of the city of Florence. He helped decorate the Salone Grande
between 1578 and 1582 in the Medici Villa located in Poggio a Caiano
and supervised the work of his assistants in the *Grotesques* painted on the
top floor of the Uffizi in 1581.[58]

Allori's works in the 1580s were strongly influenced by the painter Andrea del Sarto, just as were the works by Michele Tosini in the 1570s.
Mannerist artists seem to be attracted to the elegance of the Vasarian
maniera, the monumental drapery style of Andrea and the complex body
positions of Michelangelo. Allori executed three versions of the Last Supper
between 1582 and 1583, combining elements of these three masters.[59]

When painting religious works in the 1590s, he adopted the style of Santa
di Tito (1536–1602), who grew up with Allori as a fellow pupil of Bronzino's.
Santi di Tito's works can be characterized as narrative, pure, simple, and

direct. He was part of the Counter-Reformation revival of a pre-Mannerist style. Allori fluctuated between the style of Santi and the Mannerism of the mid-century. The Salviati family called on him again from 1583 to 1588 to decorate their family church in San Marco, Florence. Allori painted a fresco cycle of S. Antonio (Anthony) and an altarpiece of the *Descent into Limbo*. This altarpiece is considered one of Allori's masterpieces, and along with the *Pearl Fishers* exhibits two facets of Mannerism. The *Descent into Limbo* shows the necessary skill at rendering a composition on the contemporary *maniera* style. The *Pearl Fishers* characterizes the artificial elegance, and unnatural qualities sometimes found in Mannerist commissions.

Although Allori's influence was limited and his work has been recognized as more imitative than innovative, he remained open to several styles occurring contemporaneously as the story of art moved from the high Renaissance into Mannerism and finally, in the late sixteenth century, into the Baroque.[60] His son Cristofano Allori (1577–1621), in his mature works, paints in the new style of the day, today called the Baroque. Allori died in Florence on September 22, 1607, at a time when most scholars would agree that the Baroque style was in place.

The Painting

Jacopo Salviati hired Allori from 1574 to 1580 to do a series of projects in the renovation of his palace. Jacopo Salviati was the nephew of Cardinal Giovanni Salviati and the cousin of the Grand Duke of Tuscany, Francesco I de'Medici. Thus, because of his family relations, Jacopo had influential connections with the Catholic Church and with local political leaders.

Eventually, Jacopo Salviati developed his own sphere of influence. By the time Jacopo hired Allori, Jacopo was serving as one of nine operai who were responsible for overseeing the Santa Croce.[61] His service to the Catholic Church and the pope eventually resulted in Jacopo being named as the grand duke of Tuscany.[62]

Jacopo decided to renovate the Palazzo Salviati (1572–80) shortly after he purchased his family palace. Part of this renovation included the creation of a family chapel dedicated to St. Mary Magdalen within the palace.[63] Allori executed the chapel dedicated to Saint Mary Magdalen within the Palazzo Salviati between 1578 and 1580).[64] *Christ in the Home of Mary and Martha* is the altarpiece and the focal point for this program.

Upon entering the family chapel, this altarpiece is the first thing that a viewer sees. To the right of the altar but on the same wall, Allori began his fresco scenes (Figure 5-3). The three Magdalene frescoes, working clockwise and beginning next to the oil altar painting, are *The Magdalen*

Figure 5-3. Alessandro Allori. *View of Altar Wall.* 1578–80.
Fresco. Palazzo Portinari-Salviati, Florence. Photo.
Collezione Privata Palazzo Portinari-Salviati–sede Banca
Toscana, Florence.

Washes the Feet of Christ in the House of Simon (Figure 5-4), *Noli mi Tangere*
(Figure 5-5) on the wall perpendicular to the altar wall, and *Mary Mag-*
dalen Receives Communion on the wall opposite the *Magdalen Washing the*
Feet of Christ fresco (Figure 5-6). On the ceiling are Sibyls, Prophets, and
the four sacrifices of the Old Testament. Above the doorway facing the
altar is a fresco of Jesus' dead body on a Communion table with the cup
in front of him and two angels supporting him.[65]

The composition of the painting places all three primary figures in
the foreground in slightly different levels as if on a stage. Christ is in
the center wearing a rose gown with green mantle. This color palette is
quite typical for late sixteenth-century Florentine Mannerist art. Martha
wears a beautiful, contemporary Florentine dress and raises her right hand
in surprise at the words being spoken to her by a seated Christ who
points to Mary, the subject of his words. Mary is seated diagonally to
the left of Christ and her light pink and cream dress with gold brocad-
ing is partially covered by a green mantle (the same color as Christ's)
draped over her lap. Her hands are resting on her lap as she holds an
open book.

Figure 5-4. Alessandro Allori. *The Magdalen Washes the Feet of Christ in the House of Simon.* 1578–80. Fresco. Palazzo Portinari-Salviati, Florence. Photo. Collezione Privata Palazzo Portinari-Salviati–sede Banca Toscana, Florence.

There is an open window in the left background that opens onto a land-scape active with various workers carrying things and taking water from a well. In addition, he includes columns and that statuesque little boy whom we saw in *Christ and the Samaritan Woman* (1575), thereby fusing the arts. Allori also includes vivid colors and a significant amount of movement in the courtyard. Yet, the emotion of the characters is restrained, and the primary focus is on the biblical narrative in the foreground. The elegance of the Mannerist style learned from Bronzino is apparent in this paint-ing. The works in oil, even more luxurious than the muted fresco palette, convinces the viewer of the glory of the scene. Again, Allori's religious style seems to align him with the Catholic Church's Counter-Reformation convictions about the purpose of religious art. Thus, Allori's painting can easily be viewed without searching for a more complex or paradoxical message that is associated with the works of Bronzino, as discussed below.

Sources and Precedents

It is actually easier to find sources for Allori's program than it is to find sources for *Christ in the Home of Mary and Martha*. There were two fresco

Figure 5-5. Alessandro Allori. *Noli mi tangere*. 1578–80. Fresco. Palazzo Portinari-Salviati, Florence. Photo. Collezione Privata Palazzo Portinari-Salviati–sede Banca Toscana, Florence.

cycles of Mary Magdalen present in Florence during Allori's lifetime. First, Giotto's frescoes were in the Bargello chapel. Second, Giovanni da Milano produced a fresco cycle of Mary Magdalen in the Rinuccini chapel of Santa Croce, Florence, in 1365 (Figure 5-7).[66] One must remember that both Allori and this patron, Jacopo Salviati, had ties and experience with the church of Santa Croce and would certainly have been familiar with this fresco.

In Giovanni's *Christ in the Home of Mary and Martha*, Mary is seated facing Jesus with her back to Martha and four of Jesus' disciples. Martha is pointing to the kitchen,[67] and a real tension between Mary and Martha can be perceived.[68] While Mary and Christ are united structurally, Martha and several disciples are separated from Jesus, and they are expressing strong disapproval.[69]

Allori's altarpiece of *Christ in the House of Mary and Martha* is not complex or paradoxical like his more Mannerist works. Mary, Martha, and Jesus are all united structurally. There is no conflict.

Iconography of the Painting

The patron Jacopo Salviati would have known of the Giovanni da Milano painting as would Allori. Salviati probably also would have

Figure 5-6. Alessandro Allori. View of Entire Chapel. 1578–80. Palazzo Portinari-Salviati, Florence. Photo. Fresco. Collezione Privata Palazzo Portinari-Salviati–sede Banca Toscana, Florence.

been aware of the debate about Mary Magdalen and approved of the Counter-Reformation theology.

Alessandro Allori was influenced by the Counter-Reformation while in Rome. He maintained the Catholic tradition about Mary Magdalen. He also relied on the Gospel of Luke rather than the Giovanni da Milano precedent, which exposes elements of conflict and rebuke in the scene. Martha is depicted as a virtuous host and Jesus is not rebuking her. Mary is doing something even better than being a host. She listens like a disciple sitting at Christ's feet.

Haskins observes: "Although it was the episode in Luke 10 (vv. 38–42) which established Mary Magdalen as the patron and symbol of the contemplative life, and although there was constant reference to this aspect of her in devotional literature of the period, it was rarely illustrated until the sixteenth century except as cycles of her life."[70]

Jane Couchman argues that the iconography of Martha and Mary divides over whether or not the roles of Martha and Mary (active and

Figure 5-7. Giovanni da Milano. *Christ in the House of Mary and Martha.* 1365. Fresco. Rinuccini Chapel, Santa Croce, Florence. Photo. Chiesa di Santa Croce, Florence.

contemplative) are seen as competing (so Giovanni da Milano 1365) or complementary.[71]

Couchman also argues that the presence of other characters in the scene (especially apostles or religious leaders), who of course are absent from the biblical story, can contribute to the tension between the figures (as in the case of Giovanni da Milano). Whether or not these additional figures always contribute to a sense of tension between Mary and Martha, there were those who objected to their presence not simply because they are not recorded in the Scriptures but because of what they were often depicted as doing.

Erasmus, for example, objected to the way in which artists depicted scenes from the Gospels in an impious fashion and cites the scene in the house of Mary and Martha in particular:

> ....as for example, when they portray Mary and Martha receiving Our Lord to supper, the Lord speaking with Mary and John as a youth talking secretly in a corner with Martha, while Peter drains a tankard. Or again, at the feast, Martha standing behind by John, with one arm over his shoulders, while with the other she seems to mock at Christ, [who is] unaware of all this. Or again, Peter already rubicund with wine, yet holding the goblet to his lips.[72]

Couchman concludes:

> Of all the scenes from the life of Christ and of the Magdalene, this one appears to have the least stable, the least predictable iconog-

raphy. The illuminations, the frescoes, the windows, and the altar pieces . . . present a mixed message, reflecting the debate surrounding the choices of the two sisters, reinforced by the problems raised in the scenes that conflated with the scenes involving Mary and Martha. The sixteenth-century depictions of the scene show the same variety and ambiguity.[73]

However ambiguous the iconography may have been in the history of this particular scene, the meaning in our particular painting is clear. Allori fits the complementary pattern, with both Martha and Mary's actions — action and contemplation — being commended.[74]

Concluding Hermeneutical Reflections

Ironically, the more connected we become to the "world," through the Internet, cell phones, and satellites, the more tempting it is to disconnect from our immediate communities, and even ourselves. The story of Mary and Martha has much to say to us in our (post)modern condition.

Here during the early twenty-first century, interest is renewed in Protestant circles, even evangelical ones, in the Christian contemplative life.[75] We would do well to draw on the rich resources of the Christian tradition to engage in theological reflection on God, God's world, and our role in that world. Certainly reflection on the soteriological effects of Jesus' death have been and continue to be crucial to the formation of Christian identity. In this volume, we suggest that contemplation, assisted by the visual arts, on the public ministry of Jesus — his teachings, his acts of mercy and healing — might also contribute to our spiritual formation. That formation will take place in quiet solitude and in community with like-minded believers.

Of course, the Christian church is also called to action, to engage in compassionate acts that contribute to the mending of a broken world. In light of the example of Martha, the church should engage in specific acts of hospitality, concrete acts of kindness and compassion to the stranger, the traveler, the "other" in our midst.[76]

Jesus knew, however, that Mary's example was "the better part," because action, if it is to be sustained and consistent, always follows being — that is, what we do should flow naturally from who we are. The episodes immediately following this story in Luke illustrate this point. Jesus, in response to the disciples' request, teaches them how to pray (11:1–4). To sit and listen with Mary is not a passive act. It is, rather, to choose the

better part; to converse with God. We love God when we actively engage
with God in prayer with our heart, soul, strength, and mind.

The Lord's Prayer is immediately followed by the Parable of the Friend
at Midnight, a concrete example of the practice of hospitality (11:5–8).
Just as the disciples are to pray for God to supply their "daily bread," the
friend in the parable understands it as his duty as hospitable host to provide bread for the traveler who has stopped (inconveniently, it turns out)
to take up lodging in his home. The actions of the friend at midnight
remind us that it is through the hospitality of the church that God has
chosen to provide sustenance — physical substance through acts of charity and justice; spiritual bounty through the church's ministry of Word
and Eucharist — to those traveling the journey with us, both friend and
stranger. Martha's hospitable activities as host provide the paradigm.

As Allori evocatively suggests in his painting, these two activities are
complementary. Life of discipleship requires both action and meditation,
but the action should be examined; thoughtful action and the meditation
are rigorous activity. Therefore, let us choose the "better part."

Notes

1. See Walter Grundmann, *Evangelium nach Lukas* (Berlin: Evangelische Verlags-
anstalt, 1961), 225. Furthermore, this theme is continued into the next chapter, where
both love of God and neighbor (now defined as friend) are explored in both the Lord's
Prayer and the parable of the Friend at Midnight. Here we disagree with Joseph Fitzmyer,
The Gospel According to Luke (AB 28–28A; 2 vols.; Garden City, N.Y.: Doubleday, 1981,
1982), 2:891, who claims that the Mary and Martha episode "is unrelated to the preceding
passages . . ."

2. Material in the following paragraphs is taken from a paper by Andrew Arterbury
written for our class, The Gospels in Art, offered at Baylor University in fall 2001. Gratitude
is expressed to Dr. Arterbury (now our colleague at Baylor) for permission to use material
from that paper.

3. John Nolland, *Luke 9:51–18:34* (WBC 35B; Dallas: Word, 1993), 605.

4. R. Alan Culpepper, *The Gospel of Luke* (NIB 9; Nashville: Abingdon, 1995), 231.

5. In addition to the standard commentaries on Luke (Bock, Bovon, Fitzmyer,
Johnson, Talbert, Tannehill, etc.), recent literature includes: Erling Laland, "Die Martha-
Maria-Perikope Lukas 10, 38–42: Ihre kerygmatische Aktualität für das Leben der
Urkirche," *Studia Theologica* 13 (1959): 70–85; François Castel, "Luc 10:38–42," *Études
théologiques et religieuses* 55 (1980): 560–65; E. Jane Via, "Women, the Discipleship of
Service, and the Early Christian Ritual Meal in the Gospel of Luke," *Saint Luke's Journal
of Theology* 29 (1985): 37–60; Elizabeth Schüssler Fiorenza, "A Feminist Interpretation for
Liberation: Martha and Mary: Luke 10:38–42," *Religion and Intellectual Life* 3 (1986): 21–
36; Adele Reinhartz, "From Narrative to History: the Resurrection of Mary and Martha,"
Women Like This (Atlanta: Scholars Press, 1991), 161–84; Pamela Thimmes, "Memory and
Re-vision: Mary Magdalene Research Since 1975," *Currents in Research: Biblical Studies* 6
(1998): 193–226; Pamela Thimmes, "Narrative and Rhetorical Conflict in Luke 10:38–
42: A Cautionary Tale," *Proceedings — Eastern Great Lakes and Midwest Biblical Societies*

20 (2000): 51–60; Robert W. Wall, "Martha and Mary (Luke 10:38–42) in the Context of a Christian Deuteronomy," *Journal for the Study of the New Testament* 35 (1989): 19–35; Warren Carter, "Getting Martha Out of the Kitchen: Luke 10:38–42," *Catholic Biblical Quarterly* 58 (1996): 264–80; Boyo G. Ockinga, "The Tradition History of the Mary-Martha Pericope in Luke (10:38–42)," *Ancient History in a Modern University* (vol. 2; Grand Rapids: Eerdmans, 1998), 93–97; Veronica Koperski, "Luke 10,38–42 and Acts 6,1–7: Women and Discipleship in the Literary Context of Luke-Acts," *Unity of Luke-Acts* (Louvain: Leuven University Press, 1999), 517–44.

6. On the relationship of Luke to the ancient practice of hospitality, see Andrew Arterbury, "Acts 10–11 and the Custom of Hospitality" (Ph.D. dissertation, Baylor University, 2003). The phrase "welcomed (*hupedexato*) into [her] home" is conventional hospitality language. On hospitality in the ancient world, see, e.g., Ladislaus J. Bolchazy, *Hospitality in Antiquity: Livy's Concept of Its Humanizing Force* (Chicago: Ares Publishers, 1977); John Koenig, *New Testament Hospitality: Partnership with Strangers as Promise and Mission* (Philadelphia: Fortress Press, 1985).

7. Donald Wayne Riddle, "Early Christian Hospitality: A Factor in the Gospel Transmission," *Journal of Biblical Literature* 57 (1938): 143–45; Helga Rusche, "Gastfreundschaft und Mission in Apostelgeschichte und Apostelbriefen," *Zeitschrift fur Missionswissenschaft und Religionswissenschaft* 41 (1957): 254.

8. Although Brendan Byrne (*The Hospitality of God: A Reading of Luke's Gospel* [Collegeville, Minn.: Liturgical Press, 2000], 103) claims "Martha has gone overboard in the duties of hospitality."

9. In John 11:1, these two sisters figure in the raising of their brother Lazarus from the dead, though Lazarus does not appear anywhere in the Third Gospel. This Mary in Luke's Gospel is probably not to be identified with Mary Magdalen (pace Fitzmyer's note on Luke 8:2), despite later proclivities in the early and medieval church to do so. See Susan Haskins, *Mary Magdalene: Myth and Metaphor* (San Francisco: HarperCollins, 1993), chap. 3, and below under "Subsequent History of Interpretation." Occasionally in later tradition, the Lazarus of John was confused with the Lazarus mentioned in the parable in Luke 16. On this confusion, see our preceding chapter on Bassano's *Good Samaritan* and *Rich Man and Lazarus*.

10. On the textual problems associated with this verse, see Gordon Fee, "'One Thing Is Needful?' Luke 10:42," *New Testament Textual Criticism* (ed. Eldon J. Epp and Gordon Fee; Oxford: Oxford University Press, 1981), 61–75.

11. Fitzmyer, *Luke*, 2:892.

12. See Via, "Women," 55–56.

13. And such Christian hospitality *was* important; see Andrew Arterbury, "The Ancient Custom of Hospitality, The Greek Novels, and Acts 10:1–11:18," *Perspectives in Religious Studies* 29 (2002): 53–72.

14. Arterbury, "Acts 10–11 and the Custom of Hospitality," 17–18.

15. For more on this term, see Kathleen Corley, "Women and Meals in the Gospel of Luke," *Private Women, Public Meals: Social Conflict in the Synoptic Tradition* (Peabody, Mass.: Hendrickson, 1993), 140.

16. Pamela Thimmes, "Narrative and Rhetorical Conflict in Luke 10:38–42: A Cautionary Tale," *Proceedings: Eastern Great Lakes and Midwest Biblical Societies* 20 (2000): 51–60; contra Fiorenza, "Feminist Interpretation for Liberation," 32, who argues that "Lu. 10:38–42 pits the apostolic women of the Jesus movement against each other and appeals to a revelatory word of the resurrected Lord in order to restrict women's ministry and authority." For a rebuttal of Fiorenza's reading from a feminist's perspective, see Reinhartz, "From Narrative to History," 166–71.

17. Fitzmyer, *Luke*, 2:892.

18. Reinhartz, "From Narrative to History," 172.

19. For more see Ockinga, "Tradition History of the Mary-Martha Pericope," 93–97.

20. Ambrose, "M. Magdalenae an plures personae fuerint?" PL 15, cols. 1616–17. Ambrose himself (1617) allows the possibility of a connection between these two Marys.

21. Augustine, *In Joannis Evangelium*, PL 35, col. 1748; cited by Haskins, *Mary Magdalene*, 94. Augustine did not, however, identify the sinful woman of Luke 7 with Mary Magdalen.

22. Haskins, *Mary Magdalene*, 94–95. For more on these various exegetical traditions, see U. Holzmeister, "Die Magdalenfrage in der kirchlichen Uberlieferung," *Zeitschrift für katholische Theologie* 46 (1922): 558–84; Victor Saxer, "Santa Maria Maddalena dalla storia evangelica alla leggenda e all'arte," in *La Maddalena tra Sacro e Profano* (ed. Marilena Mosca; Milan: Arnoldo Mondadori Editore, 1986), 24–28.

23. Gregory the Great, *Homily XXXIII*, PL 76, col. 1239; cited by Haskins, *Mary Magdalene*, 96.

24. Gregory the Great, *Homily XXV*, PL 74, col. 1180; cited by Haskins, *Mary Magdalene*, 96.

25. The situation in Eastern orthodoxy, however, is very different. Most Greek fathers, following John Chrysostom, opt for three, or at least two, different women, even opting for three different feast days: July 22 for Mary Magdalen; March 18 for Mary, Martha's sister; and March 31 for the sinful woman who anointed Jesus. On this see, Sister Magdalen LaRow, S.S.J., "The Iconography of Mary Magdalen: The Evolution of a Western Tradition" (Ph.D. dissertation, New York University, 1982), 6–7.

26. Haskins, *Mary Magdalene*, 96.

27. See Jacobus de Voragine, *The Golden Legend: Readings on the Saints* (trans. William Granger Ryan; Princeton, N.J.: Princeton University Press, 1993), 1:379–80.

28. Esther De Boer (*Mary Magdalene: Beyond the Myth* [London: SCM Press, 1996], 8) notes that Mary Magdalen was also identified as the patron saint of those who tended vineyards, gardeners, apothecaries, glove-makers, perfume manufacturers, hatters, weavers, seafarers, prisoners, and gypsies.

29. Renewed interest in academic circles is coincidental to the popular but spurious claims regarding Mary's role as mother of Jesus' offspring made in the notoriously popular novel, *The Da Vinci Code*, by Dan Brown. Representative of this reassessment of Mary Magdalen's role(s) in early Christianity (which pay generous and critical attention to mention of her in apocryphal sources), see Ann Graham Brock, *Mary Magdalen, the First Apostle: The Struggle for Identity* (Harvard Theological Studies 51; Cambridge, Mass.: Harvard Divinity School, 2003), and F. Stanley Jones, ed., *Which Mary? The Marys of Early Christian Tradition* (Leiden: Brill, 2002).

30. Fitzmyer, *Luke*, 2:892–93.

31. Haskins, *Mary Magdalene*, 22. For more on the medieval interpretations of Luke 10:38–42, along the lines of the contemplative/active life, see Daniel A. Csányi, "Optima pars. Die Auslegungsgeschichte von Lk 19:38–42 bei den Kirchenvätern der ersten vier Janrunderte," *Studia Monastica* 2 (1960): 5–78 (despite the fact that Csányi himself disavows this interpretation).

32. Cited by LaRow, "The Iconography of Mary Magdalen," 35.

33. Jerome, *Epistola XXII*, Ad Eustochium, Paulae Filliam, PL 32, cols. 410–11.

34. LaRow, "The Iconography of Mary Magdalen," 36. LaRow cites Augustine, *Sermons*: ciii, civ, clxxix, cclv. Also *de Trinitas* xii, 22, *Civ. Dei* viii 4; Migne PL 37, 28, 39, 41; Augustine, *de Trinitas* 1, 20; Migne PL 42, col. 834. For more on Augustine's interpretation of the complementarity of the active and contemplative lives based on the examples

of Martha and Mary, see James Halporn, "Saint Augustine Sermon 104 and the Epulae Vernerales," *Jahrbuch für Antike und Christentum* 19 (1976): 82–108.

35. Ambrose, *Exposition of the Gospel of Luke*, 7.85–86; *Exposition of the Holy Gospel According to Saint Luke with Fragments on the Prophecy of Isaias* (trans. T. Tomkinson; Etna, Calif.: Center for Traditional Orthodox Studies, 1998), 265–66; cited by Ancient Christian Commentary on Scripture (ACC) on Luke, 183.

36. Ephrem the Syrian, *Commentary on Tatian's Diatessaron*, 8.15; cited in *Saint Ephraem's Commentary on Tatian's Diatessaron: An English Translation of Chester Beatty Syriac MS 709* (trans. and ed. C. McCarthy; Journal of Semitic Studies Supplemental 2; Oxford: Oxford University Press, 1993), 153; cited by ACC on Luke, 183.

37. Gregory, *Moralia* in Job, VI, ch. 28; Migne PL 75, col. 754.

38. John Cassian, *Collationes*, I, 8. Migne, PL 49, cols. 491–92.

39. Jacobus de Voragine, *Golden Legend*, 1:374, 375. It should nonetheless be pointed out that Mary as penitent receives the most attention in this section.

40. Ps.-Bonaventure, *Meditations on the Life of Christ* (ed. I. Ragusa and R. B. Green; Princeton, N.J.: Princeton University Press, 1961), 247.

41. John Calvin, *A Harmony of the Gospels: Matthew, Mark and Luke* (ed. David W. Torrance and Thomas F. Torrance; trans. T. H. L. Parker; Edinburgh: St. Andrews Press, 1972), 89. De Boer, *Mary Magdalene*, 9, traces the criticism of the composite Mary to Jacques Lefevre d'Etaples, a Protestant humanist, who in 1517 published *De Maria Magdalena et triduo Christi disceptatione* (On Mary Magdalen and the Departure of Christ after Three Days), in which he asserted that the woman who was a sinner (Luke 7:36–50), Mary the sister of Martha, and Mary Magdalen were three distinct biblical figures. Margaret Hannay, "Mary Magdalene," in *A Dictionary of Biblical Tradition in English Literature* (ed. David Lyle Jeffrey; Grand Rapids: Eerdmans, 1992), 487.

42. See John B. Knipping, *Iconography of the Counter Reformation in the Netherlands: Heaven on Earth* (Leiden: A. W. Sijthoff, 1974), 314–20.

43. De Boer, *Mary Magdalene*, 14–15. De Boer (15) further notes that the Roman Catholic Church does not change its official position on Mary Magdalen until 1970.

44. Hannay, "Mary Magdalene," 487. Legend holds that Mary Magdalen was put on a ship and landed at Marseilles, France. There she evangelized the people and performed many miracles. She died after spending thirty years in solitude while not eating, but only depending upon the nourishment she received from the angels while communing with Christ (see de Voragine, *The Golden Legend*, 1:376–81). Her relics were housed in the basilica of Vezelay in France. The Giovanni da Milano fresco cycle in S. Croce, Florence, shows the final fresco scene of the deceased Mary Magdalen in the foreground and a ship on the water in the background.

45. Diane Apostolos-Cappadona, "Saint Mary Magdalene," in *Dictionary of Christian Art* (New York: Continuum, 1994), 236.

46. For general information regarding this palace and its collections, see Mario Bucci and Raffaello Bencini, *I Palazzi di Firenze, Quartiere di Santa Croce* (Florence: Vallecchi editore, 1971), 85–90; Patriza Fabbri and Francesco Gurrieri, *Palazzi a Firenze* (Venice: Arsenale Editrice 1995), 282–93; Guido Pampaloni, *Il Palazzo Portinari-Salviati* (Firenze: Banca Toscana, 1960) 45, 50–52; Marcello Vannucci, *Splendidi palazzi di Firenze* (Firenze: Le Lettere, 1995), 300–304.

For various views of the chapel decorated by Allori, see Claudia Nardini and Laura Amadori Gori, *Banca Toscana: Storia e collezioni* (Florence: Nardini Editore, 1982), 247–93; Mina Gregori, ed., *Mostra dei tesori segreti della Case Fiorentine* (Firenze, 1960), n. 52; fig. 42; *Italian 16th Century Drawings from British Private Collections. Catalogo della mostra* (Edinburgh: Edinburgh Festival Society, 1969), 2, fig. 55; Leonardo Ginori Lisci, *I Palazzi di Firenze nella storia e nell'arte* (Firenze: Cassa di Risparmio, 1972), 475, fig. 383; Piero Bargellini, *Paintings by Alessandro Allori. The Palazzo Salviati-da Cepperello Formerly Houses of the Portinari Property and Seat of the Banca Toscana, Florence* (Florence: Banca Toscana, 1953).

47. Many thanks to Robert Simon for his bibliographic assistance related to Alessandro Allori. See Simona Lecchini Giovannoni, *Alessandro Allori*, 247, 315–28, figs. 140–44.

48. Jack Spalding, "Alessandro Allori," in the *The Dictionary of Art* (ed. J. Turner; 34 vols.; London: Macmillan, 1996), 1:670–71. Given Spalding's expertise on Santi di Tito, this essay favors the influence of Santi on Allori more than most scholarship allows.

49. See Elizabeth Pilliod, "Studies on the Early Career of Alessandro Allori" (Ph.D. dissertation, University of Michigan, 1989). For the relationship among the artists, see Pilliod, *Pontormo, Bronzino, Allori: A Genealogy of Florentine Art* (New Haven: Yale University Press, 2001); "Bronzino's Household," *Burlington Magazine* 134 (1992): 92–100.

50. See Giorgio Vasari, *Le Opere di Giorgio Vasari: Le Vite de'più eccellenti pittori, scultori ed architettori scritte da Giorgio Vasari pittore Aretino* (1568) (ed. Gaetano Milanesi; 9 vols.; Florence: Sansoni, 1885), 7:666–68.0

51. Spalding, "Alessandro Allori," 670.

52. See Karen-edis Barzman, *The Florentine Academy and the Early Modern State: The Discipline of Disegno* (Cambridge: Cambridge University Press, 2000), 29–31.

53. Vasari, *Le vite*, 6:281–83, 71–85; 7:596.

54. Spalding, "Alessandro Allori," 670.

55. For a comparison of differences within the Florentine Mannerist style in the late 1570s, see chap. 2, this volume.

56. See Heidi J. Hornik and Mikeal C. Parsons, *Illuminating Luke: The Infancy Narrative in Italian Renaissance Painting* (Harrisburg, Pa.: Trinity Press International, 2003), fig. 5.

57. See http://www.Getty.edu/art/collections/bio/a730-1.html (accessed July 8, 2004).

58. Spalding, "Alessandro Allori," 671.

59. These *Last Supper* paintings are located in the following locations: Accademia Carrara, Bergamo (1582); S. Maria del Carmine, Florence, fresco (1582); S. Maria Novella, Florence (1584). Another religious painting in this style is the *Virgin and Child with Saints*, 1583, National Museum, Cardiff.

60. Spalding, "Alessandro Allori," 671.

61. Marcia B. Hall, *Renovation and Counter-Reformation: Vasari and Duke Cosimo in Sta. Maria Novella and Santa Croce* (Oxford: Oxford University Press, 1979), 22.

62. Chiara Stefani, "Salviati," in *The Dictionary of Art* (ed. J. Turner; 34 vols.; London: Macmillan, 1996), 27:648.

63. The Banca Toscana has placed a virtual tour of the palazzo, including color images of the chapel, at http://www.bancatoscana.it/banca/virtualtour.htm (accessed July 8, 2004).

64. The fresco depicting the Communion table is signed and dated 1580 in the lower right corner: "Hoc sacellum pingebat Alessandro Allori MDLXXX." See Bargellini, *Paintings by Alessandro Allori*, 2.

65. For additional photos of the chapel, see Leonardo Ginori Lisci, *I Palazzi di Firenze nella storia e nell'arte*, 475; Mario Bucci and Raffaello Bencini, *I Palazzi di Firenze, Quartiere di Santa Croce*, 85–90; Bargellini, *Paintings by Alessandro Allori*, 41–47.

66. George Kaftal, *Iconography of the Saints in Tuscan Painting* (Firenze: Casa Editrice Le Lettere, 1986), 717.

67. G. Schiller, *Iconography of Christian Art* (Greenwich, Conn.: New York Graphic Society, 1972), 159.

68. Jane Couchman, "*Actio* and *Passio:* The Iconography of the Scene of Christ at the Home of Mary and Martha," *Studi Medievali* 26, no. 2 (1985): 716. Couchman's article traces the development of this scene in art, but the only painting that she discusses that could effectively serve as a source for Allori is Giovanni da Milano's.

69. Ibid.

70. Haskins, *Mary Magdalene*, 198. L. Réau, *Iconographie de l'art Chretien* (Paris: Universitaires de France, 1955–59), 2:328, lists only six examples before 1600, four of which come from the 1500s. Likewise G. Schiller, *Iconography of Christian Art* (Greenwich, Conn., 1972), 1:158–59, calls it "a very rare theme," listing only three examples before 1600. For more on the history of the iconography of the Mary/Martha scene, see in addition to Haskins, LaRow, "The Iconography of Mary Magdalen," and Marga Janssen, "Maria Magdalena in der abendlandischen Kunst" (Inaugural-Dissertation, Philosophy Faculty of the Albert-Ludwigs-Universität zu Freiburg im Breisgau, 1961). See, especially, Marilena Mosco, "Gesu in casa di Marta," in *La Maddalena Tra Sacro e Profano*, (ed. Marilena Mosca; Milan: Arnoldo Mondadori Editore, 1986), 97–101 (which includes a discussion of Allori). Also in that volume, see Luciano Berti, "Le belle immagini," 14; Sergio Salvi, "Una Maddalena europea," 15–16; Maria Pia Mannini, "La diffusione de culto in Toscana: lazzareti, conventi, case delle Convertite e Malmaritate," 60–64.

71. Jane Couchman, "*Actio* and *Passio*," 711–19. See also David Mycoff, *The Life of Saint Mary Magdalen and of her Sister Saint Martha: A Medieval Biography* (Kalamazoo, Mich.: Cistercian Publications, 1989).

72. Desiderius Erasmus, Christian Matrimonii Institutio, Opera Omnia (Antwerp, 1733), v. 695; cited by P. K. F. Moxey, "Erasmus and the Iconography of Pieter Aertsen's *Christ in the House of Martha and Mary* in the Boymans-Van Beuningen Museum," *Journal of the Warburg Institute* 34 (1971): 336. This treatise on marriage was first published in 1526. For Erasmus's views in general on religious art (which also cites this same passage, see 211), see Erwin Panofsky, "Erasmus and the Visual Arts," *Journal of the Warburg Institute* 32 (1969): 200–227.

73. Jane Couchman, "*Actio* and *Passio*," 718.

74. The complementary nature of Mary and Martha's roles is seen even more clearly in Allori's other version of *Christ in the House of Mary and Martha* (Kunsthistorisches Museum, Vienna, oil on canvas, 124 x 104 cm, 1603) where Mary and Martha are positioned together on the same side of Jesus. See Simona Lecchini Giovannoni, *Alessandro Allori* (Torino: U. Allemandi, 1991), no. 403. For discussion of a related painting, see Teresa Pugliatti, "La 'Vergine Odigitria' di Alessandro Allori," in *Modelli di lettura iconografia* (ed. Mario Alberto Pavone; Napoli: Liguori, 1999), 159–76.

75. For many evangelicals and free church Protestants, Richard Foster's *Celebration of Discipline: The Path to Spiritual Growth* (San Francisco: Harper & Row, 1978) was an oasis in the desert. Since then, the category of Christian spirituality (to be distinguished from popular Christian self-help books) has burgeoned. Among those recent works that also include hospitality as a dimension of Christian spirituality, see W. Paul Jones, *Facets of Faith: Living the Dimensions of Christian Spirituality* (Cambridge, Mass.: Cowley Press, 2003), and David M. McCarthy, *The Good Life: Genuine Christianity for the Middle Class* (Grand Rapids: Brazos Press, 2004).

76. On Christian hospitality as an activity of the contemporary church, see especially Christine D. Pohl, *Making Room: Recovering Hospitality as a Christian Tradition* (Grand Rapids: Eerdmans, 1999).

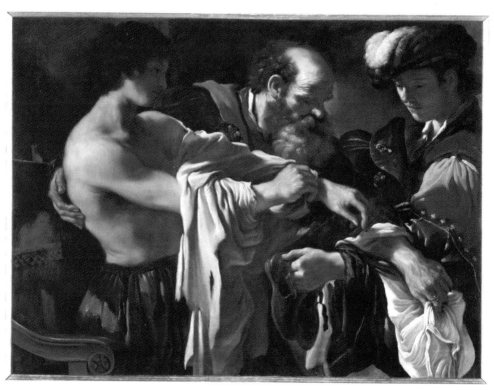

Figure 6-1. Guercino. *Return of the Prodigal Son.* 1619. Oil on canvas. Kunsthistorisches Museum, Vienna. Photo. Kunsthistorisches Museum, Wien oder KHM, Vienna.

Chapter Six

The Prodigal Son by Guercino

(Luke 15:11–32)

Sometimes a text from Scripture so engages its audience that a reader returns many times to it over the course of his or her life. The Parable of the Prodigal Son has no doubt had that kind of impact on many readers over the centuries.[1] Such certainly seems to be the case for the subject of this chapter, Guercino, who rendered the story of the Prodigal no fewer than seven times, two of which are now lost, over a period of nearly forty years.[2] We explore the meaning of several of these versions, not only in relationship to each other and their place in Guercino's evolving *oeuvre*, but in terms of their interaction with the prevailing social and religious views of Guercino's day.

Overview of the Biblical Text

[11]And he said: A certain man had two sons: [12]And the younger of them said to his father: Father, give me the portion of substance that falleth to me. And he divided unto them his substance. [13]And not many days after, the younger son, gathering all together, went abroad into a far country: and there wasted his substance, living riotously. [14]And after he had spent all, there came a mighty famine in that country: and he began to be in want. [15]And he went and cleaved to one of the citizens of that country. And he sent him into his farm to feed swine. [16]And he would fain have filled his belly with the husks the swine did eat: and no man gave unto him. [17]And returning to himself, he said: How many hired servants in my father's house abound with bread, and I here perish with hunger? [18]I will arise and will go to my father and say to him: Father, I have sinned against heaven and before thee: [19]I am not worthy to be called thy son: make me as one of thy hired servants. [20]And rising up, he came to his father. And when he was yet a great way off, his father saw him

and was moved with compassion and running to him fell upon his neck and kissed him. [21]And the son said to him: Father, I have sinned against heaven and before thee I am not now worthy to be called thy son. [22]And the father said to his servants: Bring forth quickly the first robe and put it on him; and put a ring on his hand and shoes on his feet. [23]And bring hither the fatted calf, and kill it: and let us eat and make merry: [24]Because this my son was dead, and is come to life again, was lost and is found. And they began to be merry. [25]Now his elder son was in the field, and when he came and drew nigh to the house, he heard music and dancing: [26]And he called one of the servants, and asked what these things meant. [27]And he said to him: Thy brother is come and thy father hath killed the fatted calf, because he hath received him safe. [28]And he was angry and would not go in. His father therefore coming out began to entreat him. [29]And he answering, said to his father: Behold, for so many years do I serve thee and I have never transgressed thy commandment: and yet thou hast never given me a kid to make merry with my friends: [30]But as soon as this thy son is come, who hath devoured his substance with harlots, thou hast killed for him the fatted calf. [31]But he said to him: Son, thou art always with me; and all I have is thine. [32]But it was fit that we should make merry and be glad; for this thy brother was dead and is come to life again; he was lost, and is found. (Luke 15:11–32, Douay-Rheims Bible)

The familiar and well-loved parable in Luke 15:11–32 has long been known in English as the Parable of the Prodigal Son, and this is probably still its most popular title.[3] No less a prominent figure in biblical studies than Joachim Jeremias, however, in his classic study of the parables, suggested that this parable is more aptly described as a "parable of the Father's Love."[4] But even Jeremias's judgment could not derail the tide of subsequent interpreters, many of whom still see the parable as predominately about the prodigal younger brother. Joel Green's comments are characteristic: "as important as the father is to this parable, center stage belongs to the younger son."[5]

Does the grammar of the passage help us understand better how the authorial audience may have heard this parable? Every beginning language student is aware that Greek is a highly inflected language, but, in light of the Progymnasmata, the significance of that fact for New Testament interpretation has not been fully appreciated.[6]

The Progymnasmata, introduced earlier in this volume, were "handbooks that outlined 'preliminary exercises' designed to introduce students who had completed basic grammar and literary studies to the fundamentals of rhetoric that they would then put to use in composing speeches and prose."[7] As such, these graded series of exercises were probably intended to facilitate the transition from grammar school to the more advanced study of rhetoric.[8] Four of these Progymnasmata from the first to fifth centuries C.E. have survived.[9] What is important about these writings is that some of the exercises in the Progymnasmata are clearly intended to embrace both written and oral forms of communication.

About the progymnasmata, George Kennedy observed:

> The curriculum described in these works, featuring a series of set exercises of increasing difficulty, was the source of facility in written and oral expression for many persons and training for speech in public life. . . . Not only the secular literature of the Greeks and Romans, but *the writings of early Christians beginning with the gospels* and continuing through the patristic age, and of some Jewish writers as well, *were molded by the habits of thinking and writing learned in schools* (emphasis added).[10]

Our arguments about the rhetorical shape of the parable in Luke 15 are drawn primarily from the *Progymnasmata* of Aelius Theon of Alexandria (c. 50–100 C.E.), the only textbook roughly contemporary to Luke.[11] We are not, of course, suggesting any kind of literary dependence between Luke and Theon, but rather that Theon's text conveniently represents the type of rhetorical exercises practiced in the first century, many of which, in fact, had been practiced as early as the first or second centuries B.C.E.[12] Thus, we assume that most, but not all, of what Theon says about these rhetorical exercises was not unique to Theon. This assumption is buttressed by occasional appeal to the discussions in the rhetorical handbook tradition, which, while discussing specifically rhetorical speech, have remarkable similarity to a number of Theon's points.

Inflecting the main subject or topic (*klisis*) was one of the first exercises taught to beginning students of elementary rhetoric and provided a transition from the study of grammar to the study of rhetoric given that the exercise focused on the rhetorical function of inflection.[13] Theon gives a rather full description of how such inflection is to take place in his discussion of chreia and fable and refers back to it in his discussion of narrative (85.29–31; Patillon, 48). In his chapter on "Fables," Theon asserts:

> Fables should be inflected, like chreia, in different grammatical numbers and oblique cases. . . . The original grammatical construction must not always be maintained as though by some necessary law, but

one should introduce some things and use a mixture (of construc-
tions); for example, start with one case and change in what follows to
another, for this variety is very pleasing. (74.24–35, 74.75; Patillon,
33; cf. also 101.10–103.2)

Quintilian (*Institutio Oratoria*, 9.1.34) also comments briefly on the use
of inflection as a rhetorical device.[14] Following a discussion of the effects of repetition, he suggests: "Other effects may be obtained by the
graduation or contrast of clauses, by the elegant inversion of words, by
arguments drawn from opposites, asyndeton, paraleipsis, correction, ex-
clamation, meiosis, the employment of a *word in different cases* (in multis
casibus), moods and tenses...." And again at 9.3.37:

At times the cases and genders of the words repeated may be varied, as in 'Great is the goal of speaking, and great the task, etc.'; a
similar instance is found in Rutilius, but in a long period. I therefore merely cite the beginnings of the clauses. Pater hic tuus? Patrem
nunc appellas? Patris tui filius es? [Is this your father? Do you still
call him father? Are you your father's son?] This figure may also be
effected solely by change of cases, a proceeding which the Greeks
call *poluptôton.*

What Theon calls *klisis*, Quintilian refers to as *poluptôton*]; but the
phenomenon is the same. Inflection was more than just an ornamental
figure of style designed to please the aesthetic tastes of the audience. In
fact, Quintilian included inflection in his discussion of figures of thought,
a "class of figure, which does not merely depend on the form of the language for its effect, but lends both charm and force to the thought as well"
(9.3.28; Loeb Classical Library). The function of inflection was for emphasis (see Quintilian, *Inst.* 9.3.67) and to attract the audience's attention to
the subject under discussion (Quintilian, *Inst.* 9.3.27).

Any student of elementary rhetoric then would have been accustomed
to inflecting the main topic or subject of a chreia, fable, or narrative, and
presumably an ancient audience would have been naturally, almost in-
stinctively, able to identify the main subject by hearing the topic inflected
in the various cases of the Greek noun. If true and if Luke were the student
of rhetoric that we think him to have been, then we might expect Luke to
have used this inflection convention to provide rhetorical markers as to
the topic or subject of various parts of the Lukan narrative. We think we
see this phenomenon clearly exhibited in the parable of the father's love,
recorded in Luke 15.

The term "son" occurs eight times in Luke 15:11–32, once in the accusative case (and plural, v. 11) and seven times in the nominative singular, in reference to the prodigal (15:13, 19, 21 [twice], 24, 25, 30). We might reasonably expect that the subject of a parable or story would occur most frequently in the nominative case; however, if we take seriously the role of grammatical inflection in the educational system of late antiquity, then we might not be surprised to learn that not only does the word "father" occur twelve times in the parable, it appears in all five cases at least once, and in four cases, including the vocative (a rarity in Luke) at least twice: nominative — vv. 20, 22, 27, 28; genitive — 17; dative — 12, 29; accusative — 18, 20; vocative — 12, 18, 21. The conclusion seems irresistible that an ancient audience hearing Luke 15, who were conditioned (even unconsciously) upon "hearing" a word inflected to identify that term as the subject of the story at hand, would have naturally understood that the subject of the parable was the father and his joyous response over the return of his lost, and presumed dead, son.[15] But how was the story understood by subsequent generations of hearers/interpreters?

A Brief History of Interpretation

Though interpreters often disagreed on whether there were two or three kinds of meaning beyond Scripture's literal sense, there was general agreement that the Bible's meanings could be categorized as literal and nonliteral with the latter often being referred to as the "spiritual," "mystical," or "allegorical." The allegorical interpretation of Luke 15 dominated the church's understanding throughout the Middle Ages, and was, for all practical purposes, set by three nearly contemporary discussions from the end of the fourth century C.E.: Jerome's twenty-first letter (c. 383), the Commentary on Luke by Ambrose (c. 388), and Augustine's *Questions on the Gospels* (c. 399–400).[16] Jerome and Ambrose both admit two valid readings, though they focus their attention more on one than the other: the elder and younger sons may represent Jews and the Gentiles respectively in an historical allegory (Jerome); or a penitential reading, in which the elder son signifies the self-righteous Christian, and the prodigal represents the contrite sinner (Ambrose). Augustine focuses only on the historical allegory of Jews and Gentiles.[17]

Jerome's interpretation comes in the form of a response to questions from Pope Damasus' questions: "You [Pope Damasus] say: 'Who is that father in the Gospel who divided unto his two sons his substance? Who are the two sons? Who is the elder or who is the younger?' " After an extended introduction to the parable, Jerome gives a verse-by-verse explanation, finally turning his attention to the identity of the elder brother: "now the story goes on to the older son, whom many interpret simply as the person of all the saints, but many — quite correctly — refer to the Jews." Jerome then notes the two prominent interpretations and points out difficulties with each.

From this point on, Jerome focuses on the elder brother as representative of unrepentant Israel and the prodigal son as Gentiles who are receptive to the gospel. Jerome finally rejects the claim of the elder brother to "have never transgressed your commandment" as a lie, similar in effect with the parable of the Pharisee and the Publican:

> It seems to me that the Jew boasts more than he tells the truth, and after the fashion of that Pharisee: *O God, I give thee thanks that I am not as the rest of men, extortioners, unjust, adulterers, as also is this publican.* I ask you, does not this man seem to be saying of his brother what the Pharisee had said about the publican: *he who hath devoured all his substance living with harlots?*

Jerome's conclusion is clear: The angry elder brother who refuses to go in is "Israel [who] stands outside."

Ambrose, like Jerome, admits both readings: the historical allegory and penitential reading, but he focuses on the penitential interpretation in his *Treatise on the Gospel of Luke*. "Ambrose interprets the Elder Brother as the arrogant Christian who is jealous of the sinner's reconciliation."[18] Being older is not the result of his wisdom, but his vice. Ambrose says, "He is called older because an envious person ages quickly."[19] His worldliness is manifested from his position in the fields; his selfishness in his desire for the kid: "the envious person wants the kid to be sacrificed for himself, the innocent person the lamb."[20] The elder brother is not a Jew but any Christian who is resentful of a repenting sinner.

Death and rebirth, sin and grace, departure and return, self-alienation and self-recovery — all important themes in the parable — are essential to understanding Augustine's *Confessions*.[21] Augustine establishes the interpretation that dominates medieval exegesis of the parable for the next millennium, namely, that the prodigal son and elder brother are to be understood in salvation-historical terms as referring to Gentiles and Jews: "While meanwhile his elder son, the people of Israel following the flesh, has not in fact departed into a distant region, but nevertheless is not in the house, however he is in the field, namely, he is toiling with reference to earthly things. . . ."[22] Augustine interprets the father's going out to the elder brother as an appeal for Jews to enter the church "so that all Israel — to whom, to an extent blindness, has occurred, just as to the one absent in the field may become saved."[23] But it is clear from Augustine's view of the Jews here and elsewhere that he thinks such conversion either impossible or highly improbable — the elder brother/Jews will not join the great feast![24] The *Gloss*, an eleventh-century compilation of passages from sources as early as Tertullian and as late as authorities contemporary with the compilers, confirms the pervasiveness of Augustine's salvation-historical allegory.[25]

However, some interesting and diverse interpretations emerged from the medieval period.[26] The most interesting and disturbing reading of the elder brother at this time occurs in the medieval English version of the *Gesta Romanorum*, which offers a very unusual allegorical interpretation. About the elder brother it says:

> [T]he other sons [i.e., the elder brother in the parable], whiche betokeneth the deuyll, was euer vnkynde, & grutcheth dayly agaynst oure reconsylynge, sayenge, that by synne we oughte not to come vnto the herytage of heuen. Unto the whiche brynge vs our lorde Ihesus! Amen.[27]

During the sixteenth century, the story of the Prodigal Son enjoyed unprecedented popularity in the homiletic, dramatic, and iconographic traditions. During the period of the Reformation, though, the penitential reading of the elder brother reemerged, at least in ecclesiastical circles. This view was forcefully presented by John Calvin. Still, the historical allegory continued to be very popular in drama and art, as well as the tendency to ignore the elder brother altogether.

Calvin acknowledged those "who think that, under the figure of *the first-born son*, the Jewish nation is described, have indeed some argument on their side," but he maintained, "I do not think that they attend sufficiently to the whole of the passage."[28] Rather he argued that the section of the parable dealing with the elder brother "charges those persons with cruelty, who would wickedly choose to set limits to the grace of God, as if they envied the salvation of wretched sinners . . . If we are desirous to be reckoned the children of God, we must forgive in a brotherly manner. . . . "[29]

For Calvin, the prodigal son is the repentant sinner and the elder brother is the reluctant Christian whose negative example reminds the pious believer that it costs nothing to rejoice when God receives "into favor those who had been at variance with him." Calvin, then, is picking up on the interpretation first proposed by Ambrose (and Tertullian) and revived by Bonaventure and Albert the Great in the thirteenth century.

The Catholic Reformation affirmed that the prodigal son represented a sinner "at variance" with God. In fact, the Council of Trent (1554–63) assigned the prodigal son (along with Peter and Mary Magdalen) especially the role of penitent sinner par excellence.[30] The difference, and it was a critical one, was that in the Catholic interpretation, the father represented not only a forgiving God but also the church, the only locale sufficient for true penance. This point, as we shall see, is crucial for understanding our artist's various visual interpretations of the parable.

Introduction to the Artist

Gian Francesco Barbieri Guercino (1591–1666) was born in Cento, a small town outside the metropolis of Bologna. He became known as Guercino because he was squint-eyed, probably from a childhood accident. He had been apprenticed to Benedetto Gennari the elder (d. 1610), whose brother later married Guercino's sister in 1628. The couple had two sons who worked with Guercino. Guercino left these nephews Benedetto Gennari, the younger, and Cesare Gennari his entire estate as he did not marry and had no children.[31]

Guercino's life and works are very well documented, and many paintings have a provenance that can be traced back to the original commission.[32] The extant documents include Guercino's own meticulous account books, especially for the years 1629–66, a large number of correspondences between the artist and his patrons, and the work of his first biographer, Carlo Cesare Malvasia (1616–93), who knew him personally.[33]

Most scholars agree that despite this apprenticeship with Gennari, Guercino was practically self-trained as an artist. In 1612, when he was twenty-one, his work came to the attention of a Bolognese cleric, Canonico Antonio Mirandola, who held an ecclesiastical position at Cento. Mirandola took Guercino under his wing, so to speak, and helped him secure several important commissions that were noticed by Bolognese patrons. When he arrived in Bologna in 1617, he was already an accomplished painter at age twenty-six. Ludovico Carracci (1555–1619), a contemporary Bolognese painter, writes a letter about him in 1617 and describes "a great draughtsman and a most felicitous colorist; he is a prodigy of nature, a miracle . . . who astonishes the leading painters."[34]

Guercino was a painter of the third-generation Bolognese style. He preferred a pictorial, rather violently Baroque manner that creates a deep impression and hastens a change in the prevailing classicism. Guercino visited the artistic centers of Venice (1618), Ferrara (1619 and 1620), and Mantua (1620). The works by Ludovico Carracci and Scarsellino (1550–1620) influenced Guercino greatly. He may also have traveled to Modena and Parma and seen paintings by Correggio.[35] His prestigious group of patrons included Cosimo II, grand duke of Tuscany; Cardinal Alessandro Ludovisi, archbishop of Bologna; Pope Gregory XV; Cardinal Jacopo Serra, papal legate of Ferrara; and Ferdinando Gonzaga, duke of Mantua. Despite being sought after by the kings of England and France, Guercino opted to work relatively close to home.[36] Bologna is the nearest city to Cento, and people would frequently visit Bologna from Cento. Cento itself belonged to the papal territory of Ferrara in the seventeenth century.[37]

Guercino's work is usually characterized by the Aurora ceiling fresco, 1621–23, in the Casino Ludovisi, Rome. Cardinal Ludovico Ludovisi, nephew to Gregory XV, commissioned the painting from Guercino. Guercino had worked for the cardinal archbishop of Bologna, Alessandro Ludovisi, before he was elected pope in 1621 and selected the name of Gregory XV, so the patronage line with this important Bolognese family was established early in the artist's career.[38] The new pope brought his nephew to Rome and made him a cardinal. Ludovico loved art as did the pope's secretary, Monsignor Giovanni Battista Agucchi. Together these two papal assistants summoned the leading artists, Domenichino and Guercino, to Rome. Guercino left Cento for Rome on May 12, 1621.[39]

The *Aurora* was a response to a painting of the same subject by Guido Reni, a contemporary Bolognese artist. Ludovico Ludovisi purchased a villa in 1621, and Guercino was called to do the ceiling decorations. This important commission — successfully executed from everyone's point of view — should have established a fine reputation for the artist in Rome. Instead, it became apparent that Guercino had a confidence problem and did not represent himself well either socially or professionally.

In 1623, Pope Gregory XV Ludovisi died and Guercino returned to Cento. He did not establish a permanent residence in Bologna until 1642, and only then prompted by the death in the same year of Reni, who left his studio to Guercino.

The Style of Guercino

There has been no shortage of critical scholarship on Guercino, much of it sparked by the pioneering work of Sir Denis Mahon, with a flurry of exhibitions and monographs appearing in and around 1967, the third centenary of the artist's death and 1991, the four hundredth anniversary of Guercino's birth.[40] Much of the scholarship has been concerned with the ongoing debate regarding the "early" and "late" styles of Guercino.

The influence of Caravaggio and/or his works on the painting style of Guercino is also debated. Andrea Emiliani concludes that Guercino was both "exalted and oppressed by the heritage of Caravaggio" in the beginning of his life and was "forced into a confrontation with the fearful figure of Reni," on the other end of his life.[41] Other scholars disagree about any influence from Caravaggio in the career of Guercino. Michael Helston warns, "The striking use of light in Guercino's early work has often given rise to comparisons with the paintings of Caravaggio. But it should be remembered that Guercino is most unlikely to have seen any of Caravaggio's works before he went to Rome; and that the paintings of Caravaggio, who died in 1610 but who had left Rome as early as 1606, were becoming less influential when Guercino was there."[42]

Modern art-historical scholarship generally agrees with the assessment of Sybille Ebert-Schifferer: "That Guercino, in the course of his long and productive career, experienced an unusually clear change in style is in-escapably apparent, especially when one compares an early work, say from the period 1615–1620 . . . , with a late work, perhaps from the 1650s. . . ."[43] What one sees in the early Guercino is the use of light and shadows in an apparently artificial and capricious way to create a certain instabil-ity; figures' actions and facial details are left obscured with shadows. This "painterly" style, in which the painter manipulates the subject for his own evocative purposes, gives way to a more static, didactic style — a classi-cism not unknown in the Seicento, in which certain *topoi* are illustrated for instructional purposes.

What art historians do not agree upon is the reason for this radical change. In 1947, Sir Denis Mahon proposed Guercino's two-year stay in Rome (1621–23) and his exposure to the classicizing art theory prevalent in Rome at this time, and embodied in the figure Monsignor Agucci, first cultural advisor to Cardinal Ludovico Ludovisi and later, after Ludovisi's election as Pope Gregory XV, as his personal secretary.[44] A not so unim-portant element in Guercino's shift in style was, according to Mahon, his desire to please patrons, who themselves were influenced by this classi-cizing movement and were increasingly dissatisfied with the ambiguity of Guercino's figures. In an oft-cited passage, a contemporary of Guercino, Scannelli, is quoted in support of the hypothesis that Guercino's shift was, in significant part, a market-driven decision:

> Evidently the more convincing reason is that which the painter from Cento [Guercino] gave in response to this question when he ex-plained to me that it was the taste of the majority, and above all of those who ordered works [from him]; and he had often heard complaints from those who possessed works of his first manner that in these the eyes, the mouth, and other members were hidden (so

they said) in dark shadows. . . . And so, in order to satisfy the majority as far as possible, and especially those who paid money for the
requested work, he had executed the paintings in a lighter manner.[45]

Recently David M. Stone has revised Mahon's thesis, arguing that internal artistic motivations played more of a factor in Guercino's change in
style than external influences of art theory and their economic impact.[46]
Further, Stone proposed evidence from both before and after his Rome
sojourn for these "internal motivations."[47]
We need not detain ourselves further with the details of this argument
since we agree with Ebert-Schifferer's conclusion that Mahon and Stone,
differences notwithstanding, ultimately remain in agreement that in the
years following Guercino's return from Rome, between 1623 and 1630,
his style falls into a rather experimental phase that leads to the mature
style of the last two decades of his life. Guercino is thirty-two when he
returns to Cento in 1623. That his stay in Rome had consequences for
the painter ultimately remains undisputed, even if these consequences
are no longer seen as negative and even if they now seem to depend
upon the assimilation of experiences and impressions gained in Rome (and
elsewhere), rather than on direct pressure from a theoretical viewpoint or
the tastes of Roman patrons.[48]
In the other chapters of this book and in our earlier volume, our
methodology included briefly outlining the development of the style of
each artist using select paintings. We are here able to explain the chronological and stylistic development of Guercino using five paintings of the
Lukan narrative at hand — the Prodigal Son. We have been guided in our
selection of Prodigal Son paintings by Ebert-Schifferer's discussion, but
unlike Ebert-Schifferer, our primary interest is not limited solely to the
evolution of Guercino's style.[49]
Guercino (and his patrons) enjoyed the Prodigal Son story throughout
his career and, because of this fortunate fact, we are able to turn now to
a consideration of five versions of the *Return of the Prodigal Son*, executed
by Guercino over the course of his long and productive career. While
we certainly attend to the ways in which these paintings bear witness
to the transition in Guercino's style discussed above, we are even more
interested in what the paintings reveal to us about the artist's evolving
understanding of the meaning of Luke's parable, an understanding to be
recovered through iconographic analysis of the details of each painting.
Guercino painted the subject of the *Return of the Prodigal Son* on at least
seven different occasions.[50] Two of those, referenced by Malvasia, are now
lost.[51] The remaining five were executed between 1617 and 1655. The best

known now of these paintings is housed in the Kunsthistorisches Museum, Vienna, dating from 1619 (Figure 6-1). The paintings will be discussed in chronological order.

Return of the Prodigal (1617), Turin. In another letter from the painter Ludovico Carracci, dated July 19, 1617, we learn that Guercino had arrived in Bologna in order to "paint several pictures for the cardinal archbishop [Alessandro Ludovisi]" and that he "was working with outstanding success."[52] According to the biographer Conte Carlo Cesare Malvasia,[53] the paintings for Cardinal Ludovisi (later to become Pope Gregory XV) included "un miracolo di S. Pietro, che rususcita una fanciulla, . . . Una Susanna, . . . Una figliol prodigo."[54] This last painting has been identified by Sir Denis Mahon with the *Return of the Prodigal Son* (1617) in the Pinacoteca Sabauda at Turin.[55]

This painting is the earliest extant depiction of the Return of the Prodigal attributed to Guercino. Unfortunately, as Mahon notes, the condition of this painting was "fatally deteriorated when in storage during the second world war . . ."[56] Still, we are able to make out the pertinent features of the painting.

The central action occurs on the viewer's left. Three figures — a servant, the father, and the returning prodigal — are crowded into the left foreground. The prodigal, as in many renditions, is barefoot, indicating the abject state of his return, a point also made by his partially nude upper torso (clad only with a tattered shirt) and his threadbare trousers. His face is hidden from view and his hands are clasped in a pose of penance as he recites his well-rehearsed plea: "Father, I have sinned against heaven, and before thee" (Luke 15:21).

The father, on the other hand, leans forward, with arms extended, anxious to embrace this son of his, who was once lost and is now found. His face is fully illuminated as he peers intently at his son. The servant, face obscured in shadows, also watches the scene intently, presumably ready to produce a new wardrobe when so ordered by the father. In the upper background, one is able to see several musicians on a balcony, apparently making ready for the feast, which has been ordered by the jubilant father.

This depiction would make plausible the identification of the two figures on the viewer's right with the elder brother, who upon returning from the field observes the festive activities and inquires of a servant about the goings-on for the day (Luke 15:25–26). In Guercino's version, the elder brother is presumably the figure pointing, with worker's hat in hand, while a brightly dressed servant leans back, hands on hips, haughtily explaining that the prodigal has returned home and that the father has ordered a party thrown in his honor. Ironically, in both scenes, servants are better dressed than the sons!

Most noteworthy about this painting is the fact that Guercino has collapsed several distinct scenes into one. In Luke, the reunion of the prodigal and father is distinct from the feast in his honor, which in turn are separate from the return of the elder brother. Likewise, in pictorial depictions, these scenes are usually distinct. Here, though, they collapse into one flurry of activity, heightening the pathos of the scene, and underscoring the effect, on father (anxious to embrace the son), the servants (hastily preparing for the feast), and the elder brother (no doubt surprised by the day's quick turn of events). The telescoping of these various parts of the narrative underscore the parable's conclusion, "This my son was lost and is now found," and the repercussions that the prodigal's return has for so many different people. The result is an effective and evocative rendition of the reconciliation of father and prodigal and impending alienation that it will cause for the older brother.

From Malvasia's *Felsina Pittrice* again, we learn that Cardinal Archbishop Jacopo Serra of Ferrara commissioned Guercino for several paintings during 1619–20: "He was called by the Most Eminent Cardinal Legate Serra to Ferrara, where he made many pictures; they were: a wounded Saint Sebastian being succored, with various figures; a Samson with Delilah, who cuts his hair; a prodigal son received by his father."[57] The first has now been identified as *Saint Sebastian Succored* (1619), in the Pinacoteca Nazionale, Bologna; the second with *Samson Seized by the Philistines* (1619), now in the Metropolitan Museum in New York.[58] The third, *The Return of the Prodigal Son* (1619) is now in the Kunsthistorisches Museum, Vienna (Figure 6-1).[59]

This painting is part of what is generally called Guercino's "transitional period." As Mahon puts it: "The painting in Vienna is a splendid example — with its wealth of overlapping forms disposed with apparent casualness and broken up with brilliant shafts of light — of Guercino's early style at its culminating point."[60] Unlike the earlier version, which shows the more typical scene of the son's contrite return, here Guercino has chosen a slightly later scene, based on Luke 15:22, where the father tells his servants to bring the robe, ring, and shoes for his newly found son. Ebert-Schifferer observes:

All the figures are captured in spontaneous, mundane actions. As a sign of loving acceptance, the father lays his right hand on the son's sharply illuminated naked back. The son's nakedness is certainly to be understood as an allusion to his physical and spiritual need, and it stands in contrast to the sumptuous garments worn and presented by his father's servant. With his other hand the father assists his son by reaching for the rich shirt eagerly held out by the servant in a gesture that forms a contrapuntal, contrasting diagonal to the arms of the son and the father. The center of the action, although not the geometric center of the picture, lies at the point where the hands meet. While none of the faces is fully illuminated, light falls directly on the naked back at the left, on the active hands, and on the new shirt that will soon cover the nakedness of the newly returned son. All other areas lie in darkness. No figure is evenly lit or legible in all its contours. The glances of the three figures are directed toward the action in which they are presently engaged.[61]

The result is a powerfully evocative moment of intimate family reunion. There is a sense of urgency as the father intently reaches for the new garments, signifying the restored status of the son. As in Luke's parable, the father is the unifying element, this time bringing together servant and son. The characters are lovingly absorbed, not in each other as in the Turin painting, but in the symbolic action of rehabilitation. Penance and forgiveness, achieved in the moment just prior to the one depicted, lay the groundwork for this ritual of restoration. The viewer is drawn into participation in this event by the "placement of the figures close to the picture plane . . ."[62]

The Return of the Prodigal (1627–28), Rome. This image invites comparison to another painting, *The Return of the Prodigal Son* (1627–28), now in the Galleria Borghese in Rome (Figure 6-2).[63] Little is known about the patronage of this painting.[64] Denis Mahon has proposed that Tiberio Lancellotti probably commissioned the painting while Guercino was in Rome and working on another commission for Lancellotti, a tondo of the Madonna and Child for the Palazzo Lancellotti.[65]

In the Borghese painting, Guercino depicts the same moment in the parable, although this time the figures of the servant and the son are reversed, with the prodigal on the viewer's right. Ebert-Schifferer compares this painting with the Vienna image:

> Again the father, in placing his arm around his son, is the unifying element; again the son is in the act of removing his tattered shirt as the servant brings new clothing. Closer observation shows, however, that a slightly earlier moment has been chosen: the father is still completing the sentence recorded by Luke the Evangelist; the servant is not yet holding out the clothing, as the father, standing at the opposite side, points with an expressive gesture to the son, indicating

Figure 6-2. Guercino. *Return of the Prodigal.* 1627–28. Oil on canvas. Galleria Borghese, Rome. Photo. With permission from the Archivio Fotografico Soprintendenza Speciale on behalf of the Polo Museale Romano.

the person for whom the clothing is intended. This depiction combines a literal portrayal of the biblical text with the household scene imagined in the earlier picture. The lighting here stresses the arm that is being undressed and the hands bringing the new garments as well as the pointing gesture of the father. . . . [66]

Ebert-Schifferer further argues that it is this pointing gesture, unlike the action of the giving of the garment itself as in the Borghese painting, that unifies the painting and explains why the figures have been reversed, namely, to avoid having a gesture being read from right to left. Rather, with the prodigal on the viewer's right, the gesture can be read in the typical left-to-right manner.

The faces of the father and the servant are illuminated and clearly recognizable, while the prodigal's face remains obscured by the shadows. In a chiastic structure, the illuminated faces stand against a dark background, while the darkened face of the prodigal is placed before a lightened window.[67] The chiasm serves to highlight the contrast between the prodigal son, only now emerging from the darkness of his shame, and the father (and his servant), whose reconciling actions bring clarity to the moment.

Figure 6-3. Guercino. *Return of the Prodigal.* 1651. Oil on canvas.
Museo Diocesano, Wloclawek, Poland. Photo. With permission
from the Chancellor of the Curia.

Unlike the first two paintings, Guercino draws on the rhetorical conventions of gesture to unify the painting and to show that the prodigal is the
object of the father's loving actions. Guercino returns to these rhetorical
conventions in later depictions of the scene, which we discuss below.

The figure of the prodigal is slightly more emaciated than in the Vienna
painting, indicating the toll which his "riotous living" had taken on his
body. The dog in the lower register of the image may point in this same
direction. Of course, this canine presence may simply highlight the intimate domestic nature of the scene; here is the household pet joining in
the celebration of the returning prodigal. But the dog may serve another
purpose in the painting.

In the biblical tradition, as well as in post-biblical Jewish writings, the
term "dog" was often used by Jews to refer to Gentiles, since both dogs
and Gentiles were considered to be ritually unclean according to Jewish
purity laws. In Phil 3:2, Paul admonishes the Philippians to "beware of the
dogs," and is evidently referring to a certain segment of Gentiles or perhaps
ironically to Jews who, in Paul's opinion, were leading lifestyles unbefitting

those who belonged to a holy God. A more clear example may be found in the story of the Syrophonecian woman in Mark's Gospel (chap. 7), where Jesus rebuffs the Gentile woman's request for healing for her daughter by saying that it is not right to give to the dogs (Gentiles) that bread which is reserved for the children (Jews). Of course, the woman's rejoinder, "but even the little dogs deserve some crumbs from the table" (Mark 7:28) spurs Jesus to consent to her request, and the daughter is immediately healed. In that same sense, the dog here may be a reminder of the prodigal's recent inglorious past, in which he served in an occupation of feeding pigs, which was not only a shameful act, but, according to Jewish tradition, rendered him ritually unclean: *b. B. Qam 82b*: "Cursed is the man who raises pigs, and cursed be the man who teaches his son Greek wisdom."

The Return of the Prodigal (1651), Poland. More than twenty years would lapse between the painting of the Borghese Prodigal and Guercino's next extant version, *The Return of the Prodigal*, painted for Giovanni Nani in 1651 and now located in the Museo Diocesano, Wloclawek, Poland (Figure 6-3).[68] The provenance of the Poland painting begins in 1651 when it was in the collection of the Venetian Giovanni Nani (1623–79).[69] The painting was restored in 1991 and is placed in Guercino's late style. During this period, Guercino painted only two depictions of this subject each with three half figures.

In the Poland version, Guercino had chosen to paint the more commonly depicted scene of the Prodigal's repentance, recorded in Luke 15:22: "Father, I have sinned against heaven and before you; I am no longer worthy to be called your son." According to Ebert-Schifferer, "This is the central text for the Counter-Reformation concepts of contrition and conversion (which also inspired the enormous popularity of the iconography of the Penitent Magdalen)."[70]

Missing from this painting are any reference to the shoes, ring, or robe, which figure so prominently in the previous two paintings. All three of the figures' faces are fully illuminated, and the dark background focuses the viewer's attention on the action in the foreground.

The son, who presumably has just finished his speech of remorse and contrition, now dries the tears with a handkerchief held in his right hand. With his left, the prodigal holds a walking stick, which evokes the long journey he has just completed both literally and symbolically. The pilgrim/prodigal has returned home to the arms of his father, who lovingly embraces him, while he weeps. In the background on the viewer's left stands the servant. In contrast to his counterparts in the previous versions, this servant does not participate in the scene, but rather stands as

Figure 6-4. Guercino. *Return of the Prodigal Son.* 1654–55. Oil on canvas.
Timken Museum of Art, San Diego. Photo. With permission from
The Putnam Foundation, Timken Museum of Art, San Diego.

an observer to the scene — not a detached or disinterested observer, however. With tilted head and hands pensively folded, the servant's face is
clouded with tears; he is obviously moved by the intimate scene at hand.
Ebert-Schifferer observes:

> This figure functions as a mirror image, so to speak, of the viewer,
> who is thus invited to surrender to the same empathetic state inspired
> by the interaction between father and son. A passage central to
> the desired religious practice of contrition is thus conceived as a
> realistically human but narratively static moment, which, through
> the figure of the servant, is moved to the different visual level of the
> mirror image.... [71]

The scene here represents a visual exegesis, less of the Lukan parable than
of the Counter-Reformation emphasis, in response to Protestant critique,
on the necessity and benefits of true contrition. In this reading, the father has a double referent. While still referring to God, the father who

receives the penitent prodigal refers also to the church, who, as God's representative on earth, functions also through its sacraments and ministry to receive the genuinely contrite.

Return of the Prodigal (1654–55), San Diego. This same point is made, with slight variation, in our last painting (Figure 6-4). According to the *Felsina Pittrice*, in 1654–55, Girolamo Boncompagni, archbishop of Milan, commissioned Guercino to execute a Prodigal Son, in the form of three figures.[72] The archbishop in turn presented the painting as a gift to Prince Colonna. The painting is currently housed in the Timken Museum of Art, San Diego.[73] The San Diego picture came from the Colonna Collection, so its identification is not in doubt.[74]

At first glance, the two images share much in common: a contrite son, a forgiving father, an observant servant. But closer examination reveals significant variations. As Denis Mahon has commented: "That a comparison between the two late pictures themselves bears witness again to Guercino's capacity for compositional variation in treating the same theme, even when the essentials of his style remain the same."[75]

Many of the differences center around the subtle changes in gestures. In fact, Luigi Salerno has suggested that the later work of Guercino is characterized by an "iconography of gestures."[76] That certainly seems to be the case here. The hands of the father and son, for the first time in a Guercino Prodigal Son, "are entwined in a classic gesture of reconciliation and, as carriers of meaning, are positioned at the center of the composition. The hands allude to a subsequent and theologically significant verse from the Gospel of Luke in which the Father grants his forgiveness: 'for this my son was dead, and is alive again; he was lost and is found' (Luke 15:24)."[77] Furthermore the prodigal, while wiping away tears as in the Poland version, also turns his head away from the father, in a conventional gesture of shame. "Both figures face the viewer almost frontally and depict two moments in the narrative: contrition and forgiveness, climax and catharsis."[78] To return to our earliest version, Guercino has again collapsed several key moments in the narrative into one. In the first several aspects of the narrative — the reunion of father and son, the preparations for the feast, and the return of the elder brother from the fields — almost explode onto the canvas in a breathtaking flurry of activity. Here in the San Diego painting, however, the effect is different: "Because no real action is depicted, but instead two morally significant emotional states — or the 'essence' of the text — the figures, particularly that of the son, appear more artificial to modern eyes than those in any of the earlier versions. The communication of the passions is not achieved through the depiction of a real mood or a real action, but through recognized rhetorical gestures."[79]

The use of stylized gestures in this later work differs from the use of spontaneous, natural gestures in the Vienna *Prodigal Son*. The gesture in the San Diego painting, drawn from the rhetorical conventions of gesture, is intended to communicate a specific meaning, in this case, reconciliation.[80]

The comparison of painting with ancient rhetorical tradition was not unknown in Guercino's day. In 1646, Commendatore Giovanni Battista Manzini (1599–1646) wrote a letter to a Benedictine monk Giuseppe da Piacenza, in which, among other things, Manzini discussed an unnamed person's criticisms of Guercino's work. In the course of his argument, Manzini spoke of the "hardness" of Guercino's work being a laudatory aspect of his painting. He then writes:

> Hardness of manner in the painter is exactly the same as hardness of manner in the orator. By this I mean a certain raw mixture, which, combining unharmonious parts in the service of the whole, unifies these, but does not make a union; they were conceived together but are not consonant, and give an undefinable bitterness and unpleasantness to the composition, in which the ear, or the eye, not meeting that safe, low, and delicate field which it had presupposed, prepares to take offense, and not for having encountered some unpleasantness, but for not having encountered that pleasantness which it had expected.... But what have the rules of the orator to do with those of painting? These two arts are so strictly conjoined and related, that there has been no lack of masters who have prescribed the very same rules of one to the other and assigned each as the guide of the other.... Thus I conclude that in painting, and equally in eloquence, the best things are not the most tender, but the most robust, and our Signor Gio. Francesco [Guercino], who needs no Mercury to show him the way, has from his earliest days understood this....[81]

Manzini's comparison of rhetoric with painting was hardly unique or original to him. Gabriele Paleotti (1522–97), in a famous post-Tridentine treatise on painting, also compared the painter with the orator and claimed that the goal of the Christian painter (like that of the orator) was to be found in "persuading the populace and moving it to embrace something"; for the Christian painter this "something" should be "pertinent to religion."[82]

The "rules" of rhetoric that the masters, including Guercino, applied to painting also included the use of conventional gestures, as a work by Giovanni Paolo Lomazzo, written two years after Paoletti, shows.[83] According to Ebert-Schifferer, "Lamazzo in his second book methodically enumerated, chapter by chapter, all conceivable emotional states and attempted to give appropriate, but rarely practical, poses, facial expressions, and gestures for each, using figures from biblical and ancient history."[84]

Although it is unlikely that later artists drew directly from Lomazzo's catalogue of gestures, nonetheless there did exist in Guercino's day a "visual thesaurus" of gestures from which the artist could draw; the hands clasped in reconciliation and the head turned in shame in the San Diego *Prodigal Son* are but two examples. The goal of these gestures in painting seem to be the same as the goal of delivery in ancient oratory: to instruct, to please, and to move (see Quintilian, *Inst.* xi. 3).

If we accept the use of conventional gestures in Guercino's later works to signify specific meanings,[85] it is fair to inquire about the source of Guercino's knowledge of the "iconography of gestures." While it is true that grammar school in the seventeenth century still included study of the rhetorical tradition of Cicero and Quintilian, Guercino probably did not complete grammar school, much less secondary education. Still, whether through the influence of the Barberini, among Guercino's most important patrons, or the religious theatre of the Jesuits, Guercino had ample opportunity to observe the effect of conventional canons of gesture and delivery in both profane and sacred settings.[86] The connection with Jesuit theater is especially interesting. Ebert-Schifferer claims that ". . . by the mid-sixteenth century, the correlation of specific passions to specific gestures was a long-established international phenomenon, which had its roots in ancient rhetoric and was apparently propagated by the Jesuits as a means of engendering in the public feelings calculated to increase faith."[87] This connection to the theater might explain why the servant in the San Diego painting, rather than participating in reunion of father and son in the Vienna and Rome paintings or being moved to tears as in the Poland version, is seen drawing back a curtain, much like a theatrical production.

Still, tracing definitively the source of Guercino's understanding of the convention of gestures is not necessary. In fact, "it would be superficial to understand Guercino's mature style simply as influenced by the theater, even if his early interest is documented. Rather, he intuitively perceived that certain expressive gestures were becoming accepted through constant repetition and that his contemporaries increasingly believed these gestures to be unmistakably understandable."[88]

The problem, then, as Guercino must have come to understand it, was that his early works, although they were able to delight and move, were unable to instruct, "an integral component of both proper rhetoric and Counter-Reformation propaganda" and this inability to instruct "was understood as a flaw."[89] Ebert-Schifferer has drawn this conclusion about the shift from the early to later works by Guercino:

> Guercino ceased to translate freely a textual source into a mood es-tablished by purely painterly means and also ceased to break through the picture's surface plane, and thus its ontological boundedness, by using direct gestures extending beyond the frame or by bringing the picture plane close to the viewer. Instead, he tended more and more to reproduce specific passages from the Bible and other texts or to employ an orthodox exegesis. In other words, he sought to depict either the actual movement of dramatic climax as experienced in the theater or in the read/heard text, or to depict directly the cathartic passion as intended by Counter-Reformation theology.[90]

We see this shift — a shift in meaning as much as in style — clearly evidenced in the five versions of the Return of the Prodigal Son rendered by Guercino over the course of his career.

Concluding Hermeneutical Reflections

Both Luke and the later Guercino made use of the conventional rhetoric of their day as an effective vehicle of theological meaning. Luke employed, among other rhetorical devices, the tool of *klisis* or inflection to indicate to his audience that the father was the subject or topic of the parable.[91] Guercino, on the other hand, drew upon conventional gestures, known to his audience through, among other things, the avenue of the theater, both sacred and secular. In both cases, the results are the same: the author/artist is able to move, please, and instruct his audience regarding the significance of the reconciliation between father and son.

Furthermore, given Guercino's sustained treatment of the subject over a span of five decades, we might be tempted to psychoanalyze his own famil-ial relations to explain his fascination, if not obsession, with the Prodigal Son parable. However, given that we cannot overestimate the input of the various patrons into the choice of subjects, we are better off resisting attempts at such an autobiographical reading.[92]

Nonetheless, we must emphasize that Guercino's repeated return to this scene demonstrates the polyvalence of this parable (indeed all parables). While we might rightly resist the over-allegorization of the parables that plagued the church for nearly two millennia, we would hardly do the parables justice by naively embracing the historical-critical mantra that parables have only one meaning.[93] Rather we see that the same parable can produce several different but plausible interpretations.

Analogous to Guercino's multiple renditions of the Prodigal Son scene is Henri Nouwen's powerfully evocative interpretation of the parable through Rembrandt's famous *Return of the Prodigal* (1668–69; now in the Hermitage).[94] In subsequent chapters, Nouwen explores the ways in which he "sees himself" in the characters of the father, prodigal, and elder brother, respectively. Although their strategies are different, both Nouwen and Guercino remind us that the parables continue to speak to us because, at different moments in our individual lives (Nouwen) or in different historical and social contexts (Guercino), we find that the parables, and especially *this* parable, even two thousand years later continue to move, please, and instruct.

Finally, though, despite the obvious existential appeal to read the parables in light of our own changing contexts, both Luke and Guercino remind us that the central figure of this parable (and indeed of many parables) is God himself. God, the loving Father, stands with open arms ready to receive both prodigals, the one who left and the one who stayed behind. God the loving Father invites all of us to the eschatological banquet, set both for prodigals returned home and elder siblings resentful of their return. To plumb the depths of so complex a character as that of God the loving Father requires sustained engagement with the text and its message over the course of a lifetime. Guercino and his paintings bear eloquent witness to the results of such an enterprise.

Notes

1. In fact, the phrase "prodigal son" has become so popular in modern parlance that it is not uncommon to see it used in contemporary secular contexts, which are for all purposes devoid of any religious connotation. The sundry actions of various celebrities and famous athletes often earn them the title of prodigal son or daughter.

2. And not only Guercino; see, for example, the nearly 150 references cited in Robert W. Baldwin, "A Bibliography of the Prodigal Son Theme in Art and Literature," *Bulletin of Bibliography* 44 (1987): 167–71.

3. The literature on this parable is, as one might expect, voluminous, and we make no attempt to engage all of it. In addition to the standard monographs on parables and commentaries on Luke, some of the more recent periodical literature includes: Charles E. Carlston, "Reminiscence and Redaction in Luke 15:11–32," *Journal of Biblical Literature* 94 (1975): 368–90; Wolfgang Pöhlmann, "Die Absichtung des Verlorenen Sohnes (Lk 15:12f) und die erzählte Welt der Parabel," *Zeitschrift für die Neutestamentliche Wissenschaft* 70 (1979): 194–213; David Aus, "Luke 15:11–32 and R. Eliezer ben Hyrcanus's Rise to

Fame," *Journal of Biblical Literature* 104 (1985): 443–69; Wolfgang Pöhlmann, *Der verlorene Sohn und das Haus: Studien zu Lukas 15:11–32 im Horizont der antiken Lehre von Haus, Erziehung und Ackerbau* (Wissenschaftliche Untersuchungen zum Neuen Testament 68; Tübingen: Mohr-Siebeck, 1993); Kenneth E. Bailey, "Jacob and the Prodigal Son: A New Identity Story," *Theological Review* 18 (1997): 54–72; Colin Brown, "The Parable of the Rebellious Son(s)," *Scottish Journal of Theology* 51 (1998): 391–405. One of the most interesting articles is by Ronald Hock, who reads the parable in light of the ancient novels. Focusing on the use of the term "to get back" (*apolambanein*), used by the servant in reference to the prodigal's return, Hock argues that the parable refers to a "social event that includes a complex of conventional behaviors, all of them attributed to the father in the parable — seeing, running, embracing, kissing, providing clothing, sacrificing, and arranging a celebratory feast" ("Romancing the Parables of Jesus," *Perspectives in Religious Studies* 29 [2002]: 24). Though arguing from a different perspective, Hock's conclusion agrees with the one presented here, namely, that the focus of the parable is on the father, who represents God. For additional bibliography, see W. S. Kissinger, ed., *The Parables of Jesus: A History of Interpretation and Bibliography* (Metuchen, N.J.: American Theological Library Association, 1979), 351–70, and François Bovon, *Das Evangelium nach Lukas, Lk 15,1–19,27* (vol. 3; Evangelische-katholischer Kommentar zum Neuen Testament; Zürich: Benziger Verlag, 1998), 37–40.

4. Joachim Jeremias, *The Parables of Jesus* (trans. S. H. Hooke; 2nd rev. ed.; New York: Charles Scribner's Sons, 1972), 128.

5. Joel B. Green, *The Gospel of Luke* (Grand Rapids: Eerdmans, 1997), 578.

6. On the occurrence of inflection in Latin poetry (with some reference to Greek literature as well), see Jeffrey Wills, *Repetition in Latin Poetry: Figures of Allusion* (Oxford: Clarendon Press, 1996), esp. part 2 on "Polyptoton," 188–268. Much of this section is a summary of the section dealing with polyptoton in Mikeal C. Parsons, "Luke and the Progymnasmata: A Preliminary Investigation into the Preliminary Exercises," in *Contextualizing Acts: Lukan Narrative and Greco-Roman Discourse* (ed. Todd Penner and Caroline Vander Stichele; Society of Biblical Literature Symposium Series 20; Atlanta: Scholars Press, 2003), 43–63.

7. Willi Braun, *Feasting and Social Rhetoric in Luke 14* (SNTSMS 85; Cambridge: Cambridge University Press, 1995), 146.

8. Quintilian, in fact, refers to the preliminary exercises as part of the educational curriculum of young boys (*Inst.*, I.ix). On the role of rhetoric in the educational curricula of antiquity, the standard works remain S. F. Bonner, *Education in Ancient Rome* (Berkeley and Los Angeles: University of California Press, 1977); D. L. Clark, *Rhetoric in Graeco-Roman Education* (New York: Columbia University Press, 1957); H. Marrou, *A History of Education in Antiquity* (London: Sheed & Ward, 1956).

9. In addition to the text of Aelius Theon (cited below), other surviving Progymnasmata include those by Hermogenes of Tarsus (second century; critical edition in H. Rabe, ed., *Hermogenes Opera* [Rhetores Graeci 10; Leipzig: Teubner, 1913], 1–27; English translation in C. S. Baldwin, *Medieval Rhetoric and Poetic (to 1400) Interpreted from Representative Works* [New York: Macmillan, 1928], 23–38); Aphthonius of Antioch (fourth century; critical edition in H. Rabe, ed., *Aphthonii Progymnasmata* [Rhetores Graeci 10; Leipzig: Teubner, 1926], 1–51; English translation in R. E. Nadeau, "The *Progymnasmata* of Aphthonius in Translation," *Speech Monographs* 19 [1952]: 264–85); an online translation of Aphthonius by Professor Malcolm Heath, Head of the Classics Department at the University of Leeds, may also be found at www.leeds.ac.uk/classics/resources/rhetoric/index.htm; Nicholaus of Myra (fifth century; critical edition in J. Felten, ed., *Nicolai Progymnasmata* [Rhetores Graeci 11; Leipzig: Teubner, 1913]; no English translation available). English

translations of, introductions to, and notes about Theon, Hermogenes, Aphthonius, and Nicolaus (along with selections from some others) may be found in George Kennedy, trans., *Progymnasmata: Greek Textbooks of Prose Composition and Rhetoric* (Writings from the Greco-Roman World 10; Atlanta: Society of Biblical Literature, 2003). A fifth document, a commentary on Aphthonius's *Progymnasmata* attributed to John of Sardis, is available in the Teubner edition, *Ioannis Sardiani Commentarium in Aphthonii Progymnasmata* (ed. Hugo Rabe; Leipzig: Teubner, 1928).

10. Kennedy, *Progymnasmata*, v.

11. We have used the critical edition of the Greek text (along with a French translation) found in Michel Patillon and Giancarlo Bolognesi, eds., *Aelius Théon. Progymnasmata* (Paris: Les Belles Lettres, 1997). The Patillon text has replaced Leonard Spengel, ed., *Rhetores Graeci* (2 vols.; Leipzig: Teubner, 1854–56), 2:59–130, as the standard critical edition. Patillon with the aid of Bolognesi has reconstructed from the Armenian manuscripts five chapters (13–17) missing from the Greek texts. For text and translation of Theon, see also James R. Butts, "The *Progymnasmata* of Theon: A New Text with Translation and Commentary" (Ph.D. dissertation, The Claremont Graduate School, 1986). It should be noted that both Patillon and Butts have rearranged the chapters in Theon to reflect what they believe to be Theon's original order of presentation. They have also inserted "On Refutation and Confirmation," a separate chapter in all extant Greek manuscripts, into the chapter "On the Narrative," again restoring what is believed to be the original order. Hence, when we cite Theon, we have employed the Spengel numbering system (which is still the standard), supplementing it with the page number where the text can be found in the Patillon edition. For a thorough treatment of the author, text, versions, and critical editions, see Patillon, vii–clvi; also Butts, 7–95. While we have consulted the translations of Patillon, Kennedy, and Butts, unless otherwise noted we are responsible for all the translations of Theon, based on the Patillon critical edition.

12. Butts, 7. Theon himself acknowledges that others had written on the subject of preliminary exercises (I.15–16) and can even refer (I.18) to "traditional exercises" (*êdê paradedomenois gumnasmasin*).

13. Nicolaus, 4.18–19, suggests that more advanced students could skip the exercise of grammatical inflexion and move on to elaborating, condensing, refuting, or confirming.

14. Aristotle had also commented briefly on *ptôsis*, as he called it (cf. *Poetics*, 20.10; *Art of Rhetoric*, 1.7.27; 2.23.2; and esp. 3.9.9), but he used the term generally to refer to similar forms of words, whether nouns, verbs, adjectives, or adverbs. See also *Ad Herennium*, 4.22.30–31, who, like Quintilian, views *poluptôton* as a form of paronomasia.

15. Here we agree with Hock, "Romancing the Parables," 25.

16. Stephen L. Wailes, *Medieval Allegories of Jesus' Parables* (Berkeley: University of California, 1987), 238.

17. Ibid.

18. Ibid., 243.

19. Ambrose, *Traité sur l'Évangile de S. Luc* (ed. Garbriel Tissot; 2 vols.; Sources Chrétiennes 52; Paris: Éditions du Cerf, 1956–58), 2:97.

20. Ibid.

21. Jill Robbins, *Prodigal Son/Elder Brother* (Chicago: The University of Chicago Press, 1991), 39–40, argues that the Prodigal Son parable provides the structure for the Confessions.

22. Augustine, *Quaestiones*, lines 106–13.

23. Ibid., lines 131–32. Augustine dismisses the elder brother's obedience ("I have never transgressed your commandment") by arguing that this obedience is only in reference to Jewish monotheism and that the elder brother is an exception among the Israelites (cf. Robbins, *Prodigal Son/Elder Brother*, 39–40).

24. On Augustine's description of the Jews' blindness, see Augustine, *Tractatus adversus Judaeos*, chap. VII, para. 9: "*Behold Israel according to the flesh* (1 Cor. 10:18). This we know to be the carnal Israel; but the Jews do not grasp this meaning and as a result they prove themselves indisputably carnal"; and "*Let their eyes be darkened that they see not* (Ps. 69:23) . . . but you are so blind that you do not recognize yourselves for what you really are."

25. Alan Young, *The English Prodigal Son Plays: A Theatrical Fashion of the Sixteenth and Seventeenth Centuries* (Salzburg, Austria: Institut für Anglistik und Amerikanistik Universität Salzburg, 1979), 9, notes: "The continuity which one often finds between the early exegetes and those of the Middle Ages must in part be a result of the 19th Canon of the Trullan Synod (Quinisexta), summoned by Justinian II in 692," which instructed clergy "to confine their exposition of Scripture to the teaching of the Fathers, and to refrain from expositions of their own."

26. See, e.g., Gottfried of Admont, who suggests that the father is God and the two sons stand for the human being in its two constituent parts; the younger son is the spirit, and the elder the body (*Homiliae dominicales*, PL 174, no. 31, cols. 202–10; cited by Wailes, *Medieval Allegories*, 244). For other examples of various allegorical interpretations of specific details in the parable, see Arthur A. Just Jr., ed., *Luke* (gen. ed., Thomas C. Oden; Ancient Christian Commentary on Scripture 3; Downers Grove, Ill.: InterVarsity Press, 2003), 246–53; see also François Bovon, *Das Evangelium nach Lukas*, 3:54–65.

27. *The Early English Versions of the Gesta Romanorum* (ed. Sidney J. Herrtage; London: Trübner, 1879), 444; cited by Young, *The English Prodigal Son Plays*, 11–12. In identifying the elder brother with the devil, the final (perversely) logical step in objectifying the elder brother as the personification of evil and the other is complete.

28. John Calvin, *Commentary on a Harmony of the Evangelists, Matthew, Mark, and Luke* (trans. William Pringle; vol. 2; Edinburgh: The Calvin Translation Society, 1845), 349–50.

29. Calvin, *Commentary*, 350. Calvin did note that in the Lukan context:

The discourse was occasioned by *the murmuring of the scribes*, who took offence at the kindness of Christ towards wretched persons who had led a wicked life. He therefore compares the scribes, who were swelled with presumption, to good and modest men, who had always lived with decency and sobriety, and honourably supported their family; any, even to obedient children, who throughout their whole life had patiently submitted to their father's control. And though they were utterly unworthy of the commendation, yet Christ, speaking according to their belief, attributes to them, by way of concession, their pretended holiness, as if it had been virtue; as if he had said, Though I were to grant to you what you falsely boast of, that you have always been obedient children to God, still you ought not so haughtily and cruelly to reject your brethren, when they repent of their wicked life. (350)

30. See John B. Knipping, *Iconography of the Counter Reformation in the Netherlands: Heaven on Earth* (Leiden: A. W. Sijthoff, 1974), 314–20. See also the comments in chap. 3, this volume.

31. Nicholas Turner, "Guercino," in *The Dictionary of Art* (ed. J. Turner; 34 vols.; London: Macmillan, 1996), 13:785.

32. Michael Helston, "An Outline of Guercino's Life," in *Guercino in Britain: Paintings from British Collections* (catalogue, Michael Helston and Tom Henry; London: National Gallery Publications, 1991), 1.

33. Ibid.

34. For the text of the letter, see Giovanni Bottari, *Raccolta di lettere sulla pittura*, vol. 1 (two printings: Rome, 1754), 198–99 and 208–9 in the two printings. The English translation is from Sir Denis Mahon, ed., *Guercino: Master Painter of the Baroque* (Washington, D.C.: National Gallery of Art, 1992), 156

35. Helston, "An Outline of Guercino's Life," 1.

36. Ibid., 3, states:

In 1626 King Charles I of England, after attempting in vain to secure the services of Guido Reni, then the most renowned Italian painter, tried to persuade Guercino to visit London. Similar attempts were made by Louis XIII of France, again without success. In 1629 Guercino was visited at Cento by the great Spanish painter, Velázquez. One of the reasons for the latter's Italian journey was to try to secure the services of important Italian painters to work at the court of Philip IV in Madrid. However that may be, it is clear that Guercino had no wish to travel. Indeed he had no need for extra or more prestigious work, for commissions continued to arrive.

37. Ibid., 1.

38. Ibid.

39. Ibid., 2.

40. So much recent attention has been paid to Guercino that Nicholas Turner ("Guercino," 13:789) claimed that Guercino's "paintings and drawings are now probably better published than those of any other Italian Baroque painter." Turner (789), himself a one-time collaborator with Mahon, likewise credits Mahon with championing a reappraisal of the "importance of Guercino's place in the history of Italian painting."

41. Andrea Emiliani, "Guercino: From Natural Talent to the Romanticism of Reality," in Mahon, *Guercino: Master Painter*, 17.

42. Helston, "An Outline of Guercino's Life," 3.

43. Sybille Ebert-Schifferer, "'Ma c'hanno da fare I precetti dell'oratore con quelli della pittura?': Reflections on Guercino's Narrative Structure," in *Guercino: Master Painter of the Baroque* (ed. Sir Denis Mahon; Washington, D.C.: National Gallery of Art, 1992), 75.

44. See Denis Mahon, *Studies in Seicento Art and Theory* (London: The Warburg Institute, 1947). Part one of Mahon's study is devoted to an analysis of the origins of the shift in Guercino's style; part two considers in detail the classicizing art theory of Giovanni Battista Agucchi.

45. The English translation is by Ebert-Schifferer, "Reflections on Guercino's Narrative Structure," 76. Francesco Scannelli, *Il microcosmo della pittura* (Cesena, 1657, facsimile edition; ed. Guido Giubbini; Milan: Edizioni Labor, 1966), 115.

46. David Marshall Stone, "Theory and Practice in Seicento Art: The Example of Guercino" (Ph.D. dissertation, Harvard University, 1989). Although the dissertation remains unpublished, much of Stone's study was refined and integrated into an exhibition catalog, see David M. Stone, *Guercino: Master Draftsman. Works from North American Collections* (Bologna: Nuova Alfa Editoriale, 1991). Donald Posner, "The Guercino Exhibition at Bologna," *Burlington Magazine* 110 (1968): 600, earlier had disputed Mahon's theory.

47. Stone, "Theory and Practice in Seicento Art," 26–35. Stone's arguments have received nuanced support from Ebert-Schifferer, "Reflections on Guercino's Narrative Structure," 76.

48. Ebert-Schifferer, "Reflections on Guercino's Narrative Structure," 75–76. We also leave aside assessments, both modern and medieval, of whether or not this marked change in style in Guercino's painting from "painterly" to "classicizing" is to be viewed positively or negatively (76).

49. Ebert-Schifferer, "Reflections on Guercino's Narrative Structure," 83–87.

50. *Important Italian Baroque Paintings 1600–1700* (London: Matthiesen Fine Art Ltd., 1981), 74.

51. According to Carlo Cesare Malvasia (*Felsina pittrice: vite de' pittori bolognesi* [orig. ed. 1648; Bologna: Forni, 1967], 265, 323), one was commissioned by Prince Taddeo Barberini and given to Pope Urban VII (paid for on June 21, 1642); the other was commissioned by Padre D. Gregorio Maffone and paid for on October 12, 1642. Cf. *Important Italian Baroque Paintings*, 76.

52. See the facsimile reproduction of the original letter in A. W. Thibaudeau, *Catalogue of the Collection of Autograph Letters and Historical Documents Formed . . . by Alfred Morrison*, vol. 1 (London: 1883), pl. 36, opposite 167. English translation is that of Mahon, *Guercino: Master Painter*, 156.

53. For an assessment of Malvasia's reliability, see inter alia, Denis Mahon, *Guercino: Master Painter*, 113–18.

54. See Carlo Cesare Malvasia, *Felsina Pittrice: Vite de'pittori bolognesi* (2 vols., Bologna, 1678), 2:363. Malvasia deals with the life of Guercino in 2:358–86. Mahon (*Guercino: Master Painter*, 157) identifies the first as *The Raising of Tabitha* (1618, Galleria Palatina, Palazzo Pitti, Florence). The second is likely *Susanna and the Elders*, now in the Prado at Madrid (1617). A fourth painting, not mentioned in the Felsina Pittrice but found listed in Malvasia's manuscript notes along with the Susanna and the Prodigal Son, was *Lot and His Daughters* (1617), now located at the Monasterio de San Lorenzo, El Escorial. For Malvasia's notes, see ms. B16 in the Biblioteca Communale dell'Archiginnasio at Bologna; cited by Mahon, *Guercino: Master Painter*, 157 n. 10.

55. Mahon, *Guercino: Master Painter*, 157. The painting is oil on canvas and measures 192 x 203 cm. The image is found in Luigi Salerno, *I Dipinti del Guercino* (Rome: Ugo Bozzi Editore, 1988), cat. 33. Three preparatory drawings for this painting have been identified by Mahon, *Designi*, 54, 56. The figures are:

23. Monaco, Staatliche Graphische Sammlung (Inv. 10546). 266/268 x 420 mm.

24. Vienna, Staatliche Graphische Sammlung Albertina (Cat. B 217; Inv. 2325) 201 x2 68 mm.

25. Firenze, Gabinetto Disegni E Stampe Degli Uffizi (Inv. 1686 E.)

Return of Prodigal. Pen and brown ink. 203 X 176 mm (formerly of Christie's, London, Turner and Plazzotta, 154).

56. Mahon, *Guercino: Master Painter*, 157.

57. Malvasia, *Felsina Pittrice*, 2:364. The English translation is from Mahon (*Guercino: Master Painter*, 180), who points out that Guercino's Ferrara commission most likely included several more paintings than those listed by Malvasia.

58. The *Saint Sebastian Succored* is an oil on canvas image and is 179.5 x 225 cm. Discussions of it may be found in Mahon (*Guercino: Master Painter*, cat. 17) and Salerno, *I Dipinti del Guercino*, cat. 54. The *Samson Seized by the Philistines* is also oil on canvas and is 189 x 235 cm. Discussion of it is found in Salerno, cat. 58.

59. This painting is oil on canvas and is 106.5 x 143.5 cm. Further discussions may be found in Mahon, *Dipinti*, 1968, cat. 36; Salerno, *Dipinti del Guercino*, cat. 57; Mahon, *Il Guercino. Giovanni Francesco Barbieri, 1591–1666. Dipinti e Disegni*, 112–13; Stone, *Guercino: Catalogo completo dei dipinti* (Florence: Cantini, 1991), 78. Most recently, see Denis Mahon, Massimo Pulini, and Vittorio Sgarbi, *Guercino. Poesia e sentimento nella pittura del'600* (Rome: DeAgostini, 2003), cat. 60. Salerno (*I Dipinti del Guercino*, 134) mentions an early copy by a Dutch Caravaggesque artist now in the Galleria Corsini, Florence. On the political and social context of Ferrara during the time of or just prior to Guercino's residence there, see Shelley Karen Perlove, "Power and Religious Authority in Papal Ferrara: Cardinal Serra and Guercino," *Konsthistorisk tidskrift* 68 (1999): 19–30; Charmarie Jenkins Blaisdell, "Politics and Heresy in Ferrara, 1534–1559," *Sixteenth Century Journal* 6 (1975): 67–93.

60. Mahon, *Guercino: Master Painter*, 182.

61. Ebert-Schiffer, "Reflections on Guercino's Narrative Structure," 84.

62. Ibid.

63. The painting (Inv. N. 42 in the Borghese gallery) is oil on canvas and measures 125 x 163 cm. See Salerno, *I Dipinti del Guercino*, cat. 130. See also, Paola Della Pergola, *Galleria Borghese, I Dipinti* (Rome: Instituto Poligrafico dello Stato, 1971), I, 50; Mahon, *Il Guercino. Catalogo Critico dei Disegni*, n. 61; Salerno, *I Dipinti del Guercino*, 210; Stone, *Guercino. Catalogo Completo dei dipinti*, 134; Mahon, *Dipinti*, 151; Paolo Moreno and Chiara Stefani, *Galleria Borghese* (Milan: Touring Editore, 2000), entry n. 36, 319.

64. W. Buchanan, *Memoirs of Painting* (London, 1824), 2:86, cites a letter from an art dealer, James Irvine, to Alexander Gordon, in 1801, in which Irvine mentions "another collection" in Rome in which he found "the Prodigal Son new clothed by his Father, likewise half-length figures, by Guercino, in his fine strong manner," listed for "4000 crowns." This painting is identified by Mahon, *Dipinti*, cat. 61, and Salerno, *I Dipinti del Guercino*, 120, as the one now in the Borghese.

65. Mahon, *Dipinti*, cat. 61; on the Lancellotti, see Mahon, *Dipinti*, cat. 56.

66. Ebert-Schiffer, "Reflections on Guercino's Narrative Structure," 84.

67. Ibid., 85.

68. Denis Mahon, *Il Guercino. Giovanni Francesco Barbieri, 1591–1666. Dipinti e Disegni* (Bologna: Nuova Alfa Editorale, 1991), 342–34.

69. Ibid., 342. For the patronage of Giovanni Nani, see Mitchell Merling, "Marco Boschini's 'La carta del navegar pitoresco': Art theory and virtuoso culture in seventh-century Venice" (Ph.D. dissertation: Brown University, 1992) 144–78.

70. Ebert-Schiffer, "Reflections on Guercino's Narrative Structure," 85.

71. Ibid.

72. Malvasia, *Felsina Pittrice*, 2:380.

73. The painting is oil on canvas and measures 61 1/4″ x 57 1/2″.

74. For a discussion of the complex provenance, see Mahon, *Master Painter*, 298.

75. Mahon, *Guercino: Master Painter*, 298.

76. Salerno, *I Dipinti del Guercino*, 60, 62.

77. Ebert-Schiffer, "Reflections on Guercino's Narrative Structure," 86.

78. Ibid.

79. Ibid., 87.

80. On the various gestures recorded in the ancient rhetorical handbook tradition of Quintilian, Cicero, etc., see William David Shiell, *Reading Acts: The Lector and the Early Christian Audience* (Leiden: Brill, 2004).

81. For the text of the original, see *Delle lettere del Sig. Commendatore D. Gio. Battista Manzini, volume primo: All'Eminentiss. E Gloriosiss. Principe Il Sig. Card. D'Este* (Bologna, 1646). The English citation quoted here is by Ebert-Schifferer, "Reflections on Guercino's Narrative Structure," 80.

82. See Gabriele Paleotti, *Discorso intorno alle imagini sacre et profane* (Bologna, 1582), 66: bk. 1, chap. 21. The English translation quoted here is by Ebert-Schifferer, 96.

83. See Giovanni Paolo Lomazzo, *Trattato dell'arte de la pittura* (Milan, 1584), bk. 2, chap. 10, 105–86.

84. Ebert-Schifferer, "Reflections on Guercino's Narrative Structure," 97.

85. For other examples of such stylized gestures in Guercino's later work, see ibid., 90–95.

86. Ibid., 96–100.

87. Ibid., 100.

88. Ibid., 103.

89. Ibid., 104.

90. Ibid., 101.

91. Since neither Hebrew nor Aramaic is an inflected language, we seem right in attributing this particular literary device to the evangelist Luke. Presumably, Jesus would have had other ways of indicating the subject of his parable, which Luke then "translates" into his context with the appropriate rhetorical device.

92. This is not to say that autobiographical reading ought always to be ruled inappropriate; see Mikeal C. Parsons, "Hand in Hand: An Autobiographical Reading of the Parable of the Prodigal Son," *Semeia* 72 (1995): 125–52.

93. On this, see David Steinmetz, "The Superiority of Pre-critical Exegesis," in Donald K. McKim, ed., *A Guide to Contemporary Hermeneutics* (Grand Rapids: Eerdmans, 1986), 65–77.

94. Henri Nouwen, *Return of the Prodigal* (New York: Doubleday, 1994).

Epilogue

The title of our work, *Illuminating Luke,* is, of course, an allusion to the practice among medieval scribes of visually illustrating the manuscript being copied. The illuminations, often very detailed and elaborate, provided additional interpretive resources for the reader. We have hoped also to illumine the reader with regard both to the message of Christ's public ministry as recorded in the Third Gospel and Luke's subsequent "career" at specific moments in its reception history. To be sure, we have chosen some of the "high" moments in the visual exegesis of Luke's narrative.

Beginning with Michele Tosini's profound depiction of the baptism and temptation narratives, which built upon and extended his previous understanding of the sacrificial dimensions of Christ's baptism, we moved to Raphael's version of the *Miraculous Draught of Fishes,* with its unmistakable Petrine apologetic. With Jacopo Bassano's paintings of two parables, the *Good Samaritan* and the *Rich Man and Lazarus,* we were reminded how art can be used in the service of the church's social ministries. But Christian social action must be balanced by attention to the spiritual life, and Allori's *Christ in the House of Mary and Martha* powerfully underscores the fact that a balance between the contemplative and active life is not only possible, but perhaps, if it is to be sustained and effective, necessary. Finally, Il Guercino's several renderings over the course of his lifetime of the subject of the Prodigal Son demonstrate the power and lure of Jesus' teachings. We can return to these stories again and again, and though the words on the page never change, the message, because of our own changing circumstances or those of our culture, is nonetheless and always fresh and relevant.

By understanding how these artists and audiences of Renaissance and Baroque religious art "translated" Luke's Gospel in culturally and religiously appropriate ways, we have sought to locate each of these images within its particular historical context, to understand its iconographic significance, and briefly to comment on how this visual exegesis might inform the contemporary appropriation of both text and image. Our desire has been that our efforts here not only further clarify the interpretive history of the Lukan version of Christ's public ministry at some of its most critical moments, but also assist, as it were, in illuminating Luke.

Selected Bibliography

Abogunrin, Samuel. "The Three Variant Accounts of Peter's Call. Critical, Theological Examination of the Texts." *New Testament Studies* 31 (1985): 587–602.

Aikema, Bernard. *Jacopo Bassano and His Public: Moralizing Pictures in an Age of Reform ca. 1535–1600*. Princeton, N.J.: Princeton University Press, 1996.

Ames-Lewis, Francis. *The Draftsman Raffael*. New Haven and London: Yale University Press, 1986.

Arterbury, Andrew. "The Ancient Custom of Hospitality, The Greek Novels, and Acts 10:1–11:18." *Perspectives in Religious Studies* 29 (2002): 53–72.

Avagnina, M. Elisa. "La tecnica pittorica di Jacopo Bassano attraverso le fonti." Pages 308–10 in *Jacopo Bassano c. 1510–1592*. Fort Worth, Tex.: Kimbell Museum of Art, 1992.

Bargellini, Piero. *Paintings by Alessandro Allori. The Palazzo Salviati-da Cepperello Formerly Houses of the Portinari Property and Seat of the Banca Toscana, Florence*. Florence: Banca Toscana, 1953.

Bauckham, Richard. "The Rich Man and Lazarus: The Parable and the Parallels." *New Testament Studies* 37 (1991): 225–46.

———. "The Scrupulous and the Good Samaritan: Jesus' Parabolic Interpretation of the Law of Moses." *New Testament Studies* 44 (1998): 475–89.

Beasley-Murray, George. *Baptism in the New Testament*. Grand Rapids: Eerdmans, 1973.

Berdini, Paolo. "Parola e immagine in Jacopo Bassano." *Venezia Cinquecento* 9, no. 18 (1999): 81–106.

———. *The Religious Art of Jacopo Bassano: Painting as Visual Exegesis*. Cambridge: Cambridge University Press, 1997.

Bovon, François. *Das Evangelium nach Lukas*. 3 vols. Evangelisch-katholischer Kommentar zum Neuen Testament 3. Zürich: Benziger Verlag; Neukirchen-Vluyn: Neukirchener Verlag, 1989, 1996, 2001.

Bovon, François. *Luke: A Commentary on the Gospel of Luke 1:1–9:50*. Translated by Christine M. Thomas. Hermeneia. Minneapolis: Fortress Press, 2002.

Bucci, Mario, and Raffaello Bencini, *I Palazzi di Firenze, Quartiere di Santa Croce*. Florence: Vallecchi editore, 1971.

Charlesworth, J. H., ed. *The Old Testament Pseudepigrapha*. 2 vols. Anchor Bible Reference Library. New York: Doubleday, 1985.

Couchman, Jane. "*Actio* and *Passio*: The Iconography of the Scene of Christ at the Home of Mary and Martha." *Studi Medievali* 26 (1985): 711–19.

Da Sesso, Livia Alberton Vinco. "Jacopo Bassano." Pages 343–47 in vol. 3 of *The Dictionary of Art*. Edited by Jane Turner. 34 vols. London: Macmillan, 1996.

———. *Jacopo Bassano i Dal Ponte: una dinastia di pittori Opere ne Veneto/ the Dal Ponte: a dynasty of painters Work in the Venetian region*. Bassano dal Grappa: Ghedina & Tassotti Editori, 1992.

De Boer, Esther. *Mary Magdalene: Beyond the Myth*. London: SCM Press, 1996.

Ebert-Schifferer, Sybille. "'Ma c'hanno da fare I precetti dell'oratore con quelli della pittura?': Reflections on Guercino's Narrative Structure." Pages 75–110 in *Guercino: Master Painter of the Baroque*. Edited by Sir Denis Mahon. Washington, D.C.: National Gallery of Art, 1992.

Fermor, Sharon. "The Raphael Cartoons Re-examined." *Burlington Magazine* 140 (1998): 236–50.

———. *The Raphael Tapestry Cartoons: Narrative, Decoration, Design*. London: Scala, 1996.

Fiorenza, Elizabeth Schüssler. "A Feminist Interpretation for Liberation: Martha and Mary: Luke 10:38–42." *Religion and Intellectual Life* 3 (1986): 21–36.

Fitzmyer, Joseph. *The Gospel According to Luke*. Anchor Bible 28–28A. 2 vols. Garden City: Doubleday, 1981, 1985.

Franklin, David. "Towards a New Chronology for Ridolfo Ghirlandaio and Michele Tosini." *Burlington Magazine* 140 (1998): 445–55.

Freedberg, Sydney. *Painting in Italy 1500–1600*. New York: Penguin, 1971.

Gilbert, Creighton. "Are the Ten Tapestries a Complete Series or a Fragment?" Pages 533–50 in *Studi su Raffaello; atti del congresso internazionale di studii: Urbino-Firenze, 6–14 Aprile 1984*. Urbino: QuattroVenti, 1987.

Golzio, Vincenzo. *Raffaello nei documenti nelle testimonianze dei contemporanei e nella letteratura del suo secolo*. Vatican City: Arti Grafiche Paneto & Petrelli, 1971.

Green, Joel. "From 'John's Baptism' to 'Baptism in the Name of the Lord Jesus': The Significance of Baptism in Luke-Acts." Pages 157–72 in *Baptism, the New Testament and the Church*. Edited by Stanley E. Porter and Anthony R. Cross. Journal for the Study of the New Testament: Supplement Series 171. Sheffield: Sheffield Academic Press, 1999.

Hannay, Margaret. "Mary Magdalene." Page 487 in *A Dictionary of Biblical Tradition in English Literature*. Edited by David Lyle Jeffrey. Grand Rapids: Eerdmans, 1992.

Hartt, Frederick, and David G. Wilkins. *History of Italian Renaissance Art*. Upper Saddle River, N.J.: Prentice Hall and Harry N. Abrams, 2003.

Haskins, Susan. *Mary Magdalene: Myth and Metaphor*. San Francisco: HarperCollins, 1993.

Helston, Michael. "An Outline of Guercino's Life." Pages 1–3 in *Guercino in Britain. Paintings from British Collections*. Catalogued by Michael Helston and Tom Henry. London: National Gallery Publications, 1991.

Hock, Ronald. "Romancing the Parables of Jesus." *Perspectives in Religious Studies* 29 (2002): 11–37.

Hornik, Heidi J. "Michele di Ridolfo del Ghirlandaio (1503–1577) and the Reception of Mannerism in Florence." Ph.D. diss., Pennsylvania State University, 1990.

———. "Michele Tosini: The Artist, The Oeuvre and The Testament." Pages 22–37 in *Continuity, Innovation, and Connoisseurship: Old Master Paintings at the Palmer Museum of Art*. Edited by Mary Jane Harris and Patrick McGrady. University Park, Pa.: Penn State University Press, 2003.

———. "The Strozzi Chapel by Michele Tosini: A Visual Interpretation of Redemptive Epiphany." *Artibus et Historiae* 46 (2002): 97–118.

———. "The Testament of Michele Tosini." *Paragone* 543–45 (1995): 156–67.

Hornik, Heidi J., and Mikeal C. Parsons. *Illuminating Luke: The Infancy Narrative in Italian Renaissance Painting*. Harrisburg, Pa.: Trinity Press International, 2003.

Hornik, Heidi J., and Mikeal C. Parsons, eds. *Interpreting Christian Art*. Macon, Ga.: Mercer University Press, 2004.

Joannides, Paul. *The Drawings of Raphael with a Complete Catalogue*. Oxford: Oxford University Press, 1983.

Jones, Roger, and Nicholas Penny. *Raphael*. New Haven and London: Yale University Press, 1983.

Klein, Günter. "Die Berufung des Petrus." *Zeitschrift für die neutestamentliche Wissenschaft* 58 (1967): 1–44.

LaRow, Sister Magdalen, S.S.J. "The Iconography of Mary Magdalen: The Evolution of a Western Tradition." Ph.D. diss., New York University, 1982.

Lavin, Marilyn Aronberg. *Piero della Francesca's "Baptism of Christ."* New Haven: Yale University, 1981.

Link, Luther. *The Devil: A Mask Without a Face.* London: Reaktion Books, 1995.

Lisci, Leonardo Ginori. *I Palazzi di Firenze nella storia e nell'arte.* Firenze: Cassa di Risparmio, 1972.

Lorenzi, Lorenzo. *Devils in Art: Florence, From the Middle Ages to the Renaissance.* Florence: Centro Di della Edifimi srl, 1997.

Mahon, Denis, ed. *Guercino: Master Painter of the Baroque.* Washington, D.C.: National Gallery of Art, 1992.

Mathews, Thomas F. *The Clash of Gods: A Reinterpretation of Early Christian Art.* Rev. and exp. ed. Princeton, N.J.: Princeton University Press, 1999.

Nolland, John. *Luke.* 3 vols. Word Biblical Commentary 35A–35C. Dallas: Word, 1989, 1993.

Ockinga, Boyo G. "The Tradition History of the Mary-Martha Pericope in Luke (10:38–42)." Pages 93–97 in vol. 2 of *Ancient History in a Modern University.* 2 vols. Grand Rapids: Eerdmans, 1998.

Panofsky, Erwin. "Iconography and Iconology: An Introduction to the Study of Renaissance Art." Pages 26–54 in *Meaning in the Visual Arts.* Chicago: University of Chicago Press, 1955.

Parsons, Mikeal C. "Landmarks Along the Way: The Function of the 'L' Parables in the Lukan Travel Narrative." *Southwestern Journal of Theology* 40 (1997): 33–47.

———. "The Prodigal's Elder Brother: The History and Ethics of Reading Luke 15:11–32." *Perspectives in Religious Studies* (1996): 147–74.

Penny, Nicholas. "Raphael." Pages 896–910 in vol. 25 of *The Dictionary of Art.* Edited by Jane Turner. 34 vols. London: Macmillan, 1996.

Pietrangeli, Carlo, et al. *The Sistine Chapel. The Art, the History, and the Restoration.* New York: Harmony Books, 1986.

Pope-Hennessy, John. *The Raphael Cartoons.* London: Her Majesty's Stationery Office, 1966.

Pullan, Brian. *Rich and Poor in Renaissance Venice: The Social Institutions of a Catholic State, to 1620.* Oxford: Oxford University Press, 1971.

Rearick, William R. *Jacopo Bassano.* Bassano del Grappa: Soc. Ed. Verci Bassano, 1986.

———. "Life and Works of Jacopo dal Ponte, called Bassano." Pages 93–101 in *Jacopo Bassano c. 1510–1592.* Fort Worth, Tex.: Kimbell Museum of Art, 1992.

Réau, Louis. *Iconographie de L'Art Chrétien.* 2 vols. Paris: Universitaires de France, 1957.

Reinhartz, Adele. "From Narrative to History: the Resurrection of Mary and Martha." Pages 161–84 in *Women Like This.* Atlanta: Scholars Press, 1991.

Robbins, Jill. *Prodigal Son/Elder Brother.* Chicago: The University of Chicago Press, 1991.

Schiller, Gertrud. *Iconography of Christian Art.* Translated by Janet Seligman. 2 vols. Greenwich, Conn.: New York Graphic Society, 1971.

Sebregondi, Ludovica. "The Devil in Fifteenth- and Sixteenth-Century Florentine Engravings." Pages 111–31 in *Demons: Mediators between This World and the Other.* Edited by Ruth Petzoldt and Paul Neubauer. Frankfurt am Main: Peter Lang, 1998.

Shearman, John. *Only Connect . . . Art and the Spectator in the Italian Renaissance.* Princeton: Princeton University Press, 1992.

———. *Raphael's Cartoons in the Collection of Her Majesty the Queen and the Tapestries for the Sistine Chapel.* London and New York: Phaidon, 1972.

Simon, Robert. *Important Old Master Paintings. Discoveries . . . in una nuova luce.* New York: Piero Corsini, Inc., 1988.

Spalding, Jack. "Alessandro Allori." Pages 670–71 in vol. 1 of *The Dictionary of Art.* Edited by Jane Turner. 34 vols. London: Macmillan, 1996.

Steinmetz, David. "The Superiority of Pre-critical Exegesis." Pages 65–77 in *A Guide to Contemporary Hermeneutics.* Edited by Donald K. McKim. Grand Rapids: Eerdmans, 1986.

Stone, David. M. *Guercino. Master Draftsman. Works from North American Collections.* Bologna: Nuova Alfa Editoriale, 1991.

————. "Theory and Practice in Seicento Art: The Example of Guercino." Ph.D. diss., Harvard University, 1989.

Talbert, Charles H. *Reading Luke: A Literary and Theological Commentary on the Third Gospel.* Rev. ed. Macon: Smyth & Helwys, 2002.

Turner, Nicholas. "Guercino." Pages 785–89 in vol. 13 of *The Dictionary of Art.* Edited by Jane Turner. 34 vols. London: Macmillan, 1996.

Vasari, Giorgio. *Le Opere di Giorgio Vasari: Le Vite de'più eccellenti pittori, scultori ed architettori scritte da Giorgio Vasari pittore Aretino* (1568). Edited by Gaetano Milanesi. 9 vols. Florence: Sansoni, 1885.

Via, E. Jane. "Women, the Discipleship of Service, and the Early Christian Ritual Meal in the Gospel of Luke." *Saint Luke's Journal of Theology* 29 (1985): 37–60.

Wailes, Stephen L. *Medieval Allegories of Jesus' Parables.* Berkeley: University of California, 1987.

Young, Alan. *The English Prodigal Son Plays: A Theatrical Fashion of the Sixteenth and Seventeenth Centuries.* Salzburg: Institut für Anglistik und Amerikanistik Universität Salzburg, 1979.

Index

Accademia del Disegno, 26, 44 n. 65,
    44 n. 66, 119
Acts
  1:1, p. 4
  1:5, p. 14
  1:17, p. 113
  1:21, p. 14
  1:25, p. 113
  2:1–2, p. 14
  3:1–11, p. 61
  5, p. 70
  5:1–6, p. 61
  6:1, p. 113
  7:59, p. 70
  7:60, p. 70
  9:1–7, p. 61
  9:43–11:3, p. 112
  10:37, p. 14
  11:16–18, p. 14
  11:29, p. 113
  12:25, p. 113
  13:6–12, p. 62
  14:8–18, p. 62
  13:24–25, p. 14
  16:23–26, p. 62
  17:15–34, p. 62
  18:24–26, p. 14
  18:24–28, p. 14
  19:1–7, p. 14
  20:24, p. 113
  21:3–6, p. 112
  21:7, p. 112
  21:8–16, p. 112
  21:19, p. 113
  28:6–10, p. 112
  28:13–14, p. 112
Agucci, Monsignor, 144
Aikema, Bernard, 99–101, 103 n. 4,
    107 n. 64, 108 n. 74, 108 n. 77,
    108 nn. 80–81, 108 n. 84, 108 n. 87,
    109 n. 90
Albert the Great, 106 n. 43, 141
Alexamemos Worships His God, 2

Allori, Alessandro, 110–11, 115, 118–
    25, 127 28, 131, 132 nn 46–49,
    133 n. 68, 133 n. 70, 133 n. 74, 165
  WORKS
   Christ in the Home of Mary and Martha,
    110, 111, 118, 121, 123
   Christ and the Samaritan Woman, 123
   Descent Into Limbo, 121
   Last Judgement, 119
   *The Magdalene Washes the Feet of Christ
    in the House of Simon*, 121–22, 123
   Mary Magdalene Receives Communion,
    122
   Noli mi Tangere, 122, 124
   Pearl Fishers, 119, 120, 121
   Trinity, 119
Allori, Cristofano, 121
Ambrose, 22, 42 n. 34, 42 n. 38, 74 n. 20,
    75 n. 22, 92, 105 n. 30, 105 n. 32,
    106 n. 42, 114, 116–17, 130 n. 20,
    131 n. 35, 139–41, 159 n. 19
Angelico, Fra, xiv, 1, 36
Angelo da Vallombrosa, 68, 79 n. 115
Apostolic Constitutions, 54, 55, 74 n. 21
Ardens, Radulfus, 90, 92
Armenini, Giovan Battista, 62, 77 n. 74
  On the True Precepts of Painting, 62,
    77 n. 74
Arslan, Wart, 96, 106 n. 49
Arterbury, Andrew, xii, 113, 128 n. 2,
    129 n. 6, 130 nn. 13–14
Augustine, 23, 42 n. 39, 55, 71, 75 n. 23,
    80 nn. 128–29, 91, 92, 105 nn. 31–
    33, 106 n. 43, 114–17, 130 n. 21,
    130 n. 34, 140, 141, 159 n. 22,
    160 nn. 23–24
Avagnina, M. Elisa, 98 108 n. 73, 108 n. 76,
    108 n. 78

Baptism of Christ (see Tosini)
  Baptismal Narrative, rhetorical shape of,
    12–15
  doves in, 40 n. 6
  history of interpretation, 18ff
Baroque, xi, 3, 43 n. 55, 121, 142, 165

Bartolomeo, Fra, 25

Bassano, Jacopo (Jacopo Dal Ponte), 82–
  84, 90–102, 103 nn. 2–3, 106 nn. 49–
  51, 107 n. 53, 107 n. 65, 107 n. 67,
  108 n. 68, 108 n. 80, 111, 165
  WORKS
  Beheading of the Baptist, 99
  Flight into Egypt, 93, 94
  Good Samaritan, 82, 83, 96–99,
    107 n. 67, 108 n. 70, 129 n. 9, 165
  Iconographic analysis of, 99ff
  Miracle of the Quails and the Manna, 99
  Rich Man and Lazarus, 83, 84, 98–101,
    129 n. 9, 165
  Supper at Emmaus, 94, 95, 107 n. 53
  Two Hunting Dogs, 99
  Way to Calvary, 95, 96
Basilica of St. Peter's, 58
Bauckham, Richard, 85, 88, 89, 103 n. 5,
  103 n. 10, 104 n. 18, 105 n. 24
Berdini, Paolo, 5, 9 n. 22, 108 n. 80
Bernard of Clairvaux, 20, 42 n. 27
Bonaventure (see also ps.-Bonaventure),
  92, 141
Boncompagni, Girolamo, 153
Book of Jannes and Jambres, 88
Borghini, Vincenzo, 26, 44 n. 66
Bottari, 27
Botticelli, 36, 38, 39, 47 n. 112
  Temptations of Christ, 36
Bovon, François, 9 n. 29, 18, 21, 24,
  41 n. 14, 41 n. 18, 41 n. 20, 42 nn. 32–
  33, 42 n. 43, 43 n. 44, 73 n. 3,
  105 n. 28, 105 n. 30, 105 n. 34,
  128 n. 5, 158 n. 3, 160 n. 26
Bronzino, Agnolo, 25, 26, 44 n. 62, 118–20,
  123
Brown, Raymond, 50, 73 n. 5, 73 n. 8
Bruno of Segni, 93, 106 n. 43
Bultmann, Rudolf, 50, 51, 73 n. 4

Callixtus, Catacomb of, 55
Calvin, John, 24, 40 n. 3, 42 n. 42, 118,
  131 n. 41, 141, 160 nn. 28–29
Campagnola, Domenico, 96
Caravaggio, 143, 144
Carracci, Annibale, 95
Carracci, Ludovico, 142, 146
Cassian, John, 117, 131

Catholic Reformation (or Counter Ref-
  ormation), 24, 118, 121, 123, 125,
  131 n. 42, 141, 151, 152, 156
Ceraiolo, Antonio del, 25
Chiarini, Marco, 29, 43 n. 53
Childs, Brevard, 6, 9 n. 26
Christ in the Home of Mary and Martha (see
  Allori, Alessandro)
  iconography of, 124–27
  history and description of, 121–23
  sources and precedents, 123–24
Christ in the Home of Mary and Martha (see
  da Milano, Giovanni)
Christ Scorned, xiv
Chrysologus, Peter, 55, 74 n. 19, 92
Chrysostom, John, 34, 46 n. 94, 55, 74 n. 19,
  130 n. 25
Church as ship, 54ff
  in Church Fathers, 54
  in art, 55
Cicero, 53, 74 n. 14, 155, 163 n. 80
  De Inventione, 53, 74 n. 14
Clement, 55, 74 n. 19, 105 n. 30
  Epistle to James, 55, 74 n. 19
Comestor, Peter, 79 n. 110, 93, 106 n. 43,
  106, 47
Contarini, Gasparo, 101
Correggio, 142
Couchman, Jane, 125, 126, 133 n. 68,
  133 n. 71, 133 n. 73
Council of Trent, 118, 141
Counter Reformation (see Catholic
  Reformation)
Credi, Lorenzo di, 25
Cyprian, 19, 42 n. 25
Cyril of Alexandria, 19, 22, 42 n. 24,
  42 n. 36

De Boer, Esther, 118, 130 n. 28, 131 n. 41,
  131 n. 43
de'Pitati, Bonifazio, 93, 103 n. 2
Deuteronomy
  6:5, p. 84
Didache
  11–12, p. 112
di Tito, Santi, 120, 132 n. 48
Dodd, C. H., 51, 73 n. 7, 105 n. 31
Domenichino, 143
Domitilla, Catacomb of, 55
Donatello, 36

Dosio, Antonio, 120
Drury, John, 6, 9 n. 28
Dürer, 94

Ebert-Schifferer, Sybille, 144–45, 147–
    49, 151–52, 155–56, 161 n. 43,
    161 n. 45, 161 n. 47, 162 nn. 48–
    49, 163 n. 61, 163 n. 66, 163 n. 70,
    163 n. 77, 164 nn. 81–82, 164 n. 84
Emiliani, Andrea, 143, 161 n. 41
Epiphany, Feast of, 18, 46 n. 87, 46 n. 88
Ephrem the Syrian, 22, 42 n. 37, 71,
    80 n. 127, 116, 131 n. 36
Erasmus, 126, 133 n. 72
Exodus
    16, p. 15
    16:3, p. 15
    17, p. 15
    17:2–3, p. 15
    32, p. 15
Ezekiel
    44:25–27, p. 85

Fable, rhetorical exercise of, 74 n. 14,
    137–38
Fermor, Sharon, 60–61, 63–64, 66, 71,
    75 n. 28, 76 n. 52, 76 n. 55, 76 n. 59,
    76 n. 61, 77 n. 64, 77 n. 70, 77 n. 74,
    77 n. 77, 77 n. 83, 77 n. 89, 78 n. 91–
    92, 78 nn. 96–97, 78 n. 101, 80 n. 126
Fitzmyer, Joseph, 52, 53, 73 n. 9, 74 n. 12,
    85, 103 nn. 5–7, 104 n. 15, 105 n. 30,
    113, 115, 128 n. 1, 128 n. 5, 129 n. 9,
    129 n. 11, 130 n. 17, 130 n. 30
Francesco, Giovanni, 68, 79 n. 110
Francis I, 57

Gaetano, Cardinal, 93
Galatians
    4:14, p. 112
Gennari, Benedetto, 142
Gennari, Cesare, 142
Gesta Romanorum, 141, 160 n. 27
Ghirlandaio, Michele di Ridolfo del (see
    Tosini, Michele)
Ghirlandaio, Ridolfo del, 25, 26, 33, 36
Giaccaro, Dominican Vincenzio, 100,
    108 n. 83
Giorgione, 96

Giotto, 35, 36, 47 n. 113, 124
    WORKS
    Judas' Betrayal, 35
    Last Judgment, 35
Giovanni da Milano, 124–26, 131 n. 44,
    133 n. 68
    Christ in the Home of Mary and Martha,
    124, 126
Giovane, Palma, 96
Giuseppe da Piacenza, 154
Gloss, The, 132, 141
Golden Legend (Voragine), 20, 42 n. 27–28,
    117, 130 n. 27, 131 n. 39, 131 n. 44
Good Samaritan (see Bassano, Jacopo)
Gottfried of Admont, 91, 105 nn. 35–36,
    160 n. 26
Green, Joel, 40 n. 8, 136, 158 n. 5
Gregory XV, Pope, 143, 144, 146
Gregory the Great, Pope, 93, 106 n. 43–
    44, 114–15, 117–18, 130 nn. 23–24,
    131 n. 37
Gregory of Nazianzus, 55, 74 n. 19
Gregory of Nyssa, 71, 80 n. 129
Gressmann, H., 87, 88, 104 n. 16
Guercino, Gian Francesco Barbieri
    Life of the artist, 142ff
    style of, 143ff
    WORKS
    Aurora ceiling fresco, 143
    Return of the Prodigal Son, 134, 145ff
    on the various versions of, 145ff
    Saint Sebastian Succored, 147, 162 n. 58
    Samson Seized by the Philistines, 147,
    162 n. 58

Hampton Court, 63, 76 n. 42, 96, 98,
    107 n. 65, 107 n. 67, 108 n. 70
Haskins, Susan, 114–15, 125, 129 n. 9,
    130 nn. 21–24, 130 n. 26, 130 n. 31,
    133 n. 70
Hebrews
    4:15, p. 24
Helston, Michael, 144, 161 n. 32, 161 n. 35,
    161 n. 42
Henry VIII, 57, 58
Hippolytus of Rome. 55, 74 n. 18
Hock, Ronald, 85, 88, 103 n. 12, 104 n. 17,
    158 n. 3, 159 n. 15

Hospitality, custom of, 112ff
Hugh of Saint-Cher, 91, 92, 106 n. 37

Ignatius, *Letter to the Ephesians*
   7:1, p. 112
   9:1, p. 112
Inflection, rhetorical exercise of, 137ff
   in Latin poetry, 158 n. 6
Innocent III, Pope, 68, 70, 79 n. 120
Isaiah
   11:2, p. 18
Iser, Wolfgang, 4, 9 n. 14

Jeremias, Joachim, 136, 158 n. 4
Jerome, 13, 41 n. 19, 91, 106 n. 43, 114–15,
   130 n. 33, 139–40
Joannides, Paul, 64, 75 n. 27, 78 n. 93
John
   1:31–34, p. 13
   4:9, p. 85
   11:1, pp. 114, 129 n. 9
   21:1–11, pp. 50, 68
   21:15–17, p. 67
   21:19, p. 50
   21:22, p. 50
3 John
   5–8, p. 112
John's baptism, 14
Julius II, Pope, 56, 57, 58, 63

Kennedy, George, 74 n. 14, 137, 159 nn. 9–
   11

Lancellotti, Tiberio, 148, 163 n. 65
LaRow, Sister Magdalen, 116, 130 n. 25,
   130 n. 32, 130 n. 34, 133 n. 70
Leo X, Pope, 56, 57, 58, 61, 66, 69, 71
Leonardo da Vinci, 55, 63
Leviticus
   19:18, p. 84
Link, Luther, 35, 36, 46 n. 97, 47 n. 99,
   47 n. 104, 47 n. 108, 47 n. 111,
   47 nn. 113–14
Lomazzo, Giovanni Paolo, 155, 164 n. 83
Ludolph of Saxony, 92
Ludovisi, Cardinal Ludovico, 143, 144, 146
Luke
   1–2, p. 3
   1:5–23, p. 17
   1:5–6, p. 17

Luke (*continued*)
   1:18, p. 17
   1:19, p. 17
   1:26–28, p. 32
   2, p. 4
   3, p. 4
   3:1–20, p. 14
   3:8, p. 14
   3:19–20, p. 52
   3:21–22, pp. 11, 40 n. 3
   3:22, pp. 13, 14
   4:1–13, pp. 11, 12, 21, 40 n. 14, 42 n. 32
   4:1–9, p. 35
   4:8, p. 15
   4:9, p. 16
   4:12, p. 15
   4:16–30, pp. 17, 52
   5, pp. 4, 50, 52, 54, 55, 66, 68, 71,
     73 n. 4, 74 n. 20
   5:1–11, pp. 49–50, 52–55, 64, 68,
     73 n. 3, 74 n. 11
   5:8, pp. 70, 73 n. 3
   5:10, pp. 49, 70, 75 n. 22
   5:16, p. 14
   6:6–11, p. 17
   6:12–16, p. 52
   6:12, pp. 14, 52
   6:20–49, p. 52
   7:36–50, pp. 112, 114, 131 n. 41
   7:36–46, p. 112
   8:15, p. 113
   8:19–21, pp. 53, 113
   9:18, p. 14
   9:28–36, p. 34
   9:28–29, p. 14
   9:31, pp. 4, 15, 34
   9:51–19:27, p.
   9:51–10:42, p.
   10, pp. 4, 111, 115
   10:29, p. 85
   10:30–37, pp. 83, 100
   10:38–42, pp. 111–13, 115, 118,
     128 n. 5, 129 n. 16, 130 n. 31
   11:1–4, p. 127
   11:1, p. 14
   11:5–8, p. 128
   12:50, pp. 34, 37, 40 n. 12
   13:10–17, p. 17
   15, pp. 4, 137, 138, 139
   15:11–32, pp. 135–36, 139, 157 n. 3

Luke (*continued*)
   15:24, p. 153
   15:25–26, p. 146
   16:1–13, pp. 87, 104 n. 14
   16:14–18, p. 87
   16:19–31, pp. 83, 87, 88, 104 n. 14,
     104 n 17
   19, p. 17
   19:1–9, p. 112
   19:45–57, p. 17
   22:21–23, p. 53
   22:24–30, p. 53
   22:31–34, p. 53
   22:32, pp. 14, 69, 72
   22:35–38, p. 53
   22:39–46, p. 14
   22:54–71, p. 53
   23:46, pp. 14, 70
   24:53, p. 17

Mahon, Sir Denis, 143–48, 153,
   161 n. 34, 161 n. 40, 161 n. 44,
   161 n. 46, 162 n. 52, 162 nn. 53–55,
   162 nn. 57–58, 163 n. 59, 163 n. 64
Malvasia, Carlo Cesare, 142, 145–47,
   162 n. 51, 162 nn. 53–54, 162 n. 57
Mannerism (Mannerist), 26, 43 n. 45,
   94, 96, 98, 99, 107 n. 54, 118–24,
   132 n. 55
Manzini, Commendatore Giovanni
   Battista, 154
Marcello, Christoforo, 68, 79 n. 115
Marcovaldo, Coppo di, 35
Mark
   1:9–10, pp. 11, 32
   1:11, p. 13
   1:16–20, pp. 50, 52, 53, 68, 74 n. 11
   3:7–12, p. 52
   3:13–19, p. 52
   3:22–27, p. 13
   3:31–35, p. 53
   4:35–41, p. 54
   6:1–6, p. 52
   6:17–18, p. 52
   7:28, p. 151
   9:2–8, p. 34
   10:38, pp. 34, 37
   14:18–21, p. 53
   14:55–72, p. 53
Mathews, Thomas, 2, 8 n. 4, 8 nn. 6–7

Matthew
   2:15, p. 15
   3:13–17, pp. 11, 32
   3:14–15, p. 13
   3:17, pp. 13, 34, 46 n. 95
   4:1–11, pp. 11, 36
   4:7, p. 15
   4:8, p. 16
   4:10, pp. 15, 16
   4:11, p. 38
   5:1, p. 16
   8:18–22, p. 54
   8:23–47, p. 54
   14:23, p. 16
   15:29–31, p. 16
   15:29, p. 16
   16:16–19, pp. 52, 59, 67
   17:1–8, pp. 16, 34
   17:1, p. 16
   24:3, p. 16
   24:45–51, p. 34
   28:16, p. 16
Maximus of Turin, 18, 20, 41 n. 21,
   42 n. 26, 72, 79 n. 110, 80 n. 132
Meditations on the Life of Christ, 23, 42 n. 29,
   131 n. 40
Michelangelo, 26, 45 nn. 70–71, 55–57,
   59–60, 63, 77 n. 76, 119–20
   WORKS
   Creation of Eve, 60
   Last Judgment, 59, 60, 76 n. 53
Miles, Margaret, 1–3, 6, 7 n. 1, 8 n. 10,
   9 n. 27
Miraculous Draught of Fishes (see Raphael)
Mirandola, Canonico Antonio, 142

Nani, Giovanni, 151, 163 n. 69
Nicholas III, Pope, 58, 59
Nolland, John, 86, 103 n. 5, 104 n. 13,
   104 n. 15, 105 n. 30, 128 n. 3
Nouwen, Henri, 157, 164 n. 94
Numbers
   5:2, p. 85
   11:16, p. 15
   19:2–13, p. 85

Origen, 19, 22, 41 n. 23, 42 n. 35,
   71, 80 n. 129, 90, 105 nn. 28–29,
   106 n. 43, 115

Palazzo Portinari-Salviati
 Allori's paintings, 110, 119, 121–25
Palazzo Vecchio, 26, 28, 30, 119–20
Paleotti, Gabriele, 154, 164 n. 82
Panofsky, Erwin, 4, 5, 9 n. 15, 133 n. 72
Passion of Jesus, depiction of, 2, 7 n. 2,
 8 n. 5
Pelikan, Jaraslov, 6, 9 n. 27
Pordenone, 94
Perugino
 WORKS
 Assumption of the Virgin, 60, 62
 Baptism of Christ, 36
 Christ Giving the Keys to Peter, 59
 Finding of Moses, 62
 Nativity of Christ, 62
1 Peter
 2:22, p. 19
Philip II, 58
Philippians
 1:21, p. 34
 2, p. 38
 3:1, p. 150
Poggio a Caiano (see Strozzi chapel)
Pontormo, Jacopo da, 26, 45 n. 70, 118,
 132 n. 49
Plummer, Alfred, 51, 73 n. 6
Pope-Hennessy, John, 65, 76 n. 41, 78 n. 96,
 78 n. 104
Priuli, Domenico, 98
Progymnasmata, 53, 74 n. 14, 136–37,
 158 n. 6, 158 n. 9, 159 n. 11
ps.-Bonaventure, 20, 21, 42 n. 29, 42 n. 41,
 92, 131 n. 40, 141
Pullan, Brian, 99, 101, 108 n. 78, 108 n. 86,
 108 nn. 89–90, 109 n. 91

Quintilian, 53, 74 n. 14, 138, 155, 158 n. 8,
 159 n. 14, 163 n. 80
 Institutio Oratoria, 53, 74 n. 14, 138,
 158 n. 8
 Rhetorica ad Alexandrum, 53, 74 n. 14

Raimondi, Marcantonio, 94
Raising of Lazarus, The, 3, 8 n. 6
Raphael
 cartoons
 composition and figure style, 64ff
 Iconography of, 66ff
 life and work of, 55ff

lost cartoons of, 61
patron and commission, 56–57
Paul scenes, 61–62
Peter scenes, 61
provenance of cartoons and tapestry
 sets, 57–58
sources and technique of cartoons, 62ff
WORKS
 Adoration of the Kings, 71
 Adoration of the Shepherds, 26, 45 n. 71,
 71, 76 n. 49
 Ananias, 69
 Christ's Charge to Peter (Donation of
 Keys), 61, 65, 67–69
 Healing of the Lame Man, 61, 69
 Miraculous Draught of Fishes, 48–49, 51,
 61–72, 165
 School of Athens, 63
 Stoning of Stephen, 61, 70, 77 m 63
Rearick, William R., 97, 106 n. 49,
 108 n. 69, 108 n. 72, 108 n. 75
Reception history, 4, 5
Reformation, 60, 105 n. 34, 118, 141
Rembrandt, 157
Reni, Guido, 143, 144, 161 n. 36
Revelation
 2:1, p. 90
Rich Man and Lazarus (see Bassano, Jacopo)
Rinuccini Chapel, 124, 126
Romans
 15:22–25, p. 112

Salerno, Luigi, 153, 162 n. 55, 162 n. 58,
 163 n. 59, 163 nn. 63–64, 163 n. 76
Salviati, Alamanno, 119
Salviati, Francesco, 26
Salviati, Giuseppe Porta, 94
Salviati, Jacopo, 119, 121, 124
Sandro Foschi, Pier Francesco di, 26
Santi, Raffaello (see Raphael)
Sarto, Andrea del 25, 44 n. 59, 120
Scannelli, 144, 161 n. 45
Scarsellino, 142
Scorel, Jan van, 96
Sebregondi, Ludovica, 36, 47 nn. 100–101,
 47 n. 107
Shearman, John, 5, 9 n. 20, 57, 59, 61, 62,
 64–68, 70, 75 n. 28, 75 nn. 30–31,
 75 n. 33, 75 n. 37, 76 n. 40, 76 n. 43,
 76 nn. 48–50, 76 nn. 58–60, 77 n. 69

Shearman, John (*continued*)
    77 n. 72, 78 nn. 93–95, 78 n. 98,
    78 n. 105, 78 n. 108, 79 n. 110,
    79 n. 113, 79 n. 116, 79 n. 121,
    80 n. 124, 80 n. 128, 80 n. 131
Shepherd of Hermas, 112
Sider, Ron, 101, 109 n. 93
Simon, Robert, 96, 107 nn 63–64,
    107 n. 67, 108 n. 70, 132 n. 47
Sistine Chapel, 36, 49, 56, 69
  building, decoration, and iconography
    of, 58ff
  Tapestries, 61ff
  Tapestry narrative of, 58
Sixtus IV, Pope, 36, 56, 58, 59
Spalding, Jack, 119, 132 n. 48, 132 n. 51,
    132 n. 54, 132 n. 58, 132 n. 60
Steinmetz, David, 6, 9 n. 26, 164 n. 93
Stone, David M., 155, 161 nn. 46–47,
    163 n. 59, 163 n. 63
Stradano, Giovanni, 26
Strozzi, Matteo, 27, 46 n. 86
Strozzi Chapel, 27–30, 32–33, 35–36,
    38–39, 120
  Tosini's paintings, 28, 32

temptation of Jesus, 11
  history of interpretation, 21ff
  order of, 15–17
  portrayal of the devil in, 35ff
  rhetorical shape of narrative, 15ff
Tertullian, 19, 41 n. 22, 55, 74 n. 18,
    106 n. 43, 141
Theon, Aelius, 53–54, 74 n. 14, 137–38,
    158 n. 9, 159 nn. 11–12
tiepedezza, 98
Tintoretto, 95
Titian, 93, 94
Torquemada, 70, 79 n. 121
Tosini, Michele (see also *Baptism of Christ*)
  life of the artist, 24ff
  portraiture, 28ff

Tosini, Michele (*continued*)
  private commissions, 26ff
  public commissions, 26
  Works
  Adoration of the Shepherds, 26, 45 n. 71
  Aurora, 26
  Lamentation, 34
  Madonna and Child with Saints, 30
  *Madonna and Child with St. John the
    Baptist*, 30, 31
  *Madonna and Child with Sts. James,
    Lawrence, Francis and Clare and Bishop
    Buonafè* 33, 44 n. 59
  Marriage of Cana, 30
  Night, 26
  Sacra Conversazione, 27, 45 n. 71
  St. Mark, 28
  St. Mary Magdalen, 28, 29, 45 n. 81
  Venus and Cupid, 26, 27

Vasari, Giorgio, 25–28, 30, 43 nn. 45–46,
    43 n. 52, 43 nn. 54–57, 44 nn. 58–
    61, 44 n. 65, 44 n. 67, 45 n. 69,
    45 n. 75, 56, 62–63, 75 n. 24, 75 n. 26,
    77 nn. 74–75, 94, 119–20, 132 n. 50,
    132 n. 53, 132 n. 61
  Lives, 62
  St. Luke Painting the Virgin, 119
Vatican, Vatican Palace, 3, 51, 56, 58–59,
    63, 71, 75 n. 28, 75 n. 36, 80 n. 130
Vecchi, Pierluigi de, 60, 76 n. 53
Venerable Bede, 23, 42 n. 40, 80 n. 128, 91,
    93, 106 n. 45
Veronese, Paolo, 93, 95–96
visual exegesis, 5ff, 115, 152, 165
Voragine, Jacobus de, 20, 42 n. 28, 117,
    130 n. 27, 131 n. 39, 131 n. 44

Wailes, Stephen, 90–91, 105 nn. 26–27,
    105 n. 30, 105 nn. 32–36, 106 n. 38,
    106 n. 40, 106 nn. 43–44, 159 n. 16,
    160 n. 26
White, John, 65, 75 n. 28, 78 n. 99